7-21-80

Handbook for Job Placement of Mentally Wor

About the book

HANDBOOK FOR JOB PLACEMENT OF MENTALLY RETARDED WORKERS is the third edition of the original *Guide to Jobs for the Mentally Retarded Worker* first published in 1960. It is based on a system of job activity elements for mentally retarded people developed for the U.S. Office of Vocational Rehabilitation. This new edition has greatly benefited from comments by users of the two previous editions and reviews by nationally recognized experts in vocational rehabilitation. It is a tool of proven value in job placement of mentally retarded adults who are preparing for independent living and competitive employment.

Described are 158 job profiles arranged in six categories—merchandising occupations; office occupations; service occupations (domestic, food service, personal and public service, etc.); agriculture, fishing, and forestry; skilled trades such as construction and printing; and processing and manufacturing occupations. Each job profile lists specific work activities, skills required, a reference to the most relevant job in the fourth edition (1978) of the *Dictionary of Occupational Titles,* and reference to related jobs. The HANDBOOK also suggests an approach for designing an overall job placement program, based on the interdependent procedures of (1) locating jobs and employers, (2) redesigning jobs, (3) prevocational training, (4) vocational training, (5) evaluation, (6) placement, and (7) follow-up.

The authors encourage the users of the HANDBOOK to go beyond its confines—to amplify the job categories in the light of their own experiences and needs, add new jobs, modify those listed, develop other training and placement procedures, or

GARLAND SERIES IN MENTAL RETARDATION

Series Editor:
Eileen M. Ouellette, M.D.
Clinical Director
Eunice Kennedy Shriver Center,
Waltham, Massachusetts

(continued from front flap)

find new applications to suit their particular requirements for job placement of the mentally retarded worker.

This valuable reference work is an essential tool for training and placement personnel working with mentally retarded persons in public schools, vocational schools, vocational rehabilitation centers, and residential facilities such as hospitals or schools. It can also be a reference for personnel management staff members in business, industry, institutions, and corporations.

Handbook for Job Placement of Mentally Retarded Workers

Training, Opportunities, and Career Areas

THIRD EDITION

Angeline M. Jacobs
Judith K. Larsen
Claudette A. Smith

American Institutes for Research
in the Behavioral Sciences
Palo Alto, California

Garland STPM Press
New York & London

15 14 13 12 11 0 9 8 7 6 5 4 3 2 1

Library of Congress Cataloging in Publication Data

Jacobs, Angeline M

Handbook for job placement of the mentally retarded worker.

Edition for 1960 entered under American Institutes for Research in the Behavioral Sciences and published under title: Guide to jobs for the mentally retarded.

Bibliography: p. 320

Includes index.

1. Mentally handicapped—Employment—United States. I. Larsen, Judith K., joint author. II. Smith, Claudette A., joint author. III. American Institutes for Research in the Behavioral Sciences. Guide to jobs for the mentally retarded. IV. Title.

HV3006.A4J3 1979 331.5′9 78-20654

ISBN 0-8240-7061-5

The original research was sponsored by the Office of Vocational Rehabilitation, Grant Number RD-222. This revision was supported by general funds from the American Institutes for Research and by Biomedical Research Support Grant No. 5 SOl RR-05615-03 and -10.

Published by Garland STPM Press
545 Madison Avenue, New York, New York 10022

Printed in the United States of America

GARLAND SERIES IN MENTAL RETARDATION

The Garland Series in Mental Retardation is designed to be a multi-volume reference work in the medical and management aspects of mental retardation. The medical aspects will include volumes on the genetics, clinical and medical manifestations, detection and treatment of the syndromes themselves. The management aspects will cover both institutionalized and noninstitutionalized individuals, and will include volumes ranging from nutritional requirements to job placement and the legal issues surrounding mental retardation.

Series Editor:

Eileen M. Ouellette, M.D.
Clinical Director
Eunice Kennedy Shriver Center
Waltham, Massachusetts

Contents

Foreword

By Bernard Posner
Executive Director
The President's Committee on Employment of the Handicapped

It is a great pleasure to write the foreword to this *Handbook for Job Placement of Mentally Retarded Workers.* This completely reworked and revised edition of the *Guide to Jobs for the Mentally Retarded* is most welcome, as it represents the new government job classifications and descriptions. It reflects the trends and changes in jobs and job attitudes during the nineteen years since the *Guide* was first published.

This handbook also marks a shift in approach towards the issues of employment of individuals with mental retardation:

First, rather than trying to mold the individual into specific jobs it emphasizes the concept of jobs to fit people.

Second, the list of jobs in the handbook should be considered merely suggestive, and not all-inclusive. This list is by no means the beginning and end to placements. A recent Department of Labor project to investigate the *Dictionary of Occupational Titles* for occupations suitable for people with mental retardation uncovered more than 8000 appropriate entries and could have been expanded to include others. Hence, this handbook can inspire your own thinking to go far beyond the confines of the jobs listed here; by carefully studying its approach you can develop your own techniques for identifying jobs and job areas.

Third, the jobs described in this handbook, and others like them, are not a special category, but represent normal employment opportunities which are within the range of individuals with mental retardation.

On another note, this handbook comes at the best of times, as so much is currently being done in the realm of job placement of individuals with mental retardation:

> In the area of law, Section 503 of the Vocational Rehabilitation Act of 1973, as amended, is an affirmative action program for employment created for all handicapped people (mentally retarded included). This covers all American businesses with government contracts (half of all the businesses in the United States), making it incumbent upon them to heed the requirements of the handicapped.
>
> Section 504 of the above act is a nondiscrimination program in training and related services for all handicapped people which covers all institutions holding government grants: most schools, colleges, hospitals, nursing homes, recreational facilities, airports, and many more.

In other areas, the National Association for Retarded Citizens administers an On-the-Job-Training project, under which 20,000 men and women have found jobs.

The federal government's special hiring program for retarded persons has placed another 20,000 people, and most states and some cities also have devised special placement programs.

And finally, people with mental retardation are still the dominant category served by state and federal programs of vocational rehabilitation.

This governmental and private impetus towards providing full employment opportunities for those individuals with mental retardation can succeed only if appropriate tools are available to those concerned with their employment. In addition to being useful to individuals and their families, this handbook is one important means of helping counselors and school and program administrators assist individuals with mental retardation to realize the potential of the job market. Finding gainful employment is the greatest service any school system or institution can provide along with equal education and training opportunities.

Acknowledgments

This *Handbook* represents the contributions of a large number of people. The original research was conducted in 1959 by Richard O. Peterson and Edna M. Jones, under a grant from the U.S. Office of Vocational Rehabilitation. The purpose of the research was to develop a system for integrating and using job information in the rehabilitation of mentally retarded individuals. The research identified a series of "job activity elements." These were further analyzed, resulting in the *Guide to Jobs for the Mentally Retarded,* published in 1960. The *Guide* consisted of 131 unbound job requirements profiles and a handbook intended to provide guidelines in the training, counseling, and placement phases of a rehabilitation program. In 1964, it was extensively revised by Ruth C. Flanagan and Edythe F. Nagin. The original guide and job profiles were consolidated into one volume, and the sections dealing with training and suggestions for using the original guide were reorganized. The present version is firmly rooted in the contributions of all these individuals.

We wish to acknowledge the contributions of the many users of previous editions, who responded to surveys and many of whom were interviewed for critical comments. We are especially grateful to the following consultants, who reviewed various versions of this edition and who supplied us with valuable comments and suggestions:

Donn E. Brolin, University of Missouri, Columbia
Dan Cahn, Project to Assist Employment, Oakland, California
Alice T. Clark, University of North Dakota, Grand Forks
Cherie Faulconer, California State Personnel Board
Ruth C. Flanagan, former author of the *Guide*
Stanley Greenspan, John Swett High School, Crockett, California
Roy E. Kimbrell, Jr., formerly Director of Opportunity Training Center, Grand Forks, North Dakota
Ken Lohre, AFL-CIO Human Resources Development Institute, Oakland, California
Daniel Mills, President's Committee on Mental Retardation
Simon Olshansky, formerly Director of Community Workshops, Boston, Massachusetts
Marvin Rosen, Elwyn Institute, Elwyn, Pennsylvania
Douglas Waterman, Sacramento City Unified School District, Sacramento, California

Another group of reviewers to whom we are indebted consisted of four members of the Community Association for the Retarded (CAR) in Palo Alto, California: Roberta Gilard, Arlene Helmcke, Joyce Judd, and Edith

Rodgers. These people reviewed the *Handbook* in terms of the adequacy of the range of jobs, from the viewpoint of trainees. We are grateful to all of them, as well as to Ralph Scheer, Executive Director of CAR, and Debbie Royat, Director of the Work Activity Program, who arranged for and participated in the review.

A special note of thanks is due Dr. Donn Brolin, whose model of vocational preparation is the basis for chapter 3 of this handbook. His book *Vocational Preparation of Retarded Citizens* (Columbus, Ohio: Charles E. Merrill, 1976) presents a comprehensive conceptualization of a vocational preparation approach, and was most useful to us in organizing this version of the *Guide to Jobs.* We are grateful for Dr. Brolin's permission to use it extensively and for his critical review of two versions of the manuscript.

We are grateful to the following for permission to reprint or make use of copyrighted material:

Charles E. Merrill Publishing Co. for the model of vocational preparation from D. Brolin's *Vocational Preparation of Retarded Citizens,* © 1976, used extensively as the basis for the preparation of Chapter 3 of this book.

University Park Press and Robert B. Edgerton for the quotation on p. 25 from "Issues Relating to the Quality of Life Among Mentally Retarded Persons" in *The Mentally Retarded and Society: A Social Science Perspective,* © 1975.

Finally, we are indebted to our colleagues at the American Institutes for Research for their assistance and encouragement during this revision: to Paul Schwartz, William Clemans, and William Shanner for encouraging the project and arranging financial support; to Richard Carter for acting as liaison with the publisher and for assisting in preparation of the manuscript; to Ruth Flanagan for her careful review of several drafts; to Perry Samuels for his contributions to the Job Profile section; and to Cathy Spafford and Sharon McVicker, who patiently prepared many versions of the manuscript.

AMJ
JKL
CAS

Index of Job Profiles Included in the Handbook

Prologue

In surveys of users of earlier versions of the *Guide to Jobs,* references were made to trainees' comments about the *Guide.* It was apparent that counselors were making the book available to individuals in training programs for the purpose of expanding the trainees' knowledge about career areas and specific jobs. Since the comments from the trainees were relevant and constructive, it seemed useful to ask those who might be using the book in this way to critique it prior to final revision and publication.

Members of the People First Committee of the Expanding Experiences Club at the Community Association for the Retarded (CAR) in Palo Alto, California, agreed to do such a critique. They had all participated in vocational training programs or had been in prevocational programs, with an expressed interest in future vocational training. Five members of the committee met with CAR and AIR staff to review a draft of the manuscript. They made comments and suggestions which reflected the views of potential trainees who might use the book as a job catalog or as a tool for increasing understanding of jobs and career fields.

The review panel generally agreed that the book was useful, provided good information for counselors, and that the range of jobs was adequate and provided the opportunity for moving into better jobs as the trainees' skills developed. A specific comment regarding the last point was, "They have jobs in here where people can start. When they get better they can progress."

The panel objected to the repeated use of labels such as "mentally retarded"; the joint consensus was, "We like to know about people, not label them." One person commented, "If we're retarded that many times we should not be working!" The panel also suggested that the title of the book be changed to eliminate the term "mental retardation."

In a discussion following the panel's critique, it was agreed that the manuscript would be edited to eliminate labeling terms except where it was necessary to insure understanding by the reader. It also was agreed that for the purpose of adequately identifying what the book was about, and who could benefit by using it, the term "mental retardation" should remain in the title. The title *Handbook for Job Placement of Mentally Retarded Workers* reflects the panel's recommendation that their status as people, and as workers, be given emphasis.

The Expanding Experiences Club at CAR in Palo Alto is a group concerned with planning and participating in a variety of social and civic projects. Their valuable assistance in the preparation of the 1978 version of the *Handbook* is greatly appreciated. Participating panel members include: Edith Rodgers (Spokeswoman), Roberta Gilard, Arlene Helmcke, Joyce Judd, and Debbie Royat (CAR staff member).

1 Introduction

A. Background

The *Handbook for Job Placement of the Mentally Retarded Worker: Training, Opportunities, and Career Areas* (formerly entitled *Guide to Jobs for the Mentally Retarded*) is designed for use by those concerned with the employment of persons of limited intellectual ability. Its primary purpose is to guide, assist, and augment programs whose goal is the integration of the mentally retarded individual into the competitive work world. In this context, job placement is conceptualized as the process of specifically identifying each individual's capabilities, and then identifying with equal specificity the nature and place of the work to be done. The placement of the person with mental retardation is different only in degree from the placement of any other person. The emphasis must be on the contributions the individual can make to the employment setting. Training and placement need to reflect this philosophy.

The past several years have seen an increasing concern with the rights and problems of mentally retarded citizens. In 1961 the President's Committee on Mental Retardation was formed, and in 1962 it published *A Proposed Program to Combat Mental Retardation*. Since then, the federal government has continued to develop and increase its commitment to strengthening support to agencies and groups serving mentally retarded citizens. Under the Education for All Handicapped Children Act of 1975 (P.L. 94–142), schools are now providing related services in local classrooms.

The American Association on Mental Deficiency (AAMD), an action-oriented organization, in 1973 issued an official statement, "The Rights of Retarded Persons," which clearly and firmly supports the right of persons with mental retardation to "exercise the same rights as are available to non-retarded citizens, to the limits of their ability to do so." The impact of the principle of normalization, which stresses the right of an individual to life experiences as close to the cultural norms as possible, can be seen in current efforts toward community integration as opposed to institutionalization—the right to receive appropriate public education, the right to job training and employment, to marry, to maintain a household, and to vote. The issue of employment opportunities for mentally retarded citizens is the chief concern of this book.

In 1959 the American Institutes for Research (AIR), under a grant from the U.S. Office of Vocational Rehabilitation, conducted a study of methods for redesigning jobs for mentally retarded workers (Peterson and Jones, 1959). Techniques of task analysis and methods of deriving skill and knowledge requirements were applied to jobs known to have been successfully performed by mentally retarded persons. Job activities for each job were catalogued and categorized, and an estimate was made of their importance to the successful execution of the job. By extrapolation from these basic task data, a similar analysis was made of many semiskilled and unskilled jobs identifiable from examination of such sources as the *Dictionary of Occupational Titles* and the *United Steel Workers Job Description Manual*, from a literature survey and a nationwide agency survey, and from interviews with employers and counselors.

Upon conclusion of this initial study, research was continued under sponsorship of AIR, and in 1960 AIR published the first edition of the *Guide to Jobs for the Mentally Retarded*, containing 131 specific job descriptions (Peterson and Jones, 1960). Each job description included a Job Activities Requirements Profile, a Personal Characteristics Requirements Profile, notations on special requirements, and an indication of the best setting for specific activity training. These descriptions were on unbound cards, designed to enhance combination of jobs or deletion of irrelevant ones, and provide for the addition of new jobs to an organization's master file.

In 1964 the *Guide* was revised, incorporating suggestions from user critiques. It was reported by the users that the very specific nature of the job description format limited the usefulness of the *Guide* as a tool for the counselor. Generalization from a single profile to all jobs of a given class proved to be difficult, as requirements varied from job to job and for the same job in different employing organizations. Further, the handling of the unbound job description materials proved to be cumbersome. Thus, the 1964 revision resulted in deletion of the unbound Personal Characteristics Requirements Profiles and Job Activity Requirements sheets for each job, and incorporation of essential information into the individual job profiles.

Training suggestions were reorganized and added to the job description section of the document. Finally, the text was expanded and bound together with the job description information to provide a comprehensive tool for agencies and schools which offer training and placement.

This revision reflects the growing, and changing, needs and interests of the *Guide's* users. A nationwide questionnaire survey was conducted among users asking for their criticisms and suggestions. In addition, interviews were held with teachers, counselors, work experience education coordinators, workshop personnel, and representatives of governmental vocational rehabilitation programs. Extensive review of the revised *Guide* was solicited from experts in the field of vocational rehabilitation at two points in time—fall of 1977 and summer of 1978. *Guide* reviewers included individuals with experience in vocational rehabilitation of mentally retarded citizens at the community, state, and federal levels.

As a result of these research activities, many changes have been incorporated into this volume. Material was clarified, reorganized, expanded, or deleted to make the procedures easier to understand and use. In addition, the individual job profiles were revised to reflect job market changes. Job profiles in areas of decreasing employment were either deleted or combined, and others were added in areas of new or increased demand. There are 158 job profiles listed here. The major changes from the previous version of the *Guide* are a decrease in the number of agricultural profiles, an increase in the numbers of office occupations represented (including computer-related jobs), and a large increase in jobs for helpers in the skilled and semiskilled trades (construction, mechanics, repair, and printing).

In revising the job profiles, references to the *Dictionary of Occupational Titles* (DOT) were updated to reflect the job-title numbers in its fourth edition (United States Employment Service, 1977).

B. Description of the *Handbook*

This handbook is a reference manual designed to be used on a day-to-day basis by training and placement personnel. Specifically, it is designed to serve the needs of the following audiences: personnel in regional, state, and local vocational rehabilitation centers; counselors and teachers in special education programs in public and private schools; vocational counselors and teachers in vocational secondary programs; counselors and training personnel in residential schools or hospitals for the retarded; and counselors and training personnel in job retraining programs such as under the Comprehensive Employment and Training Act (CETA).

While some jobs might be appropriate for persons with other developmental disabilities, or for developing entry-level job placements for the nondisabled, this book is intended primarily for counselors of mentally retarded workers. The jobs are geared toward the mentally retarded individual preparing for independent living and competitive employment, and will have limited applicability to the very severely disabled. The ultimate judgment of the client's potential for employability is the counselor's; minimum levels of measured intelligence are not suggested here. Such levels would be arbitrary, given the complexity of the interaction of social, emotional, intellectual, and physical factors determining an individual's potential.

The six chapters comprising this volume cover three basic concepts related to employing the mentally retarded individual. The first two chapters ("Introduction" and "The Mentally Retarded Worker") describe past research and experience in placing mentally retarded workers in competitive jobs. The third and fourth chapters ("Prevocational Evaluation and Training" and "Vocational Training") deal with preparing the client for employment. The remaining two chapters ("Placement Procedures" and "Job Profiles") contain job information, including specific work activities and personal characteristics needed for performing a given job.

The middle section (chapters 3 and 4) offers an approach to designing a placement program for the trainees. Development of such a program is based on seven procedures which, to some extent, are interdependent—each forms the foundation of the next. They are: 1) locating jobs and employers; 2) redesigning jobs; 3) prevocational training; 4) vocational training; 5) evaluation; 6) placement; and 7) follow-up.

The sequence in which these procedures are presented can be seen in figure 1. The sequence of the chapters does not follow that in the flow chart.

The *Handbook* is arranged so that all procedures related to the job profiles in chapter 6 immediately precede that chapter. Since not all users will be interested in all seven procedures, figure 1 indicates the chapters in which each of the procedures may be found. Evaluation is shown as an integral part of each of the other six procedures, with considerable feedback occurring among all the steps.

This book is a tool for use in *placement* of mentally retarded workers into jobs. It is *not* a training manual. Training suggestions are made, inasmuch as training is an inseparable part of placement. However, the procedures described are *not* prescriptions for establishing or operating a training program. The reader who is interested in designing training programs is referred to sources especially intended for this purpose, such as the *Standards Manual for Rehabilitation Facilities* published by the Commission on Accreditation of Rehabilitation Facilities (1976).

Neither is the *Handbook* a manual for personal adjustment counseling or adult education. It is *not* intended to present methods for evaluating personal, social, or emotional characteristics of mentally retarded people. These areas are mentioned briefly because they are related to job placement. The

figure 1 STEPS IN EMPLOYMENT PROCESS

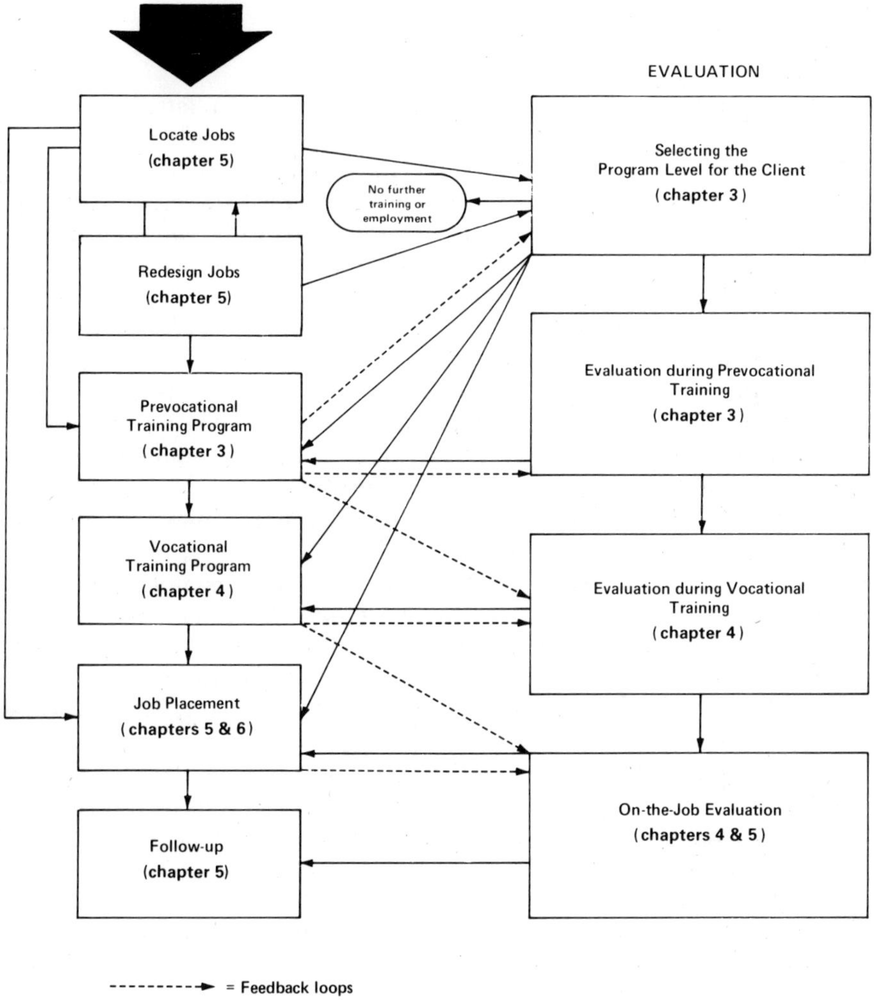

interested reader is referred to Rosen and Kivitz (1976), in *Handbook of Measurement and Evaluation in Rehabilitation,* for more information in this area.

Finally, the *Handbook* is *not* a task analysis manual. While task analyses were performed to develop the job profiles, it is not the intent of this book to teach this technique. There are many publications describing task analysis, in a number of fields. One such task analysis procedure, pertinent to mental retardation, is suggested by Gold (1976).[1]

C. How to Use the *Handbook*

This book can be used in three quite different functions related to employment: 1) job identification; 2) training; and 3) placement and follow-up.

The process of *job identification* (chapters 5 and 6) is difficult when planning for the employment of the mentally retarded worker. The *Handbook* provides a source of general information on appropriate jobs, and is designed to help the counselor locate these jobs and employers within the community. Included is a description of job redesign, which is aimed at reorganizing certain jobs and their task components to make them more suitable for the mentally retarded worker.

Suggestions for *training* (chapters 3 and 4) are given both for prevocational and vocational phases of a training program. Four types of training are discussed, which may be conducted in a variety of combinations and settings. Training in *basic* skills refers to the preparation of the trainee in fundamental academic and manual skills, such as reading, writing, and tying, which are applicable to almost all jobs. Second, training in *core* skills provides the trainee with experience in the more complex activities, common to a particular group or several groups of jobs. The third type of training relates to preparation in *specific* skills required by the job in which the trainee is to be placed. Finally *work adjustment* training pervades all aspects of vocational training and concerns such areas as motivation, work habits, work attitudes, and productivity.

The *job placement* section (chapters 5 and 6) is designed to assist in the placement of clients in competitive jobs within the community. It includes a description of specific placement activities, as well as a discussion of follow-up with both employer and client.

The 158 job profiles found in chapter 6 are arranged in related groups: 1) merchandising occupations, 2) office occupations, 3) service occupations, 4) agriculture/fishing/forestry, 5) skilled trades, and 6) processing and manufacturing occupations. For each of these groups, a master profile has been prepared, including a general description of the job category, a list of jobs described, personal/social skills usually required for that type of work, and training suggestions. Table 1 shows the number of job profiles in each job group.

Many of the 158 jobs described are designated as "helper" jobs. These are entry-level positions and are not necessarily intended as terminal placements for all clients. The positions are starting points from which some clients may move to higher-level jobs.

Job activities in each profile are presented without an indication of their

table 1 JOB PROFILES INCLUDED IN THE *HANDBOOK*, BY JOB GROUP

Job Group	Number and Types of Profiles Master Profiles	 Job Profiles
Merchandising occupations	1	15
Office occupations	1	14
Service occupations	1	49
domestic service (5)*		
food service (8)		
personal service (5)		
building services (6)		
recreation and leisure services (8)		
guest/patient services (4)		
public service (5)		
groundskeeping (4)		
other (4)		
Agriculture/fishing/forestry	1	11
Skilled trades	1	32
construction (13)		
maintenance and repair (16)		
printing (3)		
Processing and manufacturing occupations	1	37
	6	158

*Numbers in parentheses indicate number of job profiles in each subcategory.

relative importance. Since estimates of relative value can be misleading and suggest greater precision than is valid, activities usually required for a job are merely listed. If greater precision is desired, it will need to be determined relative to a specific job setting and employer.

Following the job profiles is an alphabetical index of the types of employers (or employing organizations) who may have positions matching the job descriptions mentioned in the profiles.

The master and job profiles and the index to types of employing organizations are not to be considered complete regarding job requirements, sources, or training suggestions. The reader and counselor are encouraged to write new job profiles, update present profiles, and record any other information relevant to their own specific needs and situations. In addition, these profiles lend themselves readily to computer programming and retrieval.

This book is a reference tool for training and placement, and is based on preliminary information in numerous areas of job activity; different chapters will have more relevance to some readers than to others. The reader can increase the relevance of the material by adapting the material to meet specific needs. Here are some suggestions for possible modifications:

1. add specific jobs not currently included
2. expand the list of job activities to jobs which are included
3. reorganize the broad job profiles into specific jobs reflecting skill-level differences among the various activity groupings
4. combine specific job profiles into more comprehensive and inclusive jobs
5. reorganize or select from the job profiles to suit a given community's needs and employment picture
6. add new uses and procedures to both training and job placement sections

D. Sample Case Study

Because this volume is intended as a resource tool, the reader may use as much or as little of it as needed. Earlier editions have been used to get ideas for job placement, as a training resource, as an aid in planning new curricula, to construct evaluation instruments, and in actual placement of clients in jobs. An example of one use of the *Handbook* may be helpful, especially to the new reader.

In this example, Curtis Davis, the placement counselor from a training workshop, was faced with the task of identifying potential jobs for the workshop participants. Curtis had already reviewed records of previous clients to determine where placements had been made in the past, and he contacted selected employers who had successfully hired clients before. Although these contacts resulted in expressions of interest, nothing concrete had developed in terms of placement possibilities.

Curtis decided to refer to the job profiles in the *Guide* to get some idea of what other jobs there might be in the community. The training workshop was located in a medium-sized city surrounded by a predominantly rural farming community. There were some small local industries, but no large manufacturing plants or corporations with many jobs available. After looking over the listed jobs and the index to the types of employing organizations, he decided that to discover which jobs were appropriate, it would be necessary to go into the community and determine what other kinds of activities were available. Curtis and Karen Robbins, another staff member, visited the Chamber of Commerce and got information on local industries. They also spoke with people they knew through church activities, civic groups, Little League, Girl Scouts, and the bowling team, to find out what kinds of jobs people held. They discovered that their city was a distribution and service center for the surrounding area and that this might be a job area to focus on. Specifically, they found: that there were a number of sales representatives from the city who called on clients in smaller towns in the surrounding area; that there were truckers and delivery companies, most of them small operations; and that there were service organizations such as public utilities and governmental agencies, including road maintenance, which had their central offices in the city but worked throughout the surrounding area.

Curtis began by concentrating on the trucking and delivery company jobs which might be available. Using the community survey as a basis, he prepared a master file of placement possibilities including the following information:

1. type of industry
2. jobs and job activities
3. skills required
4. list of companies (prepared from Chamber of Commerce information and from the Yellow Pages of the phone book under "Trucking")
5. size of organization
6. names of contacts

With the master file now containing basic information, Curtis turned again to the job profiles to find those which might be appropriate for the trucking and delivery industry. There were several: delivery truck helper (A-15), custodian (C-19), security guard (C-22), transportation fleet maintenance helper (E-15), and automobile mechanic helper (E-18). He now had an idea of what types of jobs might exist and the extent to which they were appropriate for the clients of the workshop.

At this point, a meeting was held with the director of the agency and selected staff to inform them of the planning activities and to get their opinions on the appropriateness of these jobs for the agency's clients. The consensus was that the clients could perform such jobs, and that if additional or specialized training were necessary, it could be provided.

Having done the necessary background work, Curtis' next step was to begin contacting some of the trucking companies who might be possible employers. In his community, personal contacts carried much more weight than group meetings, so he began calling employers and arranging for appointments. A few contacts were positive and even optimistic; other interviews were informational, but resulted in no expression of interest in employing workshop trainees.

After the initial contacts, Curtis followed up with those employers that seemed most interested. At this point their conversation progressed beyond basic information to a discussion of whether the company might have jobs for any trainees. Curtis had thought in advance of the types of jobs workshop trainees could perform in each setting, and had suggestions ready. The idea that seemed most interesting to the Boone Trucking Company was to employ a worker to do maintenance and cleaning activities in the truck docking area. The employer agreed to consider the prospect further, and after a series of additional meetings, agreed to interview some candidates.

Curtis now began dealing with potential applicants. (A job profile with specific information already existed for "custodian.") He met with the training staff to get their recommendations on possible applicants. There were two clients in the vocational training program who they felt could handle the job—John Able and Robert Fine. Client profiles were prepared for each of these applicants. By comparing the client profiles with the job profiles, it became apparent that, while both applicants were judged able to perform the job activities well, each of them was deficient in one personal/social skill. John Able was poor on the attendance factor, and Robert Fine was judged low in work independence. Both were recommended to the employer for interviews. The employer eventually decided to hire Robert Fine, since work independence was not as important to him as were punctuality and consistent attendance.

The evening of the first day on the job, Curtis called Robert at home to ask how he felt about his new job. Although Robert was nervous and somewhat unsure of the new surroundings, there were no major problems. Curtis called again later in the week and visited Robert later that month. On that occasion he spoke with Robert and his employer, and discussed a few minor matters that had come up. After several months, it seemed that the placement was working well.

With this successful placement as evidence, Curtis recontacted several of the trucking and delivery companies, pointing out the effective job Robert was doing at Boone Trucking, and again urging the employers to consider hiring a trainee from the workshop.

During the community survey, Karen had noticed that there were a number of small shops and retail stores that were unable to hire full-time help, but were looking for help for a few hours a day. She used the *Handbook* to identify jobs which might be applicable in these settings and identified clothing store helper (A-4) and floral shop assistant (A-8). These were two other areas that could then be developed for placement possibilities.

It would be ideal if all placements could be concluded as successfully as this example; unfortunately, such is not the case. For example, if Robert's placement had not been successful, Robert could have returned to the workshop for further training or training in another job. Curtis would then have met again with the employer to discuss the situation and plan future steps. Since conditions in each community and agency differ, the reader is urged to adapt the procedures and materials included here and make them appropriate and useful to the local situation.

Note

1. Gold's task analysis system is available on film from Film Productions of Indianapolis, 128 East 36th Street, Indianapolis, Indiana 46205.

2
The Mentally Retarded Worker

A. Overview of Mental Retardation

Mental retardation is a condition which affects approximately three percent of the population. Characterized by limited intellectual functioning and delayed personal and social development, mental retardation has received considerable attention from many disciplines, including medicine, law, psychology, and education. Recent advances in prevention, diagnosis and evaluation, educational strategies, and vocational training methods are largely the result of the recognition that past assumptions and techniques were not producing adequate understanding or maximum opportunities for persons with mental retardation.

The estimate of incidence of mental retardation is based on the number of children diagnosed as mentally retarded, mainly during the school years. The incidence of mental retardation among adults is more difficult to determine. It has been estimated that more than 2,000,000 adults in the United States possess the limitations, to one degree or another, which characterize this disability (Katz, 1968). Of particular interest to the rehabilitation worker, there are some 690,000 institutionalized or unemployed mentally retarded adults. Of these, approximately 400,000 could be employed if adequate services were available to them (Conley, 1973).

Mental retardation is associated with a wide range of medical, cultural, and psychological factors. The known medical causes number over 200 and include infection, birth injury, metabolic disorders, brain disease, chromosome abnormalities, premature birth, and severe environmental deprivation. When mental retardation exists with no apparent biological cause, cultural-familial causes are often cited. Cultural-familial retardation is believed to be the result of the combination of genetic and environmental influences including, among other things, poor physical health and economic poverty. The importance of maternal health, prenatal care, and early experience in promoting intellectual and social development has been well documented (Skeels and Dye, 1939; Kirk, 1958; Skeels and Skodak, 1966). Efforts to prevent cultural-familial retardation through early intervention and assistance to families appear promising, but are still in the beginning stage of development. Comprehensive diagnostic, educational, and vocational training programs can greatly enhance these individuals' chances of reaching their full potential and of assuming a productive role in the community.

Some persons who could be legitmately termed "mentally retarded" according to the criteria of the American Association on Mental Deficiency (AAMD) are actually functioning under a severe psychological disability. These individuals may appear mentally retarded, but with remission of the psychological disorder behave in a more normal manner. In any case, it is important to distinguish between the individual who is mentally retarded and has emotional problems, and the individual whose primary disability is emotional disturbance with resulting impairment of intellectual functioning and adaptive behavior.

The AAMD defines mental retardation as "significantly subaverage general intellectual functioning existing concurrently with deficits in adaptive behavior, and manifested during the developmental period" (Grossman, 1977). This definition is generally accepted, and contains the following important implications for diagnosis and classification:

1. "Significantly subaverage general intellectual functioning" refers to a measured intelligence falling two or more standard deviations below the mean. This would include those individuals with a score below 70 on a standardized IQ test.
2. "Adaptive behavior" refers to the degree to which the individual meets the standards of personal independence and social responsibility expected of his age and cultural group. Independent living skills, vocational competence, and social abilities are the main criteria for judging adequate adaptive behavior in adulthood.
3. "Existing concurrently" stresses that in order for a determination of mental retardation to be made, an individual must obtain an IQ score two or more standard deviations below the mean *and* exhibit deficits in adaptive behavior. One of these factors alone is not considered sufficient grounds for determination of mental retardation.

4. Limitations in intellectual functioning and adaptive behavior must be noted in the "developmental period" between birth and 18 years for a condition of mental retardation to exist. Although accidents or illness in adulthood can adversely affect intellectual functioning and impair an individual's ability to meet accepted standards of social behavior, such a person would not be considered mentally retarded.
5. This definition focuses on "current behavior" and does not imply future functioning or attempt to predict developmental potential. This is very important since persons who are classified as mentally retarded at one time may achieve a satisfactory adjustment with maturity and no longer be considered disabled.

Classification involves grouping those who are alike along certain dimensions, and is valuable for administrative and planning purposes. Classifying mental retardation according to the AAMD definition requires assessment along two dimensions—intelligence and adaptive behavior.

Intelligence

Early efforts to understand mental retardation contributed to the development of intelligence testing, as can be seen in the work of Binet, Terman, and Cattell (Rosen and Kivitz, 1976). Subsequent work in this area has resulted in the recognition of complex and problematic aspects of intelligence testing with mentally retarded persons. Despite the difficulties, measured intelligence still is seen as an important feature in the diagnosis and classification of mental retardation.

The AAMD classification defines four levels of mental retardation. The IQ scores associated with each level are determined using the Wechsler Adult Intelligence Scale, and could vary slightly when other standardized tests of intelligence are used.

Mild mental retardation (IQ 55–69) comprises about 89 percent of all retardation. Although minimal brain damage and less severe medical causes may be present, in most mild cases no organic pathology is known. Cultural and familial factors are felt to influence its occurrence. Mildly retarded persons are generally capable of achieving social and vocational adjustment if they receive adequate educational, vocational, and health services.

Moderate mental retardation (IQ 40–54), affecting about 6 percent of mentally retarded persons, is frequently associated with a known medical cause. Moderately retarded persons can learn some functional academic skills and can be taught to perform unskilled or semiskilled jobs. These individuals are able to profit greatly from instruction in self-help and independent living skills and can achieve a range of autonomy if they receive adequate training and support services.

Severe mental retardation (IQ 25–39), affecting about 3.5 percent of the retarded population, is generally associated with a known medical cause and deficits in motor development. Severely retarded persons do not generally profit from academic instruction, but can learn personal care and self-protection skills. Communication abilities are limited, but these individuals often perform well in a sheltered environment with adequate supervision.

Profound mental retardation (IQ 24 and below) accounts for only 1.5 percent of all mental retardation and is characterized by extreme physical and mental limitations. In cases of profound retardation, medical causes are always present. Although some motor and speech development is possible, these individuals require extensive care and supervision throughout their lives.

Adaptive Behavior

Adaptive behavior is classified in terms of performance of developmental tasks normally expected of a particular age and cultural group. The AAMD classification system lists four levels of adaptive behavior ranging from mild negative deviation (Level I) to almost complete lack of adaptation (Level IV). For a young child, adaptive behavior would include sensory-motor development, communication skills, and self-help skills. During the school years adaptive behavior includes academic proficiency and increased social participation. For the adult, working and fulfilling personal and social responsibilities are the most important criteria of adaptive behavior.

Adaptive behavior, more difficult to classify than intelligence, requires clinical observation and information from knowledgeable informants such as parents or teachers. Scales developed for measuring adaptive behavior include the AAMD Adaptive Behavior Scale and the Vineland Social Maturity Scale. It is generally felt that such measures of adaptive behavior are imprecise, thus caution is warranted in interpreting results. Changes in adaptive behavior level can occur as a result of training and maturation, and therefore frequent reassessment of individuals is desirable.

While current methods of classification adequately serve the purpose of grouping, they do not necessarily lead to effective programming. A more meaningful system, from the point of view of teachers and trainers, would lead toward effective intervention strategies and specific behavioral objectives for the individual in a training program. Current methods of evaluation and classification too often tell us not what people know, but what they do not know. They tell little about specific strengths and weaknesses, individual learning styles, or what skills are actually necessary for adequate vocational and social functioning. The process of diagnosis, classification, and the labeling which inevitably seems to follow has been much debated among professionals, parents, and mentally retarded persons themselves. Although the process implements service delivery, it is also stigmatizing and, thus, often protested.

Classification, and the labeling process which accompanies it, need not work to the disadvantage of the individual. Used as a signal that the person may need help and as a stimulus to in-depth evaluation, classification can aid in pointing the way toward effective program planning. In the final analysis, a diagnosis of mental retardation and determination of severity should be obtained by a combination of testing, clinical observation, and a careful gathering together of all relevant background information by a qualified professional. Classification is never a substitute for a complete diagnostic profile (Begab, 1975).

B. Characterisitics of the Mentally Retarded Adult

Mental retardation is a condition affecting many individuals throughout their lifespan. Until recently, however, most research and efforts at treatment concentrated on childhood, leaving the needs of mentally retarded adults misunderstood and frequently unmet.

For most people, regardless of limitations in ability, adulthood brings the hope of independent functioning—of working, maintaining a home or apartment, and perhaps marrying and having a family. By their own efforts, or with the assistance of their families or communities, many mentally retarded people have been able to fulfill the hope of independent adult living. Unfortunately, often due to a lack of personal or community resources, many who are capable of attaining independence have not done so.

Range of Personal Characteristics

The wide variation in abilities and characteristics among those who are mentally retarded is often overlooked, leading to the persistence of misleading stereotypes. In measured intelligence alone, the range of scores among persons considered to be mentally retarded can vary as much as 50 IQ points. Among the general population a range of this magnitude is clearly recognized as indicating great variation in intellectual ability. Too often the label of "mental retardation" obscures the wide range of learning and performance capabilities found among mentally retarded persons.

People with similar measured intelligence may possess great variations in communication skills, social competencies, physical capabilities, and personality characteristics. While it is not to be denied that mental retardation is limiting, sometimes very severely, the limitations it brings are far from uniform or precisely predictable.

Maladaptive behavior is often seen to be an inevitable concomitant of the disabling condition, rather than the result of poor vision or hearing, lack of training in hygiene and social skills, or a natural tendency to be unusually shy, irascible, or overly cautious. Each individual, regardless of the degree of general ability, possesses unique mental, physical, and emotional strengths and weaknesses. By recognizing individual differences as well as general similarities among clients, rehabilitation staff can develop programs which support the strengths while reducing the detrimental effects of the weaknesses.

Community Living

As a result of increased awareness and understanding, society has come to recognize the right of all persons to live in the community and exercise, to their fullest capabilities, their rights as citizens.

The principle of normalization, as stated in a publication of the President's Committee on Mental Retardation (Nirje, 1969), means "making available to the mentally retarded, patterns and conditions of everyday life which are as close as possible to the norms and patterns of the mainstream of society." The basic message is that people with mental retardation have needs very similar to those of the nonretarded. To deny them the right to live, learn, work, and participate in the community is to deny them the normal experiences which are the right of every citizen. Aspects of normalization include integrating students into regular educational programs (mainstreaming), providing career education, relevant vocational education, community work experience, normal social experiences, and the opportunity to live in the community. It has been pointed out that it is unrealistic to expect persons trained in artificial, segregated settings to adapt easily to a normal environment which may only slightly resemble the training situation (Wolfensberger, 1972).

An example of a successful community action program is ENCORE, a program of the Eastern Nebraska Community Office of Retardation (Barker, 1971).[1] It provides for the total community integration of all mentally retarded citizens in a five-county area, regardless of age or degree of handicap. The program consists of comprehensive vocational, educational, residential, and guidance services aiming at competitive employment and achievement of independent living skills. Cost analysis figures indicate that it is less costly to provide comprehensive community services of this kind than to maintain these same individuals in centralized institutions.

Although effective programs such as ENCORE exist, most communities still are not meeting the life and career development needs of mentally retarded citizens. Many moderately and severely retarded persons remain institutionalized when community placement would be possible if adequate resources were available (O'Connor *et al.*, 1970).

In examining the problem, Olshansky (1972) cites staff reluctance to practice the principle of normalization as a major deterrent to full development of a trainee's potential. He criticizes professional workers for focusing on pathology rather than normality, tending to develop an air of superiority toward those they serve, highlighting "inner" differences rather than developing adaptive behaviors, and relying on nonfunctional methods of operation.

Many mentally retarded adults living in the community have little opportunity to engage in recreation or leisure activities. In a survey of moderately retarded adults living in the community, Stanfield (1973) found that many spent much of their time alone, watching television or walking around the neighborhood. Almost half were not involved in work or activity programs and had no structured daily activities of any kind. Friendships centered around workshop participation, with little neighborhood or community involvement reported.

While it is clear that the great majority of persons with mental retardation can live and work in the community, it is also clear that without the commitment of resources, both financial and human, their doing so remains a limited reality.

Approach toward Work

Economic independence becomes important with the attainment of adult status. The development of a work personality, however, begins in childhood, and according to some theorists, continues to develop throughout the working years of the individual (Brolin, 1976). Early stages in this development are characterized by fantasies of "what I want to be when I grow up," role-playing at various occupations, and becoming aware of the wide range of existing work areas and jobs. In adolescence, the individual may work at part-time or volunteer jobs, exploring and expanding interests and understanding career options. Later stages of work personality development include career choice, education and training, employment, and perhaps job- or career-change decisions. Early environment, education, individual values and personality characteristics are important influences on the development of a work personality.

Mentally retarded persons often reach adulthood without having experienced the various stages of work personality development. Due to developmental delays, lack of exposure to a full range of life experiences, and low societal and personal expectations for achievement, they often come to vocational training with serious deficiencies in information and experience. Prevocational programs provide individuals with the opportunity to obtain necessary prework knowledge and skills that facilitate successful job training and placement.

While prevocational training can provide needed information and experience regarding the world of work, there are a number of factors that may serve to discourage the development of work competence and independent living skills. Among these factors are:

1. The fear of failure, frequently associated with school and training, is often characteristic of persons with mental retardation. The concept "if you don't try, you don't fail" can limit an individual's willingness to attempt job training or independent living. The fear of failure may appear as negativity, passivity, withdrawal, or overly aggressive behavior. By recognizing the fear for what it is, a counselor can help the individual to emphasize and augment present competencies, thus experiencing success and gaining confidence.
2. Family attitudes and support are very influential in helping or hindering a trainee's successful bid for independence. Lack of family support, or a family's need to keep the individual in a dependent state, undermines training efforts. By recognizing the family's influence and needs, the counselor can work with family members to the trainee's advantage.
3. Persons who are receiving income based on their disability status may fear the loss of that income and security if they develop work skills. The counselor needs to be aware of provisions made to safeguard financial security, such as self-support plans which enable the individual to gradually assume financial independence—and assuring that temporary or part-time work will not diminish his or her economic status.
4. Although it is stated frequently that mentally retarded persons "enjoy" repetitious work, a survey of supervisors revealed that most mentally retarded workers react in a typical way to boring, monotonous tasks (Kelly and Simon, 1969). Workers need to be given the opportunity to perform jobs they enjoy and feel are worthwhile. Incentives such as adequate salary, social opportunities at work, and economic independence can compensate for the inescapable repetition of many entry-level jobs.
5. Individuals may resist job training or choose not to work for a variety of reasons. For many, a job offers economic independence and personal freedom, but for others, the benefits may not be clear or desired. Counseling can serve to clarify the issues and enable individuals to make responsible choices regarding work readiness and job training.

C. Job Opportunities

While much progress has been made in opening up employment opportunities in a variety of situations, mentally retarded workers too often confront reluctance on the part of prospective employers or other problems which prevent them from reaching their full employment potential. The counselor or placement officer should be aware of these problems and be prepared to deal with them directly.

Barriers to Competitive Employment

Surveys of the employment situation of persons with mental retardation present what appear to be conflicting findings regarding work adjustment and employment. On the positive side, a number of programs have shown excellent attendance, longevity, and production rates by mentally retarded workers (Kelly and Simon, 1969; President's Committee on Mental Retardation, 1969).

Despite evidence that mentally retarded persons can perform well in competitive work situations, recent studies indicate that considerable employment and work adjustment problems exist. Studies by Tobias (1970), Olshansky and Beach (1974), and Brolin and others (1975) show that even after receiving special education, vocational training, and rehabilitation services, many individuals were either unemployed or had achieved only a marginal degree of work adjustment.

According to Brolin (1976), the major problem in this area is a general underestimation, by both the public and professional workers, of a trainee's potential. Mentally retarded persons are often seen as being capable only of performing simple, routine jobs, and, as part of a labor market surplus, are the first to be laid off in times of economic stress. Although there is an increasing body of research which demonstrates the ability of even severely retarded individuals to learn to perform complex manual tasks, the general applicability of new training methods and techniques has yet to achieve wide program-level acceptance (Gold, 1973).

Lack of social competence is generally acknowledged to be a major deterrent to employment in the competitive job market. Despite this, counselors and training personnel often lack familiarity with behavior management and shaping techniques which have been proven effective in changing behavior and improving social skills (Wehman, 1976). According to Gold (1973), the literature on facilitating the acquisition of new behaviors is often not specific enough to be of value to training personnel.

Other problems preventing the attainment of full employment potential include: lack of specific understanding of certain job performance requirements; employer attitudes and reluctance to hire; and the tendency of agencies to rely on past successes, thus hindering the development of new job placement opportunities.

Range of Jobs Available

In three nationwide surveys to determine the range of occupations in which placements of mentally retarded workers were being made, the data indicated a shift in prevalence of job placements away from agricultural and small manufacturing jobs to office jobs and helpers in the construction industry and in skilled trades.[2] Jobs in new technological areas, such as the computer industry, emerged. The most frequently mentioned job groups in which placements were being made in the 1977 survey were, in order of descending frequency: 1) food services, 2) building services (custodial), 3) domestic services, 4) groundskeeping, 5) office occupations, 6) merchandising occupations, 7) building trades, 8) helpers in hotels, 9) helpers in nursery schools, and 10) helpers in hospitals. While service occupations continue to head the list of placement opportunities, office and merchandising occupations now appear more frequently as options.

According to the 1977 *Guide to Jobs* survey, operative skills (such as assembly work and tending and operating mechanized equipment) are not generally offered in training programs. A survey by Goldstein (1971) indicates that in a number of European countries, moderately and severely retarded workers are employed in regular work settings and earn standard wages in assembly jobs and work requiring the use of power tools and automated equipment. Since operatives comprise a group of workers second only in size to clerical employees, this area appears promising for future training and placement efforts.

The Human Resources Development Institute (HRDI) of the AFL–CIO is engaged in promoting employment opportunities for handicapped workers in private business and industry. Established in 1968, HRDI is an integral part of the labor movement with a commitment to developing union jobs (many with the protection of collective bargaining agreements) for handicapped individuals. Through support from the Department of Labor and the Projects With Industry Placement Program of the Department of Health, Education and Welfare, HRDI offers employment counseling, training opportunities, and job development and placement services aimed at assisting individuals to get jobs with good salaries, benefits, and working conditions. In addition to direct services to clients, HRDI provides technical assistance to agencies seeking to place individuals in jobs covered by union contracts. Clients are usually referred to HRDI by a state Department of Rehabilitation office or private rehabilitation agency. Trainees participating in the Projects With Industry Program must be state rehabilitation clients. HRDI currently has 60 offices in cities throughout the nation. Information on HRDI programs may be obtained from the AFL–CIO Human Resources

Development Insititute, 815 16th Street N.W., Washington, D.C. 20006, (202) 638-3912.

In the survey conducted in 1977, users of the *Guide to Jobs for the Mentally Retarded* (1964) were asked to indicate jobs for which they did not make placements and give the reason. In general, reasons for nonplacement had to do with lack of opportunity in the agency's community. There were a few jobs indicated by some respondents as too difficult (keypunch operator, typist); demanding too much responsibility (building watchman); too dangerous (window washer); unionized (helper in transportation fleet maintenance); or seasonal (swimming pool service helper). However, many other respondents indicated that they had placed workers in these jobs. Additional jobs were suggested, many of which were closely related to existing jobs. The results of the survey were used to combine and supplement the jobs listed in the 1964 *Guide*. The final product, consisting of 158 job profiles, is included here as chapter 6.

D. Types of Rehabilitation and Training Programs Available

Education and training are provided by a variety of public and private agencies and organizations. Basically, the services can be divided into three types: 1) public school programs; 2) community rehabilitation programs serving those no longer eligible for public school; and 3) institutional programs.

Public School Programs

The schools traditionally have provided services to exceptional children through special education programs, staffed with teachers trained in methods of dealing with both general and specific learning problems. Special education has been criticized for emphasizing academic skills and failing to focus attention on more practical areas of life and career adjustment. Criticism has also been directed toward the stigmatizing effect of labeling students as handicapped and segregating them in special classes, thus focusing attention on the difference between exceptional students and regular students, rather than emphasizing the many similarities in needs and life expectations.

The integration of students into regular education programs is one answer to the criticisms against segregated classes for handicapped students. In line with the principle of normalization, this enables the handicapped student to attend classes with regular students, receiving additional services from resource persons trained to work with students having special problems.

Work-study programs, which combine academic instruction with vocational training and work experience, are another aspect of public school response to the developmental needs of special students. Work-study programs are designed to provide basic educational skills, training in personal and social competence, and vocational training and experience.

Career education is perhaps the most comprehensive approach to meeting a students' life and career development needs within the regular educational structure. The career education concept views education as more than instruction in specific academic, social, or vocational skills. Brolin (1976) suggests that career education shows a concern for the total life career development needs of the person, including personal/social skills, daily living skills, occupational development, academic education, and preparation for community working and living. Career education is a process-oriented, rather than a content-oriented approach to learning, and is aimed at assisting the student to function effectively as a consumer, a producer, a learner, and a citizen (Parnell, 1973).

Rehabilitation Programs

Rehabilitation programs generally provide services to persons of employable age (16–65) who have physical or mental handicaps. Typically vocationally oriented, rehabilitation programs have begun to broaden their approach to consider more of the personal and social needs of the individuals they serve. This is due in part to the enactment of legislation focusing attention on the needs of the severely handicapped, who, in order to function effectively, require more comprehensive service and assistance.

Rehabilitation services are provided through a variety of national and local private agencies. The primary source of public services is provided by state rehabilitation agencies under the direction of the Rehabilitation Services Administration of the Department of Health, Education and Welfare. State rehabilitation agencies provide counseling, financial assistance, and referral and follow-up with clients. They typically rely on community sources for the provision of most direct services which might include medical, psychological, and vocational evaluation; medical or psychological services for disabling conditions; prosthetic devices; vocational training; basic living costs during training; purchase of job-related equipment; and job placement services and follow-up.

Rehabilitation facilities are the primary source of vocational evaluation and training. They may be operated by state agencies, community organizations, or national organizations such as the National Association for Retarded Citizens, Easter Seal Society, and Goodwill Industries of America. In the community, facilities are mainly of four types:

1. Work activity center—provides structured work and social activities designed to develop and improve personal functioning. The emphasis is on prescriptive evaluation and remediation rather than work production.

The center may serve as the terminal placement for the more severely handicapped worker.

2. Work adjustment center—emphasizes evaluation and training in prevocational skills and work habits and attitudes. Prepares the individual for advancement to more specific job training in a vocational field.
3. Transition center—uses work as the primary method of learning job skills. Transition centers generally subcontract work from local businesses and industry, pay wages, and provide work experience similar to the competitive labor market.
4. On-the-job-training center—places trainees in actual work situations where they receive on-the-job training for a particular job. While in OJT, the trainee may continue to receive counseling and prevocational training at the rehabilitation facility or agency.

Institutional Programs

Institutional programs continue to provide services to large numbers of mentally retarded persons. Older, centralized institutions, such as state hospitals, are often seen as providing primarily custodial care and offering little opportunity for movement into the community. Other common criticisms of institutional training programs have been: 1) limited or untrained vocational staff, 2) atypical work setting which does not prepare trainees for competitive jobs, 3) need to retain capable residents to perform work in the institution, and 4) little or no opportunity for residents to earn money.

An example of positive change occurring in a long-established institution is given by Rosen and his associates (1977) in an account of the current program for residents at Elwyn Institute in Pennsylvania. In 1961 Elwyn's program emphasis shifted from segregated care to preparing residents to move into the community. A comprehensive program of education and social and vocational training, with a strong emphasis on transitional experiences, is carefully planned to maximize the individual's chances of attaining an adequate postinstitutional adjustment.

A 1975 survey of the status of vocational training in 203 state institutions for mentally retarded persons found rapid and significant changes occurring (Richardson, 1975). Compared with an earlier survey in 1957, institutions reported a 20 percent drop in residents being trained in institutional work areas. Slightly more than 50 percent of the institutions surveyed reported alternate training programs including sheltered workshops within the institution, community-based workshops, regular jobs in the community, prevocational programs, and part-time day work. Responses indicated that institutions were releasing capable workers, prompted by the legal and humanistic concern for the individual rights of the residents. Although 90 percent of resident workers reportedly received some payment for their labor (as compared with 31 percent in 1957) only 20 percent of those employed full-time received more than ten dollars a week.

Richardson points out that as capable residents move into the community, the proportion of more severely handicapped residents increases. Since these individuals are less likely to be able to meet the demands of current work programs, more sheltered workshops and work activity centers are needed to provide meaningful vocational training. The lives of mentally retarded individuals are shaped significantly by the kinds of opportunities provided to them by the agencies and facilities charged with serving their needs. If increased participation and fuller lives are the goal, then rehabilitation programs must reflect the ideals and practices set forth in the principle of normalization, the concept of career education, and the commitment to serve all persons, regardless of the degree of their disability.

E. The Future

While it cannot be denied that the past twenty years have brought increased attention to the problems of persons with mental retardation, much work remains to be done in all the areas that have been discussed. The advancing technology of instruction enables us to teach more and with greater effectiveness than before. Some progress has been made in understanding the social skills and adaptive behaviors necessary to successful community living. However, as Farber (1968) points out, the success of bringing mentally retarded persons fully into the mainstream of American life still depends on the modification of long-standing values and attitudes in our society. The pervasiveness of the latter can be seen in the kinds of programs developed and funded, the kinds of skills emphasized in training programs, and the degree of willingness to commit resources to the task of improving the lives of our retarded citizens. Gold (1973) states that the differences found between the lives of mentally retarded people in other countries (such as Sweden, Holland, and England) and in our own country are mainly the result of societal values and expectancies.

Edgerton stresses the importance and usefulness of viewing mental retardation not as a static condition but as a process—changeable, depending upon the setting, the culture, and the maturation of the person. In attempting to assess the quality of life for adults labeled mentally retarded, Edgerton and his associates engaged in first-hand observation and, whenever possible, participated in the daily lives of these persons. They attended social events, went shopping, and took weekend outings, sometimes spending a week or more in residence with those they studied.

Edgerton comments on the tendency of the research staff to reward the residents' dependency and incompetence, even though the staff's intention was to remain neutral or simply to be friendly. This points out the complexity of the relation between mentally retarded persons and those whose sincere purpose is to enable them to move toward maturity and independence. In urging professional workers to avoid reducing the complexity of mental retardation to simplicity, he cautions:

> I have come to realize that there is far more to mentally retarded persons than I had previously realized. My own writing about mentally retarded persons does not seem to me wrong, it is simply unfinished. Not only have I not got to the bottom of things, I cannot even guess where the bottom is. So I end with a cautionary note, for myself if no one else: Mentally retarded persons, even though they may have lesser skills and capacities than the rest of us, are nevertheless complex persons who live complex lives, like the rest of us. (Edgerton, 1975, p. 140)

Notes

1. Information about the program may be obtained by writing to ENCORE, 885 S. 72 Street, Omaha, Nebraska 68114.

2. The surveys were conducted by the staff of the American Institutes of Research in 1960, 1971, and 1977, in preparation for various revisions of the job profiles (chapter 6). The survey samples were selected to represent differences in: geographic location; size of community; size of agency; source of funding (public/private); and different types of programs (sheltered workshops, rehabilitation workshops, secondary and postsecondary vocational programs, and work adjustment programs).

3 Prevocational Evaluation and Training

The primary purpose of prevocational training is the acquisition of skills which support and augment subsequent specific vocational skill training. Because the trainee typically lacks many of the basic skills and understandings common to entry-level workers, the prevocational phase of training is particularly important. During this period the trainee can be helped to overcome many of the limitations which may have precluded obtaining job training and employment.

Assessment and training are components of the prevocational preparation process, which overlap and interact throughout the training program. Because the skill level of many trainees may be low, it often is difficult to obtain an accurate picture of the trainee's true capabilities until after the individual has received an extended period of prevocational remediation. Mentally retarded trainees often have difficulty working under pressure and perform poorly on first trials, thus preliminary assessment should be conducted and interpreted with this in mind. The results may not be as meaningful as an evaluation conducted later, at a time when the trainee has begun to demonstrate more clearly true performance potential. For some, prevocational evaluation and training may need to be extended for six months, a year, or longer. During this time it is important that the trainee's program be clearly related to a vocational goal, even though that goal may appear to be far in the future.

A. Selecting the Program Level for the Client

Ideally, all persons seeking admission to a program would be accepted and given instruction and training geared to their developmental level. Because of limitations of program size, stated objectives, and availability of training options, it may be necessary to delay admission or refer some clients to other, more suitable, programs. When sequenced training options are available, each program component should have specific admission requirements to insure that trainees are offered activities which build on existing competencies and suit individual needs. Admission requirements should be based on the trainee's current level of functioning as determined by a multidimensional evaluation. They should also emphasize minimum levels of competency required for participation, and be specific to the program level being considered. They should *not* be based solely on past performance, results of initial screening procedures, or predictions of future potential. General program admission standards must consider legal directives to serve particular client groups, existing wage and labor laws, safety standards, and the availability of trained staff, appropriate facilities, and equipment. Within these limitations, program admission procedures should be as open and as inclusive as possible, and attempt to place a trainee in an optimal learning or work situation.

Methods for assessing the client's capabilities are described on pages 29–33. While the evaluation should be continuous, it also is necessary to have periodic checkpoints for making decisions about the placement of the client. Depending on the results of this assessment, the client should be referred to the most appropriate program level (*see* figure 1). It is possible that some clients, after the initial prevocational evaluation, might be placed immediately in a job. Other recommendations from the initial evaluation might be referral to a vocational program; continuation in the prevocational program, with specific prescription for the types of skills which require further training; or a recommendation that the client not be continued in training or not be considered for employment. Evaluation at subsequent checkpoints would result in moving the client on to the next phase of the program if appropriate, or restructuring the existing phase to provide competence in the client's weak areas.

B. Assessment of the Client's Capabilities

The prevocational program should include an assessment of the client's abilities and limitations by qualified professional staff. This includes the client's medical history and background, intellectual functioning, interests, work adjustment (habits, attitudes, values), and work performance. Methods for making these assessments are grouped into three major categories: counseling, testing, and work evaluation. The prevocational assessment techniques discussed are based on a model developed by Brolin (1976) and described in his book *Vocational Preparation of Retarded Citizens.*

Counseling

Early in the training process, the primary purposes of vocational counseling are to establish rapport, provide the trainee with information, obtain information about the trainee, and begin to establish goals.

As in any counseling situation, trust and understanding are essential to a productive relationship between the counselor and the trainee. In the initial interview and throughout training, it is important that the trainee have a voice in the decision-making process. The level of the discussions and the information presented should be geared to the trainee's ability to understand; for many trainees a very simple explanation will be best.

The counselor should provide the trainee with information about the purpose of the interview, the process of evaluation and training, and the kinds of training programs available. The trainee should be given information about the training facility such as the hours of operation, services available, typical activities, and some idea of what individual trainees do in the program. A tour of the facilities is a concrete way of demonstrating this kind of information.

The counselor also should obtain information from the trainee in order to provide staff with an understanding of the trainee and to assist in formulating plans for vocational training and development. This information should include personal history, family history, developmental and health status, personal and social development, academic experience, vocational experience, and agency contacts. This information can come from the trainee or family members, school and health records, and records from previous agency or training contacts. Observational information also is important and should be gathered in settings other than the counselor's office. Observation of physical appearance, attitudes, personal interactions, and work behavior may give a more accurate picture of the trainee's current functioning level than can be obtained orally or from records of past performance.

Those beginning a vocational training program frequently have limited knowledge of career fields and work requirements. Because of this, the trainee may have unrealistic ideas regarding career options. On the other hand, someone who has a failure-oriented self-image may be unable to recognize personal potential for job success. If possible and appropriate, it is a good idea to involve the trainee's family in determining goals, since the family can serve as a very strong positive or negative influence on training effectiveness. Goal-setting should be introduced early in the training process and continue throughout prevocational and vocational training. Goals should be stated in practical terms with observable criteria for evaluation. The trainee should participate not only in setting goals but should also help decide how success is to be evaluated. Trainee participation in this process is considered essential to the development of a responsible work personality.

Testing

The literature reports considerable interest in the area of standardized assessment of persons with mental retardation; however, there are a number of general problems in testing this population. First, most tests require a minimum level of conceptual ability, receptive and expressive language skills, an average range of personal and social experience, and a language and cultural background similar to a norm group. Trainees frequently do not meet these criteria. In addition, most tests do not take motivation variables into account. This is a particular problem with the mentally retarded person, since a low expectation of success is characteristic and has been shown to affect performance. Tests generally are designed to compare one individual with another cognitively and emotionally. There are few tests which measure functional behavior in a school, community, or on-the-job setting. While tests are successful to some degree in measuring and classifying cognitive and functional differences among individuals, they generally lack prescriptive implications for remedial strategies and individualized program planning. Finally, psychological tests have not been shown to accurately predict the social or vocational potential of mentally retarded persons.

The test most frequently used to measure intelligence is the Wechsler Adult Intelligence Scale, which includes performance scales as well as verbal measures. Tests such as the Peabody Picture Vocabulary Test, the Leiter International Performance Scale, and the Illinois Test of Psycholinguistic Ability appear to avoid some of the problems found with language-dependent tests and are frequently used with mentally retarded persons. Achievement tests appear to offer promise in prescriptive evaluation. But, while good for quick assessment, they frequently lack specificity in defining the way an individual learns and often fail to predict accurately the ability to attain given levels of competence. Group tests are generally unsatisfactory for use with mentally retarded individuals because of problems in reading and comprehension, remembering and following directions, and the low tolerance for frustration often found among this group.

Personality assessment of mentally retarded individuals is in an early stage of development. Typical techniques and procedures of personality assessment are of questionable value with this population due to their limited conceptual ability, experience, and language skills (Gardner, 1974). Interest inventories also appear to have definite limitations for use with mentally retarded persons. Widely used tests such as the Kuder and Strong are very dependent on an average range of verbal abilities and experience.[2] Less verbally dependent inventories appear more promising, but should be checked for word difficulty if any reading is required.

Two major purposes of vocational testing are: 1) to determine a prospective trainee's current level of functioning in work-related activities; and 2) to predict vocational potential in various work areas. Major types of vocational assessment measures include evaluation scales completed by staff working with the trainee, perceptual-motor and manual dexterity tests, and standardized work evaluation techniques. Measures of vocational competence and potential can be useful when the tasks involved are clearly related to actual job tasks. Their predictive value, however, has not been established. Training and tryouts in actual work situations are generally agreed to be the best predictors of work competence.

For mentally retarded persons, training (or at least exposure to concepts and tasks involved in the testing situation) should precede actual testing. The emphasis should remain on testing for functional competencies, with clearly defined criteria for adequate performance. As part of a carefully sequenced, criterion-referenced training program, testing can provide valuable information for individual program planning.

Work Evaluation

Work evaluation—as distinguished from counseling and psychological testing—places the emphasis on real or simulated work. While still relatively undeveloped as a standardized procedure, work evaluation has come to be widely used as a method of assessing the vocational potential of mentally retarded individuals. The actual extent of the use of work samples is difficult to determine. However, it has been estimated that at least 50 percent of the workshops in the United States use this method in one form or another (Olshansky, 1975). While considerable differences of opinion exist regarding the advantages of work evaluation over other types of pretraining assessment (Sakata and Sinick, 1965), evaluation procedures undeniably provide a situation more closely resembling a real-work environment and have more face validity than do other forms of assessing work potential.

Work and job samples Work and job samples involve setting up simulated tasks which approximate the types of activities performed in a general or specific work situation. As individuals perform assigned tasks their skill, speed, perseverance, ability to follow directions, and work habits and attitudes are evaluated. The development of work samples should be done in a systematic manner with provision for validating the predictive ability of the samples used. According to Brolin (1976) work samples (compared with other forms of assessment) offer both advantages and disadvantages. Some advantages are that they are realistic; they can concentrate on simple skills within the reach of the severely disabled; they are less likely to be influenced by insufficient motivation, cultural differences, or anxiety; and generally are acceptable to employers as an indication of capability. The disadvantages of work/job samples include their current lack of predictive validity, the often subjective nature of the evaluation, the lack of standardization, and the expense and time involved in development and administration. Finally, critics claim that work/job samples may be deceptive, in that trainees believe they are actually receiving job training rather than being evaluated for a training program.

Work evaluation systems A number of work evaluation systems have been developed or adapted for use with mentally retarded individuals. These systems provide a standardized battery of work sample tasks in a wide range of vocational categories. Although predeveloped work sample batteries provide a more standardized method of evaluation and preclude the need for staff time in development, they are subject to most of the disadvantages listed previously for individually developed work samples.

Situational assessment This method of work evaluation involves observing a trainee's work behavior as the individual performs regular tasks in the training environment. While it avoids the problems inherent in a testing or obviously evaluative situation, such as a work sample task, it is a rather subjective means of assessing the trainee's work potential and depends heavily on the individual evaluator's observation and interpretation.

The focus of the situational assessment is the general work personality of the trainee rather than specific skill potential. The kinds of behavior typically assessed are: ability to work with others and to follow directions, perseverance, tolerance of frustration, speed, and accuracy. Obviously, the type of work available in the training situation limits opportunities for observing the trainee in a wide range of work situations, and as a result may leave significant gaps in the work evaluation profile. Situational work assessment can indicate general strengths and limitations in the trainee's current work behavior. This information then can be used to develop more specific evaluation procedures and training goals.

Job try-outs As part of the work evaluation process, job try-outs offer specific advantages not found in other types of evaluation. They are conducted in actual business or industry settings and can be very realistic regarding work environment, situational demands upon the trainee, and actual tasks performed. Brolin (1976) emphasizes the distinct advantages of job try-outs as part of the work evaluation process, but also stresses that considerable prevocational instruction and work adjustment training may be necessary prior to evaluation in a real work setting. Job try-outs offer the additional advantage of obtaining employer input to the evaluation process.

Employers should be encouraged to make the work situation as realistic as possible. An overly sympathetic or uninformed employer may not expect the trainee to perform according to established work requirements, or may give the trainee a high performance rating simply because the employer had low expectations regarding the trainee's capabilities.

C. Content of the Prevocational Program

The prevocational program is designed to provide a period of evaluation and remedial training before beginning actual vocational skill training. Prevocational programs may include a number of instructional and evaluative components such as skill areas, counseling and testing, work evaluation, and work adjustment. Obviously, some of these concerns overlap with the beginning of job training. While prevocational training is discussed separately from actual job-skill training, it is an important part of vocational preparation and, for many trainees, extends throughout the vocational training period.

Prevocational Skills

The prevocational curriculum can be organized in a number of ways. Basically, the essential skills fall into three categories: basic academic skills, general living skills, and orientation to occupations and work. Examples of specific skills found in each of these areas are listed in figure 2, "Prevocational Skill Areas." The basic academic skills listed are directly related to work requirements found in the job profiles and are discussed in chapter 4. The other two categories are concerned with skills and behaviors not directly related to vocational adjustment such as housekeeping, using public transportation, using community resources, and understanding the structure and activities of the competitive work environment. While not directly vocational in nature, these skills and understandings are basic to competent adult living and are part of the typical prework experience of most persons.

Whether the training is prevocational or vocational, there are certain principles that apply when working with mentally retarded persons. These principles are basic and must be incorporated into the approach of any training program if the program is to serve its client population.

Trainees are individuals While it is true that mentally retarded people typically share some developmental deficiencies, they differ as much in personality, attitudes, habits, and individual potential as do the nonretarded.

Mentally retarded people want to work The personal independence and self-respect that paid employment offers are valued highly by all workers;

figure 2 PREVOCATIONAL SKILL AREAS

Basic Academic Skills

- Reading (minimum second grade level)
- Writing (simple)
- Simple calculations
  - Counting
  - Adding and subtracting
  - Multiplying and dividing
- Ordering by letter or number
- Measuring length and quantity
  - Making simple conversions of units of measurements

Measuring (*continued*)
  - Telling time
  - Sorting into categories
  - Recognizing and counting money and making change
  - Listening and expressing ideas
  - Problem-solving
  - Making decisions
  - Applying knowledge in new situations (transfer of learning)

General Living Skills

- Housekeeping skills
- Health
  - Daily hygiene and health practices
  - Using health facilities and personnel
  - Taking medicine
- Basic communication skills
  - Asking and answering questions
  - Expressing needs
  - Obtaining information
  - Writing notes
  - Using telephone
- Handling personal funds
  - Budgeting
  - Credit buying
  - Banking and writing checks
- Finding and renting living quarters
- Paying monthly bills
- Shopping
- Using transportation
- Personal relationships
  - Self-awareness
  - Choosing friends
  - Family relationships
  - Dating
  - Sex education and preparation for marriage
- Using Community resources
  - Health agencies
  - Educational facilities
  - Welfare, employment and rehabilitation agencies
  - Recreation facilities

Orientation to Occupations and Work

- Orientation to occupations
  - Merchandising occupations
  - Clerical occupations
  - Service occupations
  - Agricultural occupations
  - Processing and manufacturing occupations
- Making career choices
  - Considering personal interests
  - Understanding capabilities and limitations
  - Exploring career fields
- Seeking and finding a job
  - Filling out applications
  - Interviewing for a job
  - Methods of job seeking
- Introduction to work
  - Work hours
  - Rest and lunch periods
  - Physical layout of work settings
  - Work areas and work stations
  - Eating areas
  - Restrooms and lockers
- Understanding work roles
  - Employee
  - Employer
  - Supervisor
  - Co-workers
  - Shop steward or employee representative
  - Safety regulations and first aid
  - Grievance procedures

those who are retarded offer no exception. They have proven to be dependable, dedicated workers in many areas and frequently express a high degree of job satisfaction.

Mentally retarded persons can learn job skills When training and placement are properly planned and carried out, trainees have proven to be capable of learning to perform a variety of job tasks at a level of competence equal to and, in some cases, surpassing that of nonretarded workers.

Mentally retarded workers are adults As adults, they are to be encouraged and expected to make responsible decisions regarding career fields, job training, and placement. The fact is that a very small percentage of them are so severely limited that they cannot assume this kind of personal responsibility. For the most part, those individuals seeking job training are capable of learning to make informed choices and decisions about training and work, as well as other important areas of their lives. Training programs should be planned to emphasize this aspect of choice and responsibility, and to optimize the trainee's capabilities in these areas.

Prevocational skills are important Persons who are deficient in verbal skills, basic academic skills, decision making and problem solving, paying attention, and working cooperatively with others can benefit from a prevocational program which stresses these and other skills not directly vocational in nature. Some may have had such training prior to seeking vocational training. For those who have not, a prevocational program is especially appropriate.

Train for success Most mentally retarded persons have experienced failure repeatedly. A negative attitude toward learning and a general expectation of failure are common. In a sense, many have been programmed for failure. Training sequences should be planned so as to provide the maximum opportunity for the trainee to do a task successfully. The trainee should be encouraged to demonstrate existing capabilities, which then form the basis for building new skills. Particularly in the initial stages of training, providing positive work experiences is more important than adhering strictly to a training schedule.

Train first, test second Training and assessment should occur concurrently, with the primary focus on training. Mentally retarded persons often perform poorly on first trials and when working under pressure. Typical testing situations should be avoided since they frequently combine unfamiliar or (what appear to the trainee to be) difficult tasks with a time limit or threat of failure. Results in a situation such as this tend to give a falsely negative picture of a trainee's current capabilities and learning potential.

Evaluation can and should be used throughout the training process to reinforce the trainee's self-confidence and as a guide for the trainer in planning and modifying the training program. When combined with background data, and observation of a trainee's performance, attitudes, and motivation, testing information can be used effectively to plan an individualized program. However, initial test scores alone are never sufficient reason to exclude an individual from a training program.

Instruction should be tailored to compensate for learning limitations Training should be specific and organized sequentially so that each task is based on skills already mastered. Tasks should be presented in small increments and employ visual and tactual experiences. Individualized motivational procedures should be used, such as tangible rewards, charts of progress, and praise and encouragement. The concept or skill to be learned should be repeated to the point of overlearning; the trainee should demonstrate mastery; and checks should be made that the learned skill is retained over time.

Work Adjustment

Work adjustment is a process all individuals experience as they enter and continue in the work world. For most persons, it is a process of trial and error as they seek a job, try a number of training options and career fields, and eventually settle into a career area which coincides with their particular interests and capabilities. For the mentally retarded worker, who may lack many of the prework experiences which aid the typical worker in finding and securing a job, work adjustment is a principal part of the vocational preparation and training process.

Work adjustment consists of an ongoing series of planned experiences, designed to help the trainee adapt to a work environment. In training for competitive employment, the necessity for work adjustment should not be underestimated. For those trainees who have not had an adequate range of experiences or who have not acquired necessary prevocational skills, some work adjustment training may be required before a valid prevocational evaluation can be obtained. This is particularly true in the case of persons with serious maladaptive behaviors which appear to preclude other aspects of vocational training.

The initial step in setting up an individualized program is to analyze all available information regarding the trainee's current level of work adjustment. This includes careful consideration of background information, information obtained during intake counseling and testing, staff observations of the trainee's attitude and behavior, and information from the trainee regarding work expectations and preferences.

In developing the work adjustment plan it is not enough to simply state that the trainee is functioning at an inadequate level personally, socially, or vocationally. Rather, it is important to specify, in functional terms, behavior and attitudes needing development or change.

After specifying work adjustment goals as precisely as possible, the counselor and the trainee should discuss how work adjustment progress will be evaluated. For example, if the goal is to be at work on time, how will successful accomplishment be measured? If the facility uses a time clock, it might be agreed that the trainee and the counselor will check the times at the end of each week and chart the results. This provides a simple and meaningful way of checking progress. In addition, it allows the trainee to receive recognition in the form of counselor approval for coming to work on time. Each work adjustment goal should be accompanied by an agreed upon evaluation procedure.

Methods used to implement the work adjustment program will necessarily depend upon staff size and capability. Four methods are discussed here: counseling, formal instruction, situational work experience, and planned behavior modification. Three of these were discussed previously as evaluation methods. The fact that these techniques serve two purposes illustrates the interrelated nature of evaluation and training.

As a method of work adjustment training, counseling should focus on developing the trainee's self-awareness and communication skills. In individual or group counseling sessions, the trainee can be provided the opportunity to discuss fears and concerns regarding the vocational program and other factors which might affect personal and vocational development. The trainee should be encouraged to participate actively. Dealing with the trainee's expressed concerns, rather than presenting issues which the counselor sees as problems, will be more likely to elicit attention and cooperation.

Formal classroom instruction should be planned in accordance with what is known about the general learning abilities and characteristics of mentally retarded individuals. Films and slides, simple charts, and pictures can help the trainee develop an understanding of punctuality, cooperation, neat appearance, consistent work performance, and other components of the work adjustment curriculum. Field trips to business and industrial settings combined with classroom discussions, bulletin board displays, and other visual aids enhance the individual's awareness and understanding of the community and actual job setting.

Situational work experience provides the trainee with realistic work in the training facility or at a community job-site with actual employers. No effort is made to provide skill training during this period. The focus is on diagnosing problems and changing inappropriate behaviors. A work situation is arranged in which aspects of the work environment are controlled, such as type of work (light, heavy, fast-paced, repetitious), interpersonal demands (needs for communication and teamwork, degree of supervision), and rewards (praise, pay, change in assignment or status).

The use of behavior modification techniques to bring about planned and systematic changes in behavior has received considerable attention in work with mentally retarded persons.[1] Behavior modification is based on the idea that most behaviors are learned, and continue because they are reinforced. In work adjustment programs the focus is on changing behaviors that interfere with work or work-related activities. Basically, the approach is to define the behavior needing modification in terms of observable actions on the part of the trainee and determine how frequently the behavior occurs (Weld, 1971). A precise statement then is made of the new behavior to be established. Next, the instructor structures a situation that will elicit the desired behavior and plans reinforcement that will be administered each time the desired behavior occurs. The behavior change program should be discussed with the client to assure understanding of the program and to gain the trainee's cooperation. Objections to using behavior modification techniques are frequently based on charges that they require too much staff time and training to conduct effectively and that they are impersonal and dehumanizing. It is often thought, however, that if such techniques enable mentally retarded persons, who would otherwise remain idle, to live in a more normal environment, participate in social situations, and engage in daily activities, then the end result is humane and the technique and staff effort worthwhile.

Evaluation of the prevocational training program should be continual, with feedback given to both the training staff and the trainee. In addition, the results of the evaluation should be used as a basis for program review and modification. The prevocational program extends into vocational training; therefore, results of evaluation activities during this period will have an impact on the overall vocational training program.

Notes

1. A thorough discussion of using behavior modification with mentally retarded persons can be found in William I. Gardner, *Behavior modification in mental retardation: The education and rehabilitation of the mentally retarded adolescent and adult* (Chicago: Oldine, 1971).

2. Kuder Occupational Interest Survey and the Strong-Campbell Vocational Blank.

4 Vocational Training

The core of the rehabilitation process is training, which brings together the two main areas of consideration—the client's capabilities and the job requirements. The objectives of the training activities discussed here are to develop the work skills and capabilities of the client in preparation for job placement. This section offers suggestions for specific content and training methods related to the jobs included elsewhere in this handbook. The organization of the materials is based on a progression from general basic skills to those that are quite specific to actual jobs. The three levels of skills are: basic, core, and specific. Work adjustment training permeates all these skill levels and probably begins even before the client is placed in a prevocational training program. (Work adjustment training is discussed in chapter 3.)

A. Definition and Overview

In this book, vocational training refers to the preparation of the mentally retarded client for employment. The client may be referred to vocational training as a result of the prevocational evaluation described in chapter 3. The outcome of this evaluation might be immediate placement in a job, referral to a vocational program, continuation in the prevocational program, or a recommendation for no further training or employment (see figure 1).

Vocational training may occur in public secondary schools, postsecondary schools, rehabilitation centers, sheltered workshops, and in the actual job setting. Brolin (1976) recommends that the bulk of vocational training be conducted in business and industry, although he concedes that it should be *initiated* in educational, institutional, or rehabilitation settings.

The principles of training and some of the methods found to be useful have been discussed in chapter 3. To recapitulate, the important steps in vocational training are:

1. Evaluation of the client's level of proficiency in the skills that will be required by the job group
2. Mutual goal-setting by the client, the counselor, and the instructor
3. Mutual planning of a flexible, individualized training program by the client, the counselor, and the instructor
4. Ongoing evaluation of the client's progress toward meeting goals, including self-evaluation
5. Modification of the training plan, as indicated by the evaluation
6. Final performance evaluation in terms of employment placement

There are certain characteristics of the mentally retarded individual that must be considered in planning methods of teaching. These include: a limited ability to transfer learning or to generalize from one activity to another, difficulty in attending to stimuli, a lack of self-confidence, and a tendency to perform poorly under pressure. The content and methods of teaching should be adapted to address these problems. Reinforcement of the concepts and specific teaching for "extending" the concepts should be planned carefully (*see* examples in Training in Core Skills, pages 53–61).

One of the most important aspects of the training situation is to make it as much like the actual work environment as possible. The training should occur in the actual work setting, but this is often not feasible. At a very basic level in school settings, realism can be achieved by extensive use of audio-visual materials rather than by demonstration and lectures. Depending on resources, simulation of a work environment in the training setting can vary from setting up one simulated work station to simulating an entire business. In selecting the work experiences appropriate to the client's capability, the counselor might choose to place the client in available transitional work experiences leading to full employment in the community, rather than to bring a simulated situation into the training facility. One possibility is for the training facility to assume responsibility for one entire operation of a business in the community, at that business's facility. This was successfully done by Marvin Rosen of the Elwyn Institute, Elwyn, Pennsylvania. The training facility would provide its own staff as supervisors and rotate trainees through the various positions.

The skills to be taught in the vocational training program may include any of the basic and core skills described later in this chapter, as well as any work adjustment skills described in chapter 3, which are appropriate to the clients in the specific training program. The suggested steps for deriving specific skills to be taught are:

1. Identify core job activity requirements from the job profiles, that is, those that are found in most of the jobs available in the community. If relevant profiles do not exist, develop them as necessary, using those in this handbook as a model.
2. Group the core requirements by training content. This involves sorting out the selected core requirements into a number of logical work segments which might possess training unity. For example, sweeping, dusting, and other similar cleaning activities constitute one group. Wrapping packages, typing, envelope stuffing, and other kinds of mailing or clerical activities make up another. Grouping serves to identify the types of work which must be created or obtained for providing training experience.
3. Develop training sequences within activity groups. Within each of the training units identified above, the order of difficulty and complexity of the activities should be determined. Trying out some of the activities with trainees may be an effective way to determine the degree of difficulty. Once such approximate sequences are established, these sequences suggest the order in which training may proceed, that is, from the least difficult to the more difficult in each unit.
4. Select training content. Some types of training units can be worked into the program through the creation of work on the training facility premises, such as cleaning, painting, refinishing, or other renovation activities. Others can be added through the development of crafts and handwork production activities. In some situations, subcontracts may be obtained, such as in mailing activities or assembling of a variety of products. Whatever the work sources, the content should be selected insofar as is economically possible to provide a context for carrying out the identified training sequences.
5. Variety in training content should be provided. The training program should not become specialized in a single type of activity, unless it is for predictably short periods of time, essential for continued existence of the program. The content of the program should be acceptable to the clients. Distasteful tasks should be introduced only when it is essential to learning the skill, and then only after the client has had some experience with more rewarding aspects.
6. Other general guidelines suggested for selection of training content include: 1) keeping the content relevant to the core activity requirements, thus enhancing direct transfer to performance of related job activities; 2) organizing the content into simple units that can be learned thoroughly before going on to more complex tasks; and 3) stressing the reality and pressure of work situations, using real or simulated work settings.

7. Sequence the presentation of the content. Find, within the available training content, a variety of segments to represent each of several possible stages of training. Early stages of training should provide basic, common and simple activities. The degree of difficulty of the activities should be increased gradually as the client demonstrates initial success at the basic level. The program also should provide for means to help the client learn to transfer abilities to new areas and to generalize, within limits.
8. Evaluate and update the work skills training program. Modifications may be necessary as the nature of the available job opportunities changes or as dictated by the success record of clients in jobs. While program revision is important, a sufficient time period should be allowed for adequate evaluation before change is instituted.

B. Training in Basic Skills

Basic skills refers to fundamental academic and work-related skills that have a direct bearing on occupational and social adjustment. Those mentioned here—reading signs and simple forms, making change, telling time, and tying knots—are considered relevant, although not necessarily essential, to all jobs listed in this book.

Training in basic skills may be provided in a public school program, a prevocational workshop, or a regular vocational training program which emphasizes total job readiness. Wherever basic skills are acquired, it is important that they be practiced extensively in simulated or actual work situations.

The Basic Skills Chart in figure 3 lists 20 basic skills identified as being common to all job categories covered in the *Handbook*. No attempt is made to provide detailed suggestions for a basic skills curriculum. However, the chart defines each skill and provides examples of practical applications for each. Although the skills listed, such as reading and counting, are basic to all jobs, the trainer may wish to gear their application to a particular work situation. For example, in learning to count, one trainee might be given exercises involving stacking boxes in groups of a given number; another might be more motivated if asked to clean and count used bricks.

The skills have not been listed in any specific order of complexity or importance since they should all be considered for inclusion in a job readiness or job training program. A trainee's inability to master particular basic skills does not mean that the individual will be unable to profit from a job training program. However, it would indicate that an extended period of basic skills training may be required, or that more specific job training should be chosen in a field which does not require competence in those skills that give the trainee greatest difficulty.

figure 3 BASIC SKILLS CHART

Basic Skill	Application of Basic Skill
1. *Read* Ability to read at second grade level. Although many jobs can be performed with no reading at all, recognition of common printed information and the ability to sound words out phonetically is very useful in any work situation.	Acquire a written survival vocabulary: signs on buildings and roads, warning signs and labels Build a reading vocabulary of key words: employees, washrooms, locker, lunchroom, drill press, social security Read simple instructions: "Remove lid," "Open this end," "Refrigerate after opening"
2. *Write* Ability to print alphabet and numbers to 100 and to copy simple words, numbers, and sentences.	Sign name, print address and phone number Fill out standard forms: receipts, credit card slips, checks, job applications Take telephone messages
3. *Count and Record Numbers* Ability to count items, arrange items in groups of a given number and record counts on standard form.	Count stock, record inventory Count copies of printed materials for distribution Count dishes, silver, knives Count tools and equipment Count prepared food items for distribution
4. *Perform Simple Calculations* Ability to add and subtract whole numbers and decimal fractions. Multiply and divide whole numbers.	Inventory stock Calculate postage Add or subtract sums of money Calculate amount of pay from hourly rate Add and convert weights and measures Calculate sales tax and add to purchase price
5. *Count Money, Make Change* Ability to recognize different coins and bills, combine coins and bills for various amounts, and make change.	Sell tickets, merchandise Collect money on newspaper route Manage personal funds, make purchases Count pay, understand deductions

figure 3 *(cont'd)*

Basic Skill	Application of Basic Skill
6. *Sort by Category* Ability to recognize and order items by size, shape, color, or function; to recognize concepts "bigger than" or "smaller than"; "rough" or "smooth."	Sort mail, library materials, stock items Organize kitchen, carpentry or mechanical tools in storage drawers or bins Sort produce Sort parts for assembly
7. *Repeat a Visual Pattern* Ability to accurately reproduce a pattern of colors, sizes, or shapes: a blue block on a red block on a yellow block, repeated five times.	String beads according to predetermined number and color pattern Assemble transformers Perform mechanical assembly, such as small toys
8. *Arrange in Order* Ability to alphabetize or to order in numerical sequence.	Sort papers into stacks or bins labeled with letters or numbers File or shelve by first letter or number Collate pages in a series
9. *Locate or Identify by Number, Word, or Symbol* Ability to recognize and match symbols. Ability to identify items necessary to the performance of a task and collect them for use.	Assemble cleaning or gardening supplies Assemble ingredients and utensils for preparing a recipe Locate seat in theatre or auditorium Locate item, such as clothing, by matching information on receipt
10. *Communicate Verbally* Ability to express observations and needs. Ability to ask and answer questions.	Run errands Deliver verbal messages Respond appropriately to requests of customers, patrons, supervisor
11. *Use Telephone* Ability to dial a number from memory or notation. Knowledge of correct phone answering procedures, telephone etiquette. Ability to conduct short information-gathering conversation.	Dial numbers as required Answer phone and record messages in store or office setting Communicate by phone with other departments or businesses

figure 3 *(cont'd)*

Basic Skill	**Application of Basic Skill**
12. *Write Simple Messages* Ability to write standardized messages and to initiate simple written information requests or responses.	Take telephone orders or messages as dictated Complete standard forms with information requested Prepare supply list Communicate by written note to other departments and employees
13. *Tell Time* Ability to read clock face or digital display accurately and to understand units of time measurement (second, minute, hour, day).	Get to work on time Use time clock to record hours worked Understand lunch and break periods Maintain delivery or route schedule
14. *Measure* Familiarity with units of linear measure and use of ruler, yardstick, tape measure. Familiarity with measures of weight and with ordinary postage scale or household scale. Familiarity with units of volume and with common measuring devices such as cup, teaspoon, tablespoon, fluid ounce measure.	Perform simple measuring and weighing in carpentry, sewing, cooking Use grocery store scale Use postal scales
15. *Read Dials, Gauges, Meters* Ability to recognize the numbers on the instruments; awareness of meaning of unnumbered calibration marks.	Read oven and meat thermometers in cooking Read mercury medical thermometer Use ammeter, fluid level gauge, air pressure gauge, and similar equipment in auto maintenance work
16. *Combine Liquids and/or Dry Materials* Ability to mix solutions or dry substances, using appropriate methods and containers.	Mix cleaning and disinfectant solutions Prepare simple food and beverage recipes Mix garden chemicals Prepare animal feeds
17. *Manipulate Small Objects* Ability to use the fingers with dexterity to handle, pick up, turn, or otherwise manipulate small items.	Thread buttons, nuts, washers, etc., for packaging Manipulate fasteners on clothing Finger tighten a small nut

figure 3 *(cont'd)*

Basic Skill	Application of Basic Skill
18. *Trace* Ability to follow a simple outline through transparent paper with a pencil. Ability to use a stencil.	Stencil designs on products Make simple signs
19. *Tie with String or Rope* Ability to wrap with the tying material and to securely fashion a knot.	Prepare items for shipping or mailing Bundle and tie supplies Secure equipment or supplies to vehicle
20. *Secure with Tape* Ability to tie up or bind with tape.	Prepare items for shipping or mailing Wrap packages

C. Training in Core Skills

The designation, core skills, refers to skills generally applicable to all jobs in a particular job group, such as clerical occupations or processing and manufacturing occupations. Training at this level concentrates on those skills specific to the job group rather than to a specific job. Although core skills are considered to be more complex than basic skills, the dividing line is flexible. For instance, a basic skill such as "folding" refers to making a neat crease in a piece of paper or material. Expanded to a core skill, the folding might be done according to much more precise specifications, such as folding linens for storage or folding inserts for mailing.

The objective of core-skill training is to develop skills that are common to a variety of jobs within the community. For example, lifting and carrying heavy objects will be relevant to a number of job groups. In chapter 6, "Lift and Carry" is found in the master profiles for every one of the occupational groups. Other core skills will be applicable to only one job group but will be relevant to more than one job within the group. An example of this is Core Skill 18, "Use Standard Office Supplies," which is appropriate for most of the jobs in job group B, Office Occupations.

Thirty-six core skills were identified by analyzing the lists of job activities in the job profiles (chapter 6). Activities that tended to occur repeatedly in many of the jobs were selected, as well as *critical* activities that were singled out in the job profiles as being hazardous or in some other way crucial to the performance of the job. These 36 core skills are presented in figure 4 along with examples of practical applications.

While core-skill training can be given in any training setting, it is particularly adaptable to work adjustment centers. Examples of five training outlines are given following figure 4: folding, handling dangerous substances (liquids), lifting and carrying, locating streets and addresses, and simple indoor cleaning.

figure 4 CORE SKILLS CHART

Core Skill	Application of Core Skill
1. *Fold* Ability to crease and arrange paper, cloth, or other materials in a prescribed manner.	Fold newspapers Fold linens, clothing Fold printed material
2. *Bundle* Ability to gather together a number of things, usually all of the same kind, and tie or bind them.	Bundle laundry or dry cleaning to place in bins Bundle hides for storage Bundle produce for shipping Bundle tree boughs for disposal
3. *Assemble* Ability to put items together in a prescribed pattern or order.	Arrange a food tray Perform simple mechanical assembly Set a table Collate printed materials Collect printed materials for mailing
4. *Fasten* Ability to use glue, pins, tape, nails, screws, staples, clips or seals to join two or more objects together.	Perform simple carpentry Wrap packages Fasten paper Pin fabric together for sewing
5. *Package and Wrap* Ability to securely and neatly wrap and tie packages with paper, tape, string, or rope.	Wrap cartons for shipping or mailing Gift wrap Package manufactured products for distribution
6. *Cut* Ability to safely use scissors, paper cutter, knife, or saw to divide into pieces.	Cut string or paper for wrapping parcels Slice fruits or vegetables Cut meat, sandwiches, and so on Perform simple carpentry tasks Cut agricultural products during harvest

figure 4 *(cont'd)*

Core Skill	Application of Core Skill
7. *Lift and Carry* Ability to pick things up from one location and move them to another, using hands if object has a handle, or using an arm carry if there is no handle. Objects may be picked up from varying heights (floor, waist-level shelf, high shelf).	Lift and carry box or crate to place on delivery truck Lift and carry pail of water Lift and carry child Handle baggage
8. *Load and Unload* Ability to safely place items in a designated place and remove them from it.	Handle merchandise Load and unload delivery trucks Load and unload food tray carts Tend conveyors
9. *Transport* Ability to move loads from one place to another by means of conveyances such as handtrucks, carts, dollies, forklifts, or other wheeled apparatus.	Load and unload delivery trucks Stack lumber in lumberyard Deliver food trays to patients on food cart Transport soiled dishes to dishwasher in restaurant Transport patient in wheelchair
10. *Stack and Shelve* Ability to place items in an orderly arrangement for storage or display.	Store wholesale or retail merchandise in warehouse Arrange attractive retail displays Maintain orderly supply or tool cabinet
11. *Pack or Crate* Ability to carefully place items in box or crate for movement or shipment, so they will not be damaged in transit. This may include perishable or fragile items requiring special care.	Package agricultural products for shipment Pack glass or other fragile merchandise for delivery to customer Pack or crate manufactured products for shipment
12. *Open and Unpack* Ability to open various kinds of cartons and other containers. Care in handling delicate or breakable items.	Uncrate produce Open boxes of supplies and equipment Unpack retail merchandise

figure 4 *(cont'd)*

Core Skill	**Application of Core Skill**
13. *Stamp and Label* Ability to mark boxes or separate items with price or other identifying information. Use stamp, stencil, printed labels, or string tags.	Price stamp merchandise Rubber stamp papers or forms Stamp designs on products Label shipping containers Stencil identification on equipment
14. *Receive and Transmit Messages* Ability to understand verbal messages, whether given in person or by telephone; to take notes if necessary; and to transmit the message in a timely and accurate manner (either orally or in a written form).	Take telephone messages in a home or office Relay customer request to sales personnel in retail store Relay patient request to nurse Transmit verbal messages as messenger in an office
15. *Run Errands* Ability to pick up and deliver messages and items and report to supervisor about outcome of errand.	Deliver copy in newspaper office Deliver messages and items in general office setting Deliver outside for retail business
16. *Find Streets and Addresses* Ability to recall travel routes to and from specific streets and buildings. Knowledge of general principles of street layout and numbering, such as: street name signs at intersections, all the addresses in one block begin with the same number and are arranged numerically.	Run errands Deliver messages or merchandise Locate potential employers Get to work
17. *Type* Ability to type by touch on manual or electric typewriter.	Perform typing tasks in an office Operate addressing machine Operate keypunch machine
18. *Use Standard Office Supplies* Ability to use stapler, staple remover, paper punch, rubber stamp, scissors, ruler, glue, paper clips, tape, erasers, correction tape or fluid, carbon paper.	Perform general office work Staple documents Prepare package for mailing Stamp books with library identification

figure 4 *(cont'd)*

Core Skill	Application of Core Skill
19. *Stuff Envelopes* Ability to fold, insert, stuff, and seal envelopes for mailing.	Assist in promotional mailings Mail voter information Prepare bulk mail Perform general office work
20. *Affix Postage* Ability to place correct amount of postage on outgoing mail. This may include weighing of the mail and calculating correct postage for different classes of mail.	Operate postage meter in office Perform general office work Assist in company mail room Assist in bulk mail preparation
21. *Use Cash Register, Adding Machine, or Calculator* Ability to operate cash register and place money correctly in drawer. Ability to perform basic operations on adding machine or calculator.	Sell tickets at amusement park Calculate postage Add inventory sheets
22. *Mix and Blend Ingredients* Ability to use correct methods and containers for mixing liquids, solids, and combinations and blend them to desired consistency.	Mix ingredients in cooking Mix beverages
23. *Use Heat and Heating Units* Ability to safely operate gas or electric stove, oven, clothes dryer, sterilizer. Proper handling of hot pans, irons, matches.	Cook Heat water Machine dry clothes Iron clothes and linens
24. *Perform Indoor Cleaning* Ability to use mop, broom, dustpan, cloths, sponges and pail for general cleaning. Understanding of cleaning methods used in kitchens, bathrooms, and other living areas. Some familiarity with electric vacuum cleaner, scrubber, and waxer.	Wash windows, walls, woodwork Mop kitchen, bathroom, hallway Clean bathroom fixtures Vacuum floors and rugs Develop general awareness of cleanliness and order

figure 4 *(cont'd)*

Core Skill	Application of Core Skill
25. *Make Beds* Ability to select linens and place sheets, blankets, spreads, and pil-low-cases neatly on bed.	Prepare room in hotel, motel, or hospital Make beds in private home Personal living skills in own home
26. *Dress and Undress Another Person* Ability to assist another, to whatever degree necessary, in getting dressed and undressed. Correct and considerate handling of infant, elderly or infirm person.	Assist nursing staff in caring for patients Assist in child care center Act as personal companion/assistant to elderly or handicapped person
27. *Set and Clear Tables* Ability to select appropriate dishes, silver, and linens and place in correct order on table. Ability to remove soiled items from table and stack for removal to kitchen.	Tend tables in dining area of restaurant Set table in private home Personal living skills
28. *Use Common Kitchen Utensils* Ability to use common kitchen utensils such as knife, ladle, grater, strainer, can opener, cutting board, funnel, spatula, stirring spoon, and so on.	Assist in private or commercial kitchen Work in fast food outlet, salad bar, etc. Make and wrap sandwiches Personal living skills
29. *Perform Kitchen Cleanup* Ability to collect, scrape, and rinse soiled dishes and cooking utensils; wash or place in dishwasher; dispose of waste; scrub equipment; sweep and scrub kitchen floors and walls.	Perform helper tasks in commercial or private kitchen Personal living skills
30. *Handle Dangerous Substances* Ability to safely pour, mix, use, and dispose of dangerous substances. Knowledge of special precautions and equipment (gloves, masks, safety-sealed containers) used in handling such substances.	Mix cleaning solutions Stir and pour hot mixtures Handle toxic or caustic substances in manufacturing or cleaning Dispose of toxic wastes

figure 4 *(cont'd)*

Core Skill	Application of Core Skill
31. *Hand Stitch* Ability to use needle and thread to do simple stitching.	Sew on buttons and fasteners Baste straight edges Mend ripped seams and tears Do decorative stitching
32. *Iron* Ability to use hand iron to press wrinkles from cloth. Set up ironing board, prepare items for pressing, operate iron with regard to personal safety and protection of items ironed.	Press linens in home or in hotel or hospital laundry Press altered garments in tailor shop Press pattern pieces or garment parts for sewing
33. *Use Hand Tools* Ability to hammer nails, set and insert screws, saw boards safely, drill holes, ream holes, plane, sand, and staple, using the appropriate hand tools.	Refinish furniture Punch paper, leather, wood Assist maintenance staff in repairs Perform simple carpentry such as making packing crates, constructing shelves, building forms for cement, erecting scaffolds
34. *Dig and Shovel* Ability to use shovel, spade, or hoe to turn the soil or make holes or ditches.	Prepare planting beds Mulch Dig trenches or foundations Mix cement, plaster, sand, or gravel Load and unload sand, topsoil, or gravel from truck
35. *Use Garden Tools* Ability to select and use appropriate tools for gardening tasks. Tools include shovels, rake, hand tools, garden hoe, wheelbarrow, sprinkler, mower, edger.	Clean lawns and flower beds Prepare planting beds Mulch Perform routine lawn maintenance
36. *Handle Live Animals and Fish* Ability to safely move and handle live animals and fish (cattle, sheep, pigs, chickens, household pets, small wild animals).	Move chickens from one coop to another Help treat injured small animals Herd livestock Transfer fish from one tank to another Groom and exercise dogs

Examples of Core Skill Training Outlines

The core-skill training outlines that follow are intended to illustrate an approach to a more specific level of training through generalizations. The generalization must be established clearly and explicitly.

Assuming that new trainees will have had a minimum of previous skill training, the program should provide a number of relatively basic, common, and simple activities in which a new trainee can begin to develop and achieve initial success. In choosing the first experiences, the teacher must evaluate the trainee's capabilities. For example, in training for "sorting," the trainee should be able to discriminate on the basis of the parameters to be used in the learning task (color, thicknesses, widths, diameters, lengths, or shapes). If the sorting task involves very small items, the trainee also must have sufficient digital dexterity to be able to handle them.

After the trainee has achieved success in these initial simple activities, the teacher can present progressively more complex activities until ultimate levels of skill proficiency can be demonstrated. Not only should the program provide this progression from simple to complex, but it should also provide the means for helping the trainee to use developed skills in new contexts, to transfer to slightly different activities, and to generalize within specifiable limits. The ability to generalize is, in itself, important to assess in the trainee and to develop if possible. Therefore, the training program should be organized so that trainees have a maximum opportunity to generalize from concepts.

Core Skill 1: Folding

The Generalization or Concept

Folding is common to many tasks, such as folding paper for stuffing into envelopes, folding linen or clothing, folding boxes for assembly, folding wrapping paper in wrapping packages, and folding nets. In each case, the material is folded to the size and shape determined by storage, assembly, or use needs. For example, the size of the envelope determines the direction and number of folds, but the part of the paper that should appear when the envelope is opened may be the prime consideration. Linen is stored on a shelf with the folded edge out for easy grasping; the size of the folded linen depends on the space allocated for it on the shelf. However, the prime determiner of the direction of fold and the ultimate shape of the folded linen may be the way the linen is to be used—for example, the mechanics involved in opening a sheet and placing it on a bed.

Presenting the Concept

Teach the trainee to fold a piece of paper along indicated lines. Show how to measure before making the final crease. Stress precision and neatness. Show how to smooth out the fold, pressing down with fingers.

Show how the folded paper fits into the envelope. Open the folded paper and show how the wrong folding results in the paper not fitting.

Demonstrate folding a small piece of linen—a towel, for example. Show how the towel fits in the space allocated on a shelf and how the folded edge is placed out, making it easy to grasp when several towels are stacked upon each other. Show how difficult it is to separate towels when the open edges face the edge of the shelf. Unfold towel, showing how unfolding only one fold will allow the towel to be hung neatly on bar without having to refold it to fit.

Enhance motivation by helping the trainee understand the merits of folding, for example, "why we fold."

Reinforcing the Concept

Let the trainee practice first on paper and linen that have guidelines, then build up to folding without them.

Extending the Concept

Give practice in folding different sizes of paper; different types of linen; boxes for assembly; making newspaper waste containers; and making paper airplanes, boats, and hats.

Show how a tri-fold leaflet might be folded differently than the same size business letter, so that the first fold presents the introductory information.

Give practice in folding and storing linen.

Core Skill 2: Handling Dangerous Substances (Liquids)

The Generalization or Concept

Potentially dangerous liquids may be handled when using cleaning solutions or disinfectants; in bathing patients; in serving or preparing hot liquids; in unloading or storing supplies in retail stores, beauty shops, and veterinarian/pet shops; and in mixing solutions in beauty shops. Concepts to be stressed include pouring, measuring, mixing, carrying, and using various solutions with accuracy and safety.

Presenting the Concept

Using water or some other safe liquid, demonstrate and give practice in pouring, measuring, and mixing without spilling and with accuracy. Use spoon measures, ounce measures, cups, and fractions of cups. Pour from containers of different sizes so that both one-handed and two-handed pouring are necessary. Show how to pour on side away from label to prevent soiling of label. Show how to wipe lip of container after pouring to prevent dripping.

Show how to carry containers to avoid spilling, slipping, and breaking. This might include carrying heavy containers of hot coffee, lifting large containers of purified water onto dispenser, or lifting down various solutions in pint or quart size bottles from a shelf.

Stress the importance of testing temperature of liquid before using it on self or others. Show how to test by feeling with finger, inside of forearm, elbow, and thermometer.

Emphasize that nothing should be tested by taste.

Introduce and educate trainees regarding poison labels. Discuss some common substances that might be toxic such as chlorine, drain uncloggers, bleaches, ammonia, alcohol, disinfectants, cleaning solutions, and medicines.

Emphasize the importance of mixing according to directions. For example, too much ammonia in the window-washing water could cause choking or eye irritation. Help the trainee learn to read simple directions, if capable; otherwise encourage asking for help in mixing.

Explain that some solutions must be stored in a certain way to prevent deterioration, possible leakage, or breakage; for example, some bleaches must be kept in brown bottles. Other substances such as cleaning solutions in aerosol cans must be kept in a cool place, away from flames.

Reinforcing the Concept

Let the trainee progress from using water to using the real solution applicable to a specific job. Help the trainee learn to read specific directions on labels, or to memorize the directions for mixing and use of each specific solution, or to ask for help.

Set up situations in which breakage or spillage is imminent and help trainee decide what actions to take to prevent the danger from actually occurring.

Set up situations to test the trainee's accuracy in identifying and choosing the correct solution from a collection of similar looking bottles.

Set up situations to test accuracy in measuring, mixing, and following prescribed directions.

Set up situations which require special effort to avoid injuring someone else, for example, taking a detour to avoid spilling coffee on someone.

Extending the Concept

Set up a simulated breakage situation and allow the trainee to decide how best to clean up the spilled liquid and shattered glass to avoid injury to self and others.

Allow the trainee to learn to generalize. For example, if household bleach used for cleaning in the beauty shop is kept in a brown or opaque container, how should we store leftover hair bleach that we want to put in a smaller container?

Core Skill 3: Lifting and Carrying

The Generalization or Concept

There are basic rules for movement when the body is at work—stooping, carrying, lifting, or pushing. If these rules are followed, there will be less fatigue and more safety:

- Keep body in balance.
  - Keep feet under pelvis and pelvis under trunk.
  - Balance is best maintained when body parts are centered over base (feet) and kept close to body.
  - If balance is threatened, spreading base will increase stability.
- External loads become part of body.
  - Keep weights close to body and over base of support.
  - Adjust new weight (body and load) as a single weight to new center of gravity without throwing body out of line to counterbalance.
- Move an object the most efficient way.
  - Most effective if moving force is applied directly through center of gravity of object in the direction in which it is to be moved.
- Center of gravity of body is approximately at level of hips.
  - Lead with thighs, not head.
  - Large movements should come from hips, not waist.
- Body should be relatively relaxed.
  - Joints should have the freedom to give with sudden motion; knees should be relaxed, not tense.

Presenting the Concept

The concepts in this case are best presented by combined demonstration and explanation proceeding from the simple (and least physically taxing) to the more complex examples of the use of good body mechanics. These demonstrations can be handled in several ways. The more formal approach would be to bring the trainees together and indicate that learning proper ways to bend, lift, and carry will be important to them in many jobs by contributing to their own safety and well-being. After a demonstration by the teacher calling specific attention to each crucial movement, the trainees may take their turns. Appropriate demonstrations are:

Picking up a small wastebasket from a standing position
- Hold body fairly erect, start down from the hips, bending at the knees.
- Separate feet, putting one a little forward.
- Move close enough to the basket so that it can be reached easily.
- Do not go down further than necessary to reach basket easily (use quarter, half, or three-quarter squat for lifting lighter objects).
- Keep knee nearest the basket out of the way by stepping back on that foot and forward on the foot farthest from the basket.
- Put arms around or under basket.
- Bring basket up and in toward body before beginning to rise.
- Extend ankle, knee, and hip joints to raise body.

Carrying the basket
- Adjust weight closer to center of gravity of body.
- Hold basket slightly down toward waist.
- Keeping trunk and pelvis aligned, let weight slip back to heels.

Picking up heavy objects from the floor from a standing position (for example, a heavy box)
- Give the body (stance) a wide base.
- Maximum lift comes from legs and hips (not from arms and back), so legs and trunk must be well balanced.
- Knees should be flexed.

Remaining in the squatting position to pick up small objects from the floor
- Go down as already indicated (hips go down with body, and so on).
- If full squat is to be held, additional support can come from sitting on heel of bent foot.
- Fatigue can be lessened by occasional shifts to kneeling position, by raising body a few inches and using entire lower leg for support.

Lifting and carrying an object with a handle (for example, a suitcase)
- Lower body so that hand reaches handle easily.
- Lift body by extending ankle, knee, hip joint.
- Keep object close to body.

Balance body by shifting weight slightly, sideward from base (not from waist).
If possible, carry two objects, one in each hand, for balance.
If one heavy object is carried away from body, extend other arm for balance.

Placing a heavy object on a high shelf
Keep feet apart with one foot in front of the other.
As object is raised to waist, body weight adjusts to balance body.
Above waist, weight settles gradually on back foot, hips stay under trunk, and back stays fairly straight.
When putting object on shelf, move from hips, not waist, by moving whole trunk forward from hips and putting weight on front foot.

Lifting a heavy object from a high shelf
Stand close enough to shelf to reach easily but not so close that body is under shelf.
Spread feet.
As arms raise forward, shift weight to back foot.
Shift body to front as the object is grasped.
As object is pulled forward, shift weight to back foot and lower object easily.
If standing on a chair or ladder, remember to move body down through hips and then step down.

Reinforcing the Concept

Any wrong motion should be corrected quickly. Reinforcement should be continued for as long a period as the trainee's interest is held. After this, consistent reinforcement should be given whenever trainees are performing any "moving" activities in the classroom or workshop, until proper sequence of movements is overlearned.

Extending the Concept

As the trainee moves into actual job assignments in the workshop training or job situation, extend the general concepts shown in a few specific situations to an ever-increasing variety of situations. For example, lifting a suitcase (which has been demonstrated) is much the same as lifting a pail full of water, because both have handles.

If the trainee is observed using poor body mechanics in moving objects, the activity should be stopped and the proper method should be demonstrated. If it is appropriate, other trainees could be involved in this impromptu demonstration, as a further means of extending the concept.

Core Skill 4: Locating Streets and Addresses

The Generalization or Concept

House or building addresses are arranged numerically (from small to large numbers). One side of the street will be odd numbers, the other side even numbers. Streets are labeled with signs at the intersections. In some communities there is an order to the street naming; for example, all the street names in a certain section may be names of trees.

Presenting the Concept

A model street might be set up to aid in explanation and discussion of addresses. Trainees could be given practice in deducing where number 115 is if the location of 114 is known.

A model of the neighborhood (or relevant communities) could be set up to show street signs at intersections and to teach the names of major streets.

Reinforcing the Concept

On a field trip trainees could learn street names, examine block numbers, and check addresses on each side of the street.

Problems could be devised in the classroom. Addresses within a several block area could be selected and trainees might take turns telling the group how these addresses can be located. If possible, the group should check the accuracy by actually walking to each address.

Extending the Concept

In either the classroom or a real job situation, practice can be provided in actual extended work-related activities such as: delivering packages, delivering messages, running errands (to the bank, the store, the post office), and getting to work (by walking, by public transportation).

Core Skill 5: Simple Indoor Cleaning

The Generalization or Concept

For each cleaning job there is an optimum sequence of tasks. Each one requires its own special equipment and is facilitated if that equipment is kept clean and in good condition.

Presenting the Concept

There are four distinct phases to present: an introduction to appropriate tools for various cleaning tasks, demonstration and practice in using the tools properly, demonstration and practice in cleaning the tools, and instruction in the proper sequence for the cleaning of a room.

1. Knowledge of tools for various cleaning tasks:
   Sweeping
      Push broom for larger, open areas
      Regular kitchen broom for smaller areas
      Whisk broom for corners, furniture
      Dust pan for collecting dust
      Vacuum cleaner for rugs and carpets (appropriate attachments)
   Furniture cleaning
      Vacuum cleaner for upholstered furniture (appropriate attachments)
      Clean, lint-free cloths for dusting
      Furniture polish and applicator, if appropriate
   Cleaning floors
      Dust mop
      Wet mop, bucket, cleaning solution
2. Suggested use of tools:
   Vacuum: run slowly and steadily in straight lines lengthwise and crosswise
   Broom: sweep from corners and sides of room towards one spot—forward stroke for push brooms, side-to-side stroke for regular fibre broom
   Dusting: dust from high objects down to lower ones, avoid shaking cloth while moving, shake cloths out-of-doors when necessary
   Dust mop: keep mop on floor and use a wiping motion, shake mop out-of-doors when necessary
   Polishing: polish small area at a time, use polish sparingly, follow grain of wood
3. Care and cleaning of tools:
   Hang brooms whenever possible
   Empty vacuum bag in newspaper after use (outdoors if possible), remove lint, hairs, other matter from brushes
   Wash mops, dust cloths in warm soapy water and let dry
   Report shortages, defects, or breakage
4. Suggested sequence for cleaning a room:
   Empty and clean ash trays and wastebaskets
   Move small or breakable pieces to a safe, out-of-way place
   Dust tops of windows and door casing

If using broom:
- Sweep floor and rug
- Let dust settle
- Dust light fixtures
- Dust around windows and sills
- Dust pictures
- Dust furniture, higher pieces first, then the legs and rungs of tables and chairs
- Dust baseboards and floor moldings
- Use dust mop on floor

If using vacuum:
- Use vacuum attachment on curtains, drapes
- Perform dusting activities (explain why dusting precedes vacuuming and follows sweeping)
- Move furniture and vacuum rug
- Replace furniture

Reinforcing the Concept

During practice sessions allow the trainee to make some decisions independently (for example, in sequencing) and immediately reinforce satisfactory decisions and correct unsatisfactory ones. In the actual work situation, consistent positive and negative feedback should be given until the trainee has grasped all the concepts.

Extending the Concept

Even in the classroom, situations can be developed to introduce new and varied experiences. For example, set up a hospital or hotel room and ask the trainee to apply the concepts learned in the cleaning of a room. In addition to the practice received in applying previously learned concepts, the trainee is confronted with new situations. Some of these are: what to say or do if the room is occupied; the necessity for straightening out the bed in a motel room—perhaps bringing in linens; the advisability of assembling and bringing all the required equipment at one time to avoid unnecessary trips; how to handle the occupant's personal belongings; and how to clean with the least disturbance to an occupant who must remain in the room.

D. Training in Specific Skills

Specific skills are those required by a specific job and may have no direct applicability to other jobs in the group. In specific-skill training, job-specific activities are introduced and emphasized; the progression being from more general job-group or core skills to very specific job skills.

Training in specific skills is tied very closely to the specific job the trainee hopes to obtain. Usually it involves preplacement training, but in many cases training in specific skills may occur directly on the job. In other cases, the training may be balanced between on-the-job activities and continued instruction at the training facility.

Because of the great variety of specific-skill requirements listed in the job profiles, and because the same job may vary greatly from setting to setting, it is impossible to present here a comprehensive list of specific skills and their applications. The ability to use price-marking devices, knowledge of local delivery routes, and the ability to properly clean and wash windows are examples listed in the job profiles.

Generally speaking, the design of specific-skill training parallels the design of both the basic and core-skill training; however, the activities are extracted from the specific job profiles for the actual job rather than from a variety of profiles or prototypical job descriptions. Work samples are established to approximate or simulate the actual job situation. Specific procedures for doing tasks may be taught; special vocabulary may be introduced; plant or office layout may be learned; and specific company policies and procedures may be presented. If the training is to be done away from the actual job setting, there also can be a simulation of some of the critical working conditions to which the employee must adjust, such as minimal supervision, pace, and demand for physical stamina.

The length of such a program is highly variable, depending upon the employer's needs and the trainee's capabilities. If the trainee progresses particularly well, it may be best to move the individual from training to the actual job quickly. If the training course is carried out on the job, company supervisors or training personnel may be able to participate in the planning of the training.

For most trainees, specific-skill training will be a necessary component of vocational preparation. Individual work situations vary greatly, and unless the trainee receives planned orientation and training on the job, it may be difficult to perform at the optimum level. On the other hand, trainees should not be given specific job training unless the probability of getting such a job is high. If this is not the case, it is preferable for the trainee to remain more flexible and adaptable through continuing development of basic skills and work adjustment skills.

E. On-the-Job Training

In many cases, the client who is hired for a specific job will have no formal training on the job, but there usually is a need for job orientation such as learning names and locations, rules and procedures, and so on. Providing this orientation should be considered a part of the training program. Where there has been close cooperation between training personnel and work supervisors, this orientation can be part of the specific-skill training just described.

It is important for the employer or trainer to assess the new employee's abilities in order to build on the employee's existing skills and knowledge. Individualization of general activities should be avoided, whenever possible. For example, if an employee has already learned certain procedures for cleaning a room and the results are adequate, the employer/trainer should be urged to permit the employee to use these procedures if at all possible. Generally speaking, on-the-job training deals with: specific job orientation, procedures (individual, general), nomenclature (names), locations (buildings, washroom, work area), hours and wages, supervisor, other employees working nearby, and care of work uniform.

In some instances the trainee just hired will need postplacement counseling to facilitate job adjustment. This activity should be planned in the placement and training program and should be continued until the client is well adjusted to the new job.

F. Evaluation

This evaluation provides a continual assessment of clients during their training. While basically an extension of the client selection techniques discussed in chapter 3, the evaluation is also concerned with more specifically identifying strengths and weaknesses, and providing a better estimate of the client's ultimate employability.

Developing Methods for Evaluation

The evaluation should be cumulative and criterion-referenced. That is, it should be a continuous process with periodic checkpoints and summaries and be clearly related to acceptable levels of performance on criterion tasks. Detailed records should be maintained throughout the training program, indicating which tasks the client is assigned, performance initially and after experience, issues or problems that arise and how they are handled, and so on. At the checkpoint periods it may be desirable to give the client a standard series of tasks so that evaluations from one checkpoint to another can be compared.

Evaluations can be both descriptive and numerical or scorable. However, they should be descriptive in each of many categories so that the results are indicative of strengths and weaknesses. For example, the client's behavior might be described in each of the personal characteristics areas and in each of the relevant work activity areas (see Client Profile, figure 5). Important behaviors will be estimates of change—for the better, one hopes—in each category. In other words, the client's evaluation is predominantly one of comparing performance and capabilities at one point with performance and capabilities at a previous point.

As the evaluation techniques are set up, attention should be given to what can be done if the client performs poorly on one or more items. If the evaluation is not associated with actions and remedies, it has limited value as a diagnostic tool.

Making Preplacement Evaluations

It may prove desirable to have a separate preplacement evaluation of client employability when it appears that the client may be ready for placement. This evaluation should emphasize activities that are most related to making the step from the training setting to a job setting. Specifically, the client should be observed in a sufficient variety of activities so that assessment can be made of performance of the job activities, whether actual or simulated.

Additional emphasis is desirable in this preplacement evaluation in two related factors: adaptability to new situations, and independence from the training environment. Adaptability may be evaluated by arranging some of the learned job activities in new groupings. It also may be desirable to set up the evaluation under a somewhat different set of work conditions than those to which the client has been accustomed. This will provide an opportunity for displaying independence as well. The new setting may be provided by conducting the evaluation in another part of the workshop, in a different room, or with a different supervisor.

Using the Evaluation Results

The evaluation of the client is not an end in itself; the results of the evaluation must be associated with remedial action. Remedial actions may be focused on the client, in the form of additional training in areas of weakness; they may be focused on improving the training methods; or they may be focused on the job if there seems no way to improve the client's deficiencies. This latter approach may include redesigning the job activities or recognizing that some aspects of the activities will be inappropriate for the particular worker.

The results of the evaluations must be shared with the client. Strengths and successes will be easy to point out; it may be more difficult to discuss areas needing improvement. However, these should be considered openly and honestly. The counselor and the client should discuss specific ways of improving, and the client should be encouraged to lead the way in this conversation. Self-direction and self-motivation are likely to result in more realistic and attainable goals than objectives imposed by the counselor.

Assessing and Updating the Evaluation Techniques

As new activities are added to the training program, the evaluation may be extended to include samples of performance on those activities. Clear and objective records of all evaluations and how they are used will be vital to determining how effective the evaluations are in the long run. As new jobs become available in the community, the methods for placement evaluation may be modified to reflect the new personal characteristics required. The need for careful assessment of the placement evaluation is essential, since this is the point at which a decision regarding placement is to be made. Judging readiness for work is difficult at times, since the quality of job supervision is unpredictable, as is the interaction with fellow workers. Therefore, it is highly recommended that continuous follow-up and checking of the validity of the placement evaluation be made, so that methods and standards can be modified as necessary to result in more appropriate placement decisions.

5 Placement Procedures

Figure 1 shows the steps in the employment process. Locating jobs in the community is often the first activity, with training, job placement, and follow-up coming later. In some communities, locating jobs may be accompanied by job redesign (described in the next section). Once the jobs have been identified, the sequential stages can be planned and introduced. Evaluation is a companion activity occurring at all stages of the process. By constantly assessing the program and making revisions where indicated, the program will be timely and responsive to individual needs and community resources and limitations.

The placement procedure suggested in this handbook is based on the use of the job profile and the client profile in preparing for employment. As described in chapter 6, the job profile presents a summary of activities and skills found in a specific job. The client profile described in this chapter contains information on the individual's strengths and limitations in various job training tasks and a summary of personal/social skills. By using these documents as a basis for planning, the placement process can be systematized and facilitated.

A. Locating Jobs and Employers

In any community it is important to assess the local employment situation so that the training and rehabilitation process can be directed realistically toward employment opportunities. Many feel that this is the first step in the job placement procedure.

Conducting a Community Job Survey

Information on what job areas are represented in the community should be collected and catalogued systematically in a master file. The file might contain information on work area, type of industry, type of jobs, skills required, size of organizations, employer organizational title, and names of contacts. The master file on job opportunities can remain a primary tool throughout the life of the program. It should be structured to allow for expansion and for elaborating notations about specific employers and employment situations. In addition, it can be coded for cross-reference to other firms and contacts.

Sources of information to use in collecting community job information include:

Chamber of Commerce
Local and state employment agencies
Local employer association
Local personnel managers' association
Civil service system
Labor unions
Service clubs and civic groups
Organizations for the disadvantaged
Sheltered workshops
Classified pages of the telephone directory
Newspapers, both advertisements and business pages

Information collected from sources such as these can then be combined into the master file, thereby integrating material on job groups into a usable form.

Preparing Additional Job Profiles

The job profiles found in chapter 6 can be used as a first step in preparing a master file. Considering their appropriateness to the local community will lead to a first estimation of possible opportunities. For example, there may be several large laundries in the area, suggesting jobs in this business; however, there may be only one hospital, so the number of opportunities there might be few. Profiles that correspond to identified opportunities can be marked, and further notes made on them as local information is obtained.

If profiles for jobs that exist in the community are not in the *Handbook*, it may be desirable to develop them, following the pattern of those given. Once the relevant profiles have been identified, the information in them can be summarized and organized for ready reference and use in training and placement. The summarization should include at least the following types of information:

Job titles and types of employing organizations, including size
Rough estimates of the number of existing jobs of each type
Summary of job activities required for all jobs, with an indication of activities common to two or more jobs
Summary of personal characteristics required by the jobs
Summary of skills, experience, and age requirements of the employer
Frequency and nature of special considerations such as safety hazards, inability to supervise, and need for special training
Availability of on-the-job training
Location
Transportation
Salaries
Work hours or shift (part-time or full-time)

Evaluating Employment Information

As experience and knowledge relating to the local job survey increase, the effectiveness of the survey procedure should be assessed. Do the existing job profiles represent a comprehensive sample of community job opportunities? Is the information in the master file accurate? Is the procedure for finding job opportunities effective or can a more effective one be developed? On the basis of answers to such questions, procedures should be adapted to the community and its particular employment situation.

The procedure for locating jobs and employers should be reevaluated periodically to determine the validity of the information and the effectiveness of its use. Opportunities for updating information include occasions such as:

Businesses open or expand, close or diminish
Employers experience success or failure with trainees
Changes occur in the scope of the training center, workshop, or school program
New training or placement procedures become available
New listings of community opportunities are prepared by other groups
New management takes over a business

It is recommended that the format for summaries and other forms of job information be relatively flexible so that changes may be made with a minimum of effort.

Reviewing Job Opportunities with Employers

Once potential jobs have been targeted, contacts should be made with employers. The exact nature of the contact depends to some extent on the community. Individual contacts are often desirable and in rural areas may be absolutely essential. However, group contacts cover more ground, and may be just as productive if handled with skill.

Meetings with groups of prospective employers should focus on a general introduction to employment. It is important to apprise the employer honestly of the general qualifications of the client and to outline what to expect regarding skills and behavior. Emphasis should be placed on matching job requirements with client capabilities; the possible attitude of hiring only for charitable reasons should be discouraged. It also may be necessary to encourage employers to think about job redesign for greater productivity. This idea, possibly unfamiliar to some employers, may need explanation and encouragement.

The employers should be involved in group discussions to generate interest in considering trainees as employees. No attempt should be made to obtain commitments from the employers at this time; rather the conversation should be oriented to the *possibility* of hiring, if and when clients meeting all the job requirements are available. Special discussion and perhaps a demonstration of the capabilities of clients would provide the employers with the background for further consideration. Later, in personalized contacts, the individual employers can be contacted to review specific clients and work prospects.

At times some employers may seem dubious about hiring a mentally retarded worker and may want basic questions answered. Is the trainee really as productive as other candidates? How much extra training will be needed, and why should the company consider providing it? How much additional supervisory time will be needed? What are the safety factors that have to be addressed? How will the trainee get along with other employees? These are common questions asked by companies and corporations, and the counselor should be prepared for such questions when meeting with employers.

The best way to respond to these concerns is to report on the experiences other local employers have had and to answer the questions by providing actual examples of cases where the same issues were faced by others. If there is no record of successful placements in the community, it may be best to refer to available follow-up studies in the literature. One such study conducted by Kelly and Simon (1969) found that when properly placed, the majority of mentally retarded employees perform tasks as efficiently and as rapidly as other employees. The authors also stated that in repetitive kinds of jobs, labor costs caused by tardiness, absenteeism, and high turnover were reduced. In general, the point to be stressed with employers is that the same factors need to be considered as in hiring any employee: the individual's skill in performing job activities, and personal and social skills.

B. Redesigning Jobs

The purpose of job redesign is to define jobs in cases where relevant jobs are not known to exist, where there is concern regarding their complete appropriateness, or where there is not a match between client and job. This procedure is most likely to be used with employers who have indicated a willingness to consider hiring a trainee, but who feel they do not have suitable jobs available. Job redesign would permit client placement following some reorganization of an employer's present job categories.

A job can be described as a composite of tasks requiring various skills, sequenced to produce a certain result. Task analysis has been used in the job profiles in chapter 6 to identify component job activities for similar skill levels. In communities with a limited number of job opportunities, a similar procedure may be used to analyze job groups.

Job redesign must give primary consideration to overall improvement in production; few employers will be interested in job redesign if there is not some payoff for their company. The redesign of jobs does not necessarily result in the creation of additional jobs, but it can result in greater productivity, because it releases more skilled personnel to perform jobs with higher skill requirements. The cost of redesigning jobs can, therefore, be absorbed in expanded production capability. Current government programs to reduce unemployment through retraining may tend to encourage the application of job redesign techniques.

The first step in redesigning jobs is to survey the employer's job situation. Through discussions with the employer and staff, job information can be obtained on entry-level positions, generally involving semiskilled or unskilled areas. Many of these jobs may be the same as, or parallel to, those in the job profiles developed previously and therefore may be obvious employment possibilities.

After a general survey, a smaller group of jobs should be selected for more intensive study. These should include four or five suggested by the employer that have some functional or physical relationship to one another. The employer should affirm that there are occasional openings for such jobs, and that there would be a minimum number of problems involved in slightly reorganizing the duties and activities of these jobs.

Within the job group, the specific activity requirements are then identified. Most of these activities can be found in the job profiles. A list should be compiled of all the activities found in the job group, with some indication of percentages of time spent in each activity. Estimates will need to be made of the personal and social skills required for each of the revised jobs.

Next, job activities and other requirements are sorted and redistributed into a new series containing the same number of jobs. The new jobs should be constructed to contain elements that are as homogeneous as possible. At least one of the jobs will include the lowest levels of ability requirements of all the previous jobs in the group. There will be many ability requirements that are not at all appropriate for the mentally retarded worker. It may be possible to concentrate all such requirements in one job, or it may be necessary to distribute them over two or three jobs, depending on homogeneity and similarity among these more skilled requirements and the proportion of total job time necessary for these activities.

Ultimately, if the job activities from four or five jobs are arranged in an ascending order of difficulty, and four or five new jobs evolve on the basis of this listing, it may be possible for a client to undertake those activities occurring at the bottom of the list. In essence, the trainee probably would perform some unskilled functions formerly done by a number of semiskilled workers.

The final step is to implement the new series of jobs on a trial basis, probably with present employees. This trial will provide information on how effective the redesigned jobs actually are in the organization. It may be that the increase in homogeneity of job duties will result in increased effectiveness, or it may be that further job revisions are necessary. The ultimate test of the new structure is to place a client in one of the new jobs at an appropriate level and determine both client and employer satisfaction.

While job redesign has been used effectively in many locations, it is not a panacea to employment difficulties, and its limitations should be acknowledged. Job redesign presumes the employer is highly motivated, willing to redesign job categories, and willing to consider the expense involved in equipment, work sites, or job environments necessary to accommodate the new organization. It also presumes that local staff working with the trainees in job placement have time, skills, and resources to do a job analysis, follow up on the reorganization, and match the skills of their clients to those openings. This is not meant to suggest that job redesign is an impractical alternative, but it is one requiring both work and resources.

C. Placement—Matching Candidates and Jobs

The placement phase is the crux of the rehabilitation process; therefore it is characterized by a number of approaches, any of which may be effective in various situations or with various clients. It is generally accepted that when client training, job selection, placement, and follow-up are done well, the probability of a successful adjustment is greatest (Goldstein, 1964). Professional placement assistance can be used to obtain and sustain employment (Usdane, 1976).

In some communities it may not be possible to provide all these services to the highest degree. The placement situation can differ markedly from the ideal, especially if the community is rural or depressed and a variety of jobs are not available. In such situations it may be necessary to redefine placement as encouraging and assisting the trainee to accept and succeed at the jobs that are available (Clark, 1973). At times, clients may be working beneath their potential or in jobs for which they are minimally suited. In such cases, there needs to be more attention given to what seems to be working for each specific client and less consideration of groups or classes of clients. Highest priority may be given to determining which clients have the most immediate need for employment. The specific placement decision may be based on what jobs are available at that time.

Matching the candidates to the jobs is facilitated by having information readily available on both. The job profiles described earlier provide information on jobs existing in the community. Specific information on trainees can be organized into client profiles.

Preparing Client Profiles

The format of the client profile (figure 5) may be similar to that of the job profile (figure 6). One section summarizes the job activities on which the trainee has been working, with performance estimates of each one. Another section, in like manner, summarizes personal/social skills.

The major section of the client profile on job activity training should be based on records and information maintained during the client's training. A systematic review of these records should indicate areas in which the individual has reached and consistently maintained satisfactory levels of performance, and other areas in which progress has not been made or has been inconsistent. To provide additional objectivity, various staff members might complete profiles for the client. For example, the placement counselor may base a profile on accumulated records and data; the training supervisor may base a profile on a combination of written information and a current evaluation of the client. Considerably more weight should be given to continuous records of evaluation than to the momentary, subjective evaluations of a staff member working closely with a client, undoubtedly wanting the trainee to succeed.

The section of the client profile dealing with personal and social skills should include information such as that described in chapter 6. It should also include space for client information relevant to employment such as health status, physical limitations, present medications, and relevant secondary handicaps. Personal/social skill profiles are not included for each specific job; however, they can be prepared from the master profile which

figure 5 EXAMPLE OF CLIENT PROFILE

CLIENT PROFILE

PART I

Client's Name Dorothy Norris Date 1/6/80

Counselor Curtis Davis

Job Profile: A-1 Food Store Helper
Job Activities (*List Below:*)

1. Unload and store grocery items in stockroom
2. Mark with stamp or tag
3. Display grocery items for sale
4. Stock grocery shelves
5. Set up advertising signs
6. Clean and display produce for sale
7. Keep displayed produce misted
8. Sack grocery orders for customers
9. Transport purchases to customer's car
10. Sweep, mop and dust display and stockroom areas

Client's Proficiency in skills required for job performance. *Check appropriate rating.*

	Proficiency			
	Minimal	Moderate	Considerable	Not yet covered
Basic Skills:				
Do simple reading		✓ (2nd grade level)		
Count and record numbers		✓		
Write numbers and copy simple words		✓		
Sort by category			✓	
Core Skills:				
Load and unload stock		✓		
Stamp or label grocery items		✓		
Stack and shelve grocery items		✓		
Lift and carry		✓		
Transport by cart		✓		
Indoor Cleaning				✓
Specific Skills:				
Knowledge of stockroom organization				✓
Use of price marking device				✓
Ability to sort, clean and display produce				✓
Sacking grocery orders			✓	
Interaction with customers			✓	
Ability to carry 40 pounds			✓ very strong	

figure 5 *(cont'd)*

CLIENT PROFILE
PART 2

Client's Name Dorothy Norris Date 1/6/80

Counselor Curtis Davis

	Personal/Social Skill Requirements	Extent Exhibited: Minimal	Moderate	Major
Social Skills	1. *SELF-EXPRESSION* - communicate, ask for assistance, question			✓
	2. *SOCIABILITY* - interact with other employees or public			✓
	3. *WORK INDEPENDENCE* - work without supervision or guidance		✓	
	4. *APPEARANCE/HYGIENE* - cleanliness, good manners, neatness in appearance			✓
	5. *TEAMWORK* - perform in close coordination with other jobs		✓	
Time Factors	6. *PACE* - perform at a consistent rate of speed		✓	
	7. *ATTENDANCE* - be reliable in attendance and punctuality		✓	
	8. *SIMULTANEITY* - perform several activities at near same time	✓		
	9. *TIMING* - perform timed, scheduled activities; be aware of time		✓	
Performance Skills	10. *ACCURACY* - perform within well-defined tolerances		✓	
	11. *DEXTERITY* - make fine manipulations, coordinated movements			✓
	12. *CHOICES* - select among alternatives, make decisions	✓		
	13. *DIRECTION* - follow procedures, instructions, or directions			✓
	14. *MEMORY* - remember locations, procedures, nomenclatures, etc.	✓		
	15. *CAUTION* - use care in activities which pose personal hazard		✓	
	16. *NEATNESS* - work in a neat, orderly manner		✓	
	17. *CONCENTRATION* - attend to task despite environmental distraction		✓	
Tolerance	18. *REPETITION* - tolerate repetitive work assignments		✓	
	19. *PERSEVERANCE* - perform continuously, over normal periods		✓	
	20. *STAMINA* - have physical stamina, strength, resist fatigue			✓

figure 6 JOB PROFILE A-1 (SAMPLE)

JOB PROFILE A-1
Food Store Helper

General Description

Assists in receiving and displaying grocery items, packaging orders, and performing cleaning duties in a supermarket, neighborhood grocery, quick-stop market, or produce store. Usually these retail stores are self-service, but the same job activities and skill requirements would apply in other stores as well. If the job activities include making deliveries, see job profile A-14.

Job Activities

Unload and store grocery items in stockroom area
Mark grocery items with stamp or tag
Display grocery items for sale
Stock grocery shelves with new or transferred merchandise
Set up advertising signs
Clean and display produce for sale
Keep displayed produce misted
Sack grocery orders for customers
Transport purchases to customer's car
Sweep, mop and dust display and stockroom areas

Specific Skill Requirements

Knowledge of stockroom organization
Ability to use price-marking devices
Ability to safely handle and display cans, boxes, dairy products
Ability to sort, clean, and display produce
Ability to make choices in sorting produce
Knowledge of special handling and sorting procedures
Knowledge of correct procedure for sacking grocery items
Ability to interact with customers
Ability to lift and carry heavy loads

Relevant DOT Reference

Stock Clerk, Self-Service Store 299.367-014

Related Job

Sales Clerk, Food 290.477-018

gives a general description of the characteristics appropriate to the job group. (Figure 7 is an example of a specific personal/social skill requirements profile.)

It is essential to include in the client profile whatever information can be obtained from the client directly about personal interests, motivations, and job preferences. Assuming that these interests are realistic, they should play an important role in the final placement. Consultation with parents, guardians, and institutions regarding their ambitions for the client also may be appropriate. This information may be summarized as part of the profile.

From the client profile it should be possible to identify individual patterns of strengths and weaknesses in the client's performance of job activities and attainment of personal/social skills. These individual profiles may suggest job-related patterns. If training has been set up adequately, it should be possible to identify various patterns emerging in the client, and develop these individual characteristics in a way likely to facilitate eventual employment possibilities.

Matching Clients and Jobs

The placement phase may assume either of two directions requiring quite different actions on the part of the counselor. The most common placement situation is finding the job first and then selecting the best qualified candidates from among the trainees. This situation is especially common in small towns or rural settings. The second placement situation is finding an appropriate job for a given client.

Selecting from among several candidates for a specific job The objective is to identify one or more suitable candidates. Suggested steps in the selection process are:

1. Obtain a definition of job requirements. Through direct contact with the employer, the counselor should obtain sufficiently detailed information to prepare a job profile. If it is not possible to obtain the necessary information, existing related job profiles can be used.
2. Prepare client profiles. Prepare a client profile for each of the clients whose capabilities seem to most closely fit those required by the job.
3. Compare client and job profiles. The goal is to match job profiles, representing jobs available in the community, with client profiles for potential employees. This comparison seeks to identify jobs in which clients' strengths will be assets and limitations will not cause problems or can be reduced by more specific job training. This latter point is critical. The job

figure 7 EXAMPLE OF PERSONAL/SOCIAL SKILL REQUIREMENTS FOR JOB PROFILE A-1

Master Profile: **A. Merchandising Occupations**

Job Profile: A-1. *Food Store Helper*

	Personal/Social Skill Requirements	Extent Required		
		Minimal	Moderate	Major
Social Skills	1. *SELF-EXPRESSION* - communicate, ask for assistance, question			●
	2. *SOCIABILITY* - interact with other employees or public			●
	3. *WORK INDEPENDENCE* - work without supervision or guidance		●	
	4. *APPEARANCE/HYGIENE* - cleanliness, good manners, neatness in appearance			●
	5. *TEAMWORK* - perform in close coordination with other jobs		●	
Time Factors	6. *PACE* - perform at a consistent rate of speed		●	
	7. *ATTENDANCE* - be reliable in attendance and punctuality			●
	8. *SIMULTANEITY* - perform several activities at near same time	●		
	9. *TIMING* - perform timed, scheduled activities; be aware of time		●	
Performance Skills	10. *ACCURACY* - perform within well-defined tolerances			●
	11. *DEXTERITY* - make fine manipulations, coordinated movements		●	
	12. *CHOICES* - select among alternatives, make decisions		●	
	13. *DIRECTION* - follow procedures, instructions or directions			●
	14. *MEMORY* - remember locations, procedures, nomenclatures, etc.			●
	15. *CAUTION* - use care in activities which pose personal hazard			●
	16. *NEATNESS* - work in a neat, orderly manner		●	
	17. *CONCENTRATION* - attend to task despite environmental distraction		●	
Tolerance	18. *REPETITION* - tolerate repetitive work assignments		●	
	19. *PERSEVERANCE* - perform continuously, over normal periods		●	
	20. *STAMINA* - have physical stamina, strength, resist fatigue			●

profiles will indicate the areas of job activity in which job orientation and on-the-job training will substantially contribute to a new employee's effectiveness. Clients having strengths in these areas are likely first candidates; clients with limitations in these areas may require additional orientation or on-the-job training.

From the list of potential matches, those that seem to fit most closely should be reviewed first. In what areas does the client match the job, and where could there be problems? Are the limitations critical to probable success? Would the employer be likely to accept the individual with these limitations? How can the limitations be made up with additional training?

After summarizing this comparison for each client, identify the one or more clients who most closely fit the needs of the job, and meet with them to discuss their interests and personal preferences. Since the client's personal and social interests are noted on the client profile, these factors should have been noted at an earlier stage in the review. However, it is important to reconfirm that these interests still exist and that the specific job opportunity is one the client wishes to pursue.

The placement procedure described here depends on job and client profiles to provide a basis for matching prospective candidates and jobs. Other placement methods advocate having the candidate take primary responsibility for locating potential jobs and for doing preliminary screening. In practice, some combination of client and counselor participation may offer the best chance for appropriate and successful job placement.

4. Bring the clients and employer together. If there is sufficient time, it may be possible to work with the selected clients to discuss the job and the employer's needs and even to provide some very brief and highly specialized training. Clients should be prepared for the interview and other application processes. The employer also should have some preliminary background information and data on the candidates, with emphasis on client capabilities as they relate to the defined job. Finally, one or more candidates and the employer may be brought together for interviews and other processing necessary to the hiring decision.

Review of the client-employer contacts may provide additional information to the counselor on the respective capabilities of clients for the job, and the counselor may wish to make a recommendation for a specific client. Beyond this point, the decision is the employer's.

Finding a job for a specific trainee The purpose of this activity is to use what is known about a specific client to locate job prospects in the community. Once the client profiles have been developed to identify one or more appropriate job areas for a client, the job hunting can proceed systematically. A series of possible stages is:

1. Use the master file and review availability of jobs in the community appropriate for the client and make sure the information is current.
2. Identify specific employers and obtain their requirements for job application including: application forms, physical examinations, interviews, trial periods, and so on. If these procedures appear compatible with the client's abilities, work with the client to discuss the employment process and the prospects for employer contacts.
3. Contact employers for possible preliminary interviews. If the client is ready, the initial contact may be made directly by the individual. If this approach is not appropriate, it may be desirable for the counselor to talk with the employer first, especially if it is an initial contact. The counselor may want to develop client resumés to use as a basis for discussing with employers which clients are available and what abilities they have. Preliminary promotion of the client should be directed to selling capabilities rather than to making allowances for handicaps. Special strong points should be emphasized; however, the discussion should also include mention of any potential problems. An attempt should be made to arrange for a contact and interview between the employer and client.

As with the other procedures described, job-hunting activities for a specific client should be periodically examined and evaluated.

D. Follow-up

Continuous follow-up of both clients and employers should be at the core of a training and placement program, not at its fringe. Follow-up helps to insure the relevance of the program, which is a major component of its success.

Follow-up with the Employer

Whatever the outcome of the specific job-hunting or interview situation, the couselor should plan a systematic follow-up program with the employer to take advantage of future openings. If the client is hired, it is wise to keep in close contact with both employer and client during and after the initial adjustment period. If the client is not hired, the counselor will want to identify the determining factors and to evaluate whether they might be overcome. In some situations, the employer may be able to hold the job open while one or more clients are given more systematic training especially suited for the job. This would tend to increase greatly the probability of client success and employer satisfaction.

It will be important to collect additional information from the employer about the performance of the client who is hired. How does the employee perform in terms of successful task completion, speed in performing tasks, resistance to fatigue, attendance, social skills, and interpersonal relationships? Have any specific problems developed and, if so, should the counselor be actively involved in dealing with them?

The immediate identification of problems is one major advantage of conducting an employer follow-up. Especially in settings where the employer is relatively unfamiliar with having mentally retarded employees, there initially may be minor problems of adjustment and understanding. Interpersonal difficulties resulting from relationships with fellow workers are a potential problem area, but it is also an area in which the counselor may have special skills. Identifying such issues in their early stages is likely to allow for intervention with both the employer and the employee and may even prevent an early termination of employment.

While follow-up with the employer is generally beneficial, it should be noted that there are some situations where contacting the employer may be inadvisable. In cases where the employer is not aware that the employee has participated in a special training program, or in cases where the individual has found a job independent of the agency, it is best not to intrude in the employee-employer relationship (Brolin, 1976).

Follow-up with the Clients

This is a critical component of the overall program. It is important to consider the individual needs and resources of the client when scheduling follow-up contacts. Some trainees may need considerable counseling and support as they move into a more independent employment situation; others may do well with only minimal contact.

In general, the first contact with the client often occurs the first day of the new job, and may be oriented to the client's adjustment and initial reactions to the work setting and to other employees. Additional contacts may occur on a weekly basis for the first month of employment; after that time, contacts should be monthly. Most counselors feel that the follow-up activity should continue until the client has experienced six successful months of employment. After that time, contact may be intermittent and scheduled on an individual basis as needed.

At all meetings, the counselor should be sensitive to problems occurring at the time or likely to be a factor in the future, and attempt to deal with them as quickly as possible. The counselor's job cannot end when the client's job begins. The counselor must maintain contact with the employed client and with the employer to insure feedback to the program, and also must work to assist understanding between the employer and the employee so that this relationship, too, is maintained in its own right.

It would be ideal if every placement turned out to be suited to the applicant and a successful match were made. However, as every experienced staff member is well aware, such is not the case. It is not at all unusual to have a situation in which the client and employment setting are not congenial and the placement does not work. There are some clients who experience considerable difficulty in finding a permanent or long-term position, and these people may need to return to the program for additional training or for training in another job area. Many clients require several trials on the job before thay are successful.

Follow-up and Evaluation

Follow-up provides information which can be used in the evaluation of the total program. The entire training and placement program is aimed toward preparing the client for effective job adjustment and performance. The best way to insure the effectiveness of the program is to obtain accurate feedback based on actual client experience. This information then can be used to revise or restructure the program as necessary (Rosen, Clark, and Kivitz, 1977).

Nothing succeeds like success; the best evidence for how effectively a person can perform is performance. The program which attempts to be responsive to both the needs of community employers and the needs of the individual client can find no better source of feedback than the employers and employees themselves. By obtaining comments and suggestions from them, and incorporating these ideas into the program as appropriate, the program is likely to be responsive to the evolving needs of its participants.

6
Job Profiles

This part of the *Handbook* consists of three sections:

A. PERSONAL/SOCIAL SKILL REQUIREMENTS—This section contains a listing of those characteristics of the individual which are assumed to be minimum requirements for employment.

B. MASTER AND JOB PROFILES—The 158 job profiles are arranged in related groups of six similar job groups. Master profiles have been prepared for each of these groups. Immediately following each master profile are the related job profiles.

C. INDEX TO TYPES OF EMPLOYING ORGANIZATIONS—This index lists alphabetically the types of organizations that might have employment positions for trainees.

The materials in these sections are not to be considered as exhausting all of the possibilities as far as job requirements or training suggestions are concerned. The reader is encouraged to record additional notes relevant to the respective jobs.

A. Personal/Social Skill Requirements

Twenty personal/social skills have been identified, reflecting the types of demands jobs make upon the worker in terms of work habits, attitudes, tolerances, and broad skills relating to work and adjustment. They are to be considered the *minimum* characteristics required for employability in any of the jobs listed in this book. Therefore, these characteristics, at least to the degree in which they are described here, will be assumed to be part of each job's personal characteristics profile; in many job situations, some will be required to a greater degree. Whenever a personal/social skill is noted on an individual job profile (under "Specific Skills Requirements") it is considered to be crucial to successful employment in that particular job. A personal/social skills requirement profile has been prepared for each master profile, showing the pattern of skills that are required by the jobs in that group. A blank profile is included as figure 8. The information for each job group is general and not intended to discriminate among clients in predicting potential for job placement. It can be used as a guide for developing individual profiles of personal/social skills for specific jobs.

Social skills are requirements for interacting with other persons in the work environment, including other employees, supervisors, and customers.

Self-expression: This means a minimum ability to communicate so that simple questions can be answered or assistance requested by the trainee. It includes both give and take, and both oral and (minimum) written communication.

Sociability: Since any job will require a small amount of contact with at least one other person, certain basic social abilities will be required. Accepting instructions and criticism with good grace, pleasant interchange of greetings, acceptable eating habits, no extremes of shyness or aggressiveness—these would be minimum requirements for employability.

Work Independence: Even the most closely supervised job requires an ability to carry out certain activities without constant supervision.

Appearance and Hygiene: Although the requirements for good manners and lack of noticeable physical differences vary considerably, basic cleanliness and neatness are considered essential. Clothing appropriate to the work setting should be worn by the worker.

Teamwork: The need for close coordination with other workers varies greatly; however, as with sociability, all jobs require this skill to some extent.

Time factors are requirements for performing within broad implicit and explicit time limitations.

Pace: The need to work at a consistent rate of speed will vary within jobs; however, the ability to perform at a consistent pace for short periods is basic.

Attendance: Reliability in attendance is essential in all employment situations. Punctuality, although generally necessary, is more crucial in certain jobs and thus can be needed to various degrees.

figure 8 BLANK PERSONAL/SOCIAL SKILL REQUIREMENTS PROFILE

Master Profile:

	Personal/Social Skill Requirements	**Extent Required**		
		Minimal	Moderate	Major
Social Skills	1. *SELF EXPRESSION* - communicate, ask for assistance, question			
	2. *SOCIABILITY* - interact with other employees or public			
	3. *WORK INDEPENDENCE* - work without supervision or guidance			
	4. *APPEARANCE/HYGIENE* - cleanliness, good manners, neatness in appearance			
	5. *TEAMWORK* - perform in close coordination with other jobs			
Time Factors	6. *PACE* - perform at a consistent rate of speed			
	7. *ATTENDANCE* - be reliable in attendance and punctuality			
	8. *SIMULTANEITY* - perform several activities at near same time			
	9. *TIMING* - perform timed, scheduled activities; be aware of time			
Performance Skills	10. *ACCURACY* - perform within well-defined tolerances			
	11. *DEXTERITY* - make fine manipulations, coordinated movements			
	12. *CHOICES* - select among alternatives, make decisions			
	13. *DIRECTION* - follow procedures, instructions or directions			
	14. *MEMORY* - remember locations, procedures, nomenclatures, etc.			
	15. *CAUTION* - use care in activities which pose personal hazard			
	16. *NEATNESS* - work in a neat, orderly manner			
	17. *CONCENTRATION* - attend to task despite environmental distraction			
Tolerance	18. *REPETITION* - tolerate repetitive work assignments			
	19. *PERSEVERANCE* - perform continuously, over normal periods			
	20. *STAMINA* - have physical stamina, strength, resist fatigue			

Simultaneity: The ability to perform more than one activity at nearly the same time is essential to any job requiring manual movements. Certain jobs require more activities of a more complex nature to be performed simultaneously.

Timing: Some awareness of time and ability to perform activities within a schedule is basic to all jobs. Considerable variation occurs as the time element becomes more crucial and the schedule more rigid.

Performance skills are those worker characteristics related to satisfactory completion of job activities.

Accuracy: Performance within well-defined tolerance is not considered essential to many jobs appropriate to the mentally retarded person. Variation in tolerances will occur depending upon the job involved.

Dexterity: The need to make fine manipulations varies within jobs. However, certain grosser hand and finger movements are essential to performance in most of the job groups.

Choices: The need to make decisions and choices occurs on a simple level in all jobs. The example of sorting cans involves selection between alternatives. On the other hand, decision-making involving child care activities is of a much higher level.

Direction: The ability to follow simple directions or procedures is essential to any employment situation. Certain jobs involve more complex procedures or more numerous and varying instructions.

Memory: Remembering certain locations, procedures, or a special nomenclature is a basic requirement. The need for a good memory will vary with the complexity of the work area, the work procedures, and the specificity of the job.

Caution: An awareness of hazards and the ability to take normal precautions is always required, e.g., the ability to get to work safely. Caution should be used when sharp utensils, power equipment, chemicals, and other hazards are inherent in the job.

Neatness: The ability to work in a neat, orderly manner is basic. While the degree of neatness in the sense of being "tidy" will vary with the job setting, orderliness is an important skill in almost every job.

Concentration: The ability to attend to the task despite environmental distractions such as noise, distracting events, or temperature is needed to some extent in every job.

Tolerance requires both the physical and psychological ability to stick with the required job activities over normal work spans, especially under conditions of substantial repetition and physical exertion.

P. 93

Repetition: This will be inherent in many semiskilled and unskilled jobs.

Perseverance: Any employee will be expected to exhibit relatively continuous performance—working when there is work to be done and resting after normal periods of activity.

Stamina: Since physical activity is rather basic to many of the jobs found in this book, at least some physical strength and stamina must be considered to be an essential characteristic.

B. Master and Job Profiles

Description

There are 158 job profiles, arranged in six job groups.[1] A master profile precedes each of the job groupings. It contains a general description of the jobs in the family, a list of the profiles included, and a summary of the basic, core, and personal/social skills required for performance of the jobs. Each of the basic and core skills is numbered in reference to the charts in chapter 4 (figures 3 and 4). The personal/social skill requirements relevant to the jobs within the group are presented on a profile form at the end of the master profile.

The relevant job profiles are arranged immediately following the master profile. Each job profile consists of six basic divisions: 1) job title, 2) general description, 3) job activities, 4) specific skill requirements, 5) relevant DOT reference, and 6) related jobs. While each profile could represent a single job appropriate for an individual client, in general this is not realistic for the following reasons. An existing job, or one which might be developed by a specific employer, may not include all of the activities marked in the profile or it may include activities not listed. In addition, the activities marked in the job profile may not be equally appropriate for all trainees. In other words, the information is not intended to imply that this profile uniquely defines a given job such as "Cooking Assistant" (C-6). Instead, it includes the whole range of activities and requirements of a given type of job. It is obvious that there may be differences among "Cooking Assistant, Restaurant Cooking" when the comparable job is analyzed in many different restaurants. Consequently, each profile may encompass many different jobs of a given type, depending on organizational and individual differences. The organizational differences would reflect the size of the organization, degree of specialization possible, nature and amount of supervision available, and so on. The individual differences would reflect the client's individual pattern of abilities and skills.

A brief description of each of the job profile sections includes:

Job title The title has been selected to be as descriptive as possible of the job. Often the DOT title was not used if it might cause confusion by being too similar to another job in the *Handbook*.

General description This is a very brief description of the major purpose of the job.

Job activities A broad range of activities is listed. Not every client will be able to perform all the activities. Trainees represent a wide range of abilities. Some can perform the higher level job activities, others cannot. The placement officer should define the job as it exists at the prospective place of employment and make the necessary deletions or additions to the job activities. In some of the profiles the activities include assisting the journeyman or higher level worker with some rather skilled activities. It should be remembered that the trainee is expected to perform as a "Helper"[2] and with supervision.

Specific skill requirements Listed here are all job-specific skills. Basic, core, and personal/social skills are presented in the master profile as described earlier. If any personal/social skills are crucial to job performance, they also are listed under specific skills.

Relevant DOT reference This reference is to the *Dictionary of Occupational Titles,* 4th ed. (1977). Occasionally when the profile title is "Helper," the relevant DOT reference is to a higher level job because there was no helper specifically listed for that job in the DOT. The higher level DOT reference is given for the reader's convenience in examining the job to determine its applicability in the local situation.

Related jobs The job profiles in the *Handbook* represent jobs which mentally retarded people actually have been trained to perform. Many jobs have basically the same skill requirements and level of difficulty, but are not included because of the lack of evidence that mentally retarded workers have learned to do them. Related jobs include jobs within the *Handbook* and jobs which are similar in required skills and level of difficulty but are not in this book. References to related job profiles are listed first, with the profile number in parentheses. These are followed by related jobs from the DOT, with the DOT number following. The counselor is encouraged to use these numbers to identify many more relevant occupational areas in the DOT.

How to Use the Job Profiles

In deriving training implications for a given job, it may be necessary to refer to three locations in the book:

The job profile, which lists the job activities and the specific skill requirements.
The master profile, which defines the required basic, core, and personal/social skills.
The basic and core skill charts (figures 3 and 4 in chapter 4), which present more detail about the skills.

In using the job profiles for placement, the reader should refer to the procedures described in chapter 5 (fig. 5) for developing a client profile and matching it with the job requirements. The reader is reminded that the materials in this section are not exhaustive. It may be necessary to write new profiles or update those presented here to tailor the information to specific situations.

Notes

1. For a complete list, see page xiii following the Contents.
2. A "Helper" as defined in the DOT is "A worker who assists another worker, usually of a higher level of competence or expertness, by performing a variety of duties, such as furnishing another worker with materials, tools, or supplies; cleaning work areas, machines, and equipment; feeding or offbearing machines; holding materials or tools; and performing other routine duties. A 'Helper' may learn a trade but does so without an agreement with employer that such is the purpose of their relationship. Therefore it is incorrect to call a helper an apprentice."

Master Profile A: **Merchandising Occupations**

General Description

Most of the jobs in this category involve activities other than actual selling. Both retail and wholesale businesses are included. Some jobs, such as Floral Assistant or Gift Wrapper, might be seasonal, more job opportunities being available during holiday periods. Merchandise handling, housekeeping, and some customer contact are among the most common job activities. Work hours usually will be regular, and work will be indoors for most jobs in this category. Supervision may not be continuous.

Many different items will be handled, some of them fragile, and some heavy. Caution, and in some instances strength and stamina, will be required.

Job Profiles (See pages immediately following this master profile.)

A-1 Food Store Helper
A-2 Meat Market Helper
A-3 Department Store Helper
A-4 Clothing Store Helper
A-5 Dressing Room Attendant
A-6 Furniture/Appliance Store Helper
A-7 Lumber and Building Supplies Store Helper
A-8 Floral Shop Assistant
A-9 Gas Station Attendant
A-10 Fuel Sales Yard Worker
A-11 Newspaper Carrier
A-12 Gift Wrapper
A-13 Pet Shop Assistant
A-14 Merchandise Deliverer
A-15 Delivery Truck Helper

Skill Requirements

The folling basic, core, and personal/social skills are considered to apply generally to all the jobs in the merchandising occupations. In addition to these, each job profile lists specific skill requirements relevant to that particular job.

Basic skills The numbers in parentheses refer to the sequence of the skills listed in the basic skills chart beginning on page 43, which defines the individual skills and cites application for each one.

Read (simple; e.g., recognize labels) (1)
Write (simple; e.g., notations, short messages) (2)
Count and record numbers (3)
Perform simple calculations (4)
Count money, make change (5)
Sort by category (6)
Communicate verbally (10)
Use telephone (11)
Write simple messages (12)
Tell time (13)
Measure (14)
Trace (18)
Tie with string or rope (19)
Secure with tape (20)

Core skills The numbers in parentheses refer to the sequence of the skills listed in the core skills chart, beginning on page 47, which defines the individual skills and cites applications for each one.

Bundle (2)
Fasten (4)
Package and wrap (5)
Cut (6)
Lift and carry heavy items (7)
Load and unload (8)
Transport (9)
Stack and shelve merchandise (10)
Pack or crate (11)
Open and unpack boxes (12)
Stamp and label merchandise (13)
Receive and transmit messages (14)
Run errands (15)
Find streets and addresses (16)
Use cash register, adding machine, or calculator (21)
Perform indoor cleaning (24)

Personal/social skills Since contact with the public is more frequent in merchandising than in some other occupational areas, good social skills and a neat appearance are particularly important. Clothing appropriate to the sales situation should be worn.

Other personal/social skills required to a major extent in merchandising occupations are shown in the profile on the following page. Skill 15, "Caution," applies to the prevention of damage to fragile merchandise as well as to the protection of the worker from personal hazard.

Master Profile: **A: Merchandising Occupations**

	Personal/Social Skill Requirements	Extent Required: Minimal	Extent Required: Moderate	Extent Required: Major
Social Skills	1. *SELF EXPRESSION* - communicate, ask for assistance, question			●
	2. *SOCIABILITY* - interact with other employees or public			●
	3. *WORK INDEPENDENCE* - work without supervision or guidance		●	
	4. *APPEARANCE/HYGIENE* - cleanliness, good manners, neatness in appearance			●
	5. *TEAMWORK* - perform in close coordination with other jobs		●	
Time Factors	6. *PACE* - perform at a consistent rate of speed		●	
	7. *ATTENDANCE* - be reliable in attendance and punctuality			●
	8. *SIMULTANEITY* - perform several activities at near same time	●		
	9. *TIMING* - perform timed, scheduled activities; be aware of time		●	
Performance Skills	10. *ACCURACY* - perform within well-defined tolerances			●
	11. *DEXTERITY* - make fine manipulations, coordinated movements		●	
	12. *CHOICES* - select among alternatives, make decisions		●	
	13. *DIRECTION* - follow procedures, instructions or directions			●
	14. *MEMORY* - remember locations, procedures, nomenclatures, etc.			●
	15. *CAUTION* - use care in activities which pose personal hazard			●
	16. *NEATNESS* - work in a neat, orderly manner		●	
	17. *CONCENTRATION* - attend to task despite environmental distraction		●	
Tolerance	18. *REPETITION* - tolerate repetitive work assignments		●	
	19. *PERSEVERANCE* - perform continuously, over normal periods		●	
	20. *STAMINA* - have physical stamina, strength, resist fatigue			●

JOB PROFILE A-1
Food Store Helper

General Description

Assists in receiving and displaying grocery items, packaging orders, and performing cleaning duties in a supermarket, neighborhood grocery, quick-stop market, or produce store. Usually these retail stores are self-service, but the same job activities and skill requirements would apply in other stores as well. If the job activities include making deliveries, see job profile A-14.

Job Activities

Unload and store grocery items in stockroom area
Mark grocery items with stamp or tag
Display grocery items for sale
Stock grocery shelves with new or transferred merchandise
Set up advertising signs
Clean and display produce for sale
Keep displayed produce misted
Sack grocery orders for customers
Transport purchases to customer's car
Sweep, mop and dust display and stockroom areas

Specific Skill Requirements

Knowledge of stockroom organization
Ability to use price marking devices
Ability to safely handle and display cans, boxes, dairy products
Ability to sort, clean, and display produce
Ability to make choices in sorting produce
Knowledge of special handling and sorting procedures
Knowledge of correct procedure for sacking grocery items
Ability to interact with customers
Ability to lift and carry heavy loads

Relevant DOT Reference

Stock Clerk, Self-service Store 299.367-014

Related Job

Sales Clerk, Food 290.477-018

JOB PROFILE A-2
Meat Market Helper

General Description

Assists in receiving, storing, and preparing meat and poultry for sale in either a self-service meat store or a butcher shop. The meat market helper also is responsible for maintaining clean storage and sales areas. If delivery to customers is a job activity, see job profile A-14.

Job Activities

Unload fresh, cured, and boxed meats and poultry from delivery truck
Transport and store meats and poultry in storage area
Rotate meat in storage area as directed
Cut and grind meat using powered grinder
Weigh, wrap, and price packages of meat (as directed or using weighing/wrapping machine)
Arrange meat in display counter
Clean grinder, meat containers, meat counter
Clean storage and retail area
Relay customer requests for meats not on display to appropriate personnel
Sack merchandise for customers
Transport packages to customer's car

Specific Skill Requirements

Ability to handle meats and poultry in sanitary manner
Knowledge of meat storage procedures
Ability to cut and grind meat for hamburger and sausage
Ability to safely operate powered meat grinder and sharp cutting tools
Ability to operate weighing/wrapping machine
Ability to clean equipment and utensils
Knowledge of correct procedures for cleaning storage area and meat counter

Ability to lift and carry heavy carcasses
Knowledge of nomenclature, for example, meat cuts

Relevant DOT Reference

Meat Clerk 222.684-010

Related Jobs

Food Store Helper (job profile A-1)
Meat Grinder 521.685-214

JOB PROFILE A-3
Department Store Helper

General Description

Assists in handling, storing, marking, and displaying merchandise in a department store, and in minor housekeeping duties. The employee in this position is required to handle safely a wide variety of heavy, breakable, or delicate items. If merchandise delivery is part of the job requirement, see job profiles A-14 and A-15.

Job Activities

Load and unload merchandise from delivery truck
Unpack cartons of merchandise and transport to sales area
Move furniture and appliances to sales area
Sort stock
Rack or shelve merchandise
Mark merchandise with tag or stamp
Perform simple assembly of standard items
Assist in arranging items for display
Assist in inventory of items in stock
Prepare packages for shipping and mailing
Clean and maintain orderly stockroom

Specific Skill Requirements

Ability to safely handle breakable items
Ability to safely move furniture and appliances
Ability to rack or shelve merchandise appropriately
Knowledge of display procedures for certain types of merchandise
Ability to use price-marking devices
Ability to assist in assembly of furniture, display racks
Knowledge of department locations, stockroom organization, locations of specific merchandise
Ability to lift and carry heavy loads

Relevant DOT Reference

Laborer, Stores 922.687-058

Related Jobs

Clothing Store Helper (job profile A-4)
Furniture/Appliance Store Helper (job profile A-6)
Sales Clerk, Retail Trade 290.477-014

JOB PROFILE A-4
Clothing Store Helper

General Description

Assists in merchandise handling in a clothing store. The employee also may assist customers in trying on clothing and may perform housekeeping tasks. A neat appearance is important for persons working in this job. If merchandise delivery is a requirement of the job, see job profiles A-14 and A-15.

Job Activities

Transport merchandise by stock cart
Unpack boxes of clothing
Display clothing in retail area

Tag merchandise with price
Press or mend items in stock
Aid customers in locating merchandise
Direct customers to dressing rooms
Assist customers in dressing rooms
Obtain merchandise from stock room when not on floor
Keep merchandise in order
Rehang garment; refasten belts, and so on, after they have been tried on
Sack or box merchandise at time of sale
Assist in preparation of display windows
Perform light cleaning in storage and retail area

Specific Skill Requirements

Ability to unpack, sort, and display items of clothing
Ability to use hand iron safely and correctly
Ability to do simple mending (sew buttons, mend seams)
Ability to correctly attach tags to clothing
Ability to interact with customers and provide assistance when requested
Ability to correctly fold and box clothing for customers
Knowledge of window display principles and techniques

Relevant DOT Reference

Sales Attendant 299.677-010

Related Jobs

Department Store Helper (job profile A-3)
Stock Checker, Apparel 299.667-014

JOB PROFILE A-5
Dressing Room Attendant

General Description

Controls number of items customer may take into dressing room at one time, assists customers if necessary, and prepares tried-on clothing to be returned to display area.

Job Activities

Assign available dressing room to customer
Count items of clothing taken into dressing room and provide customer with correct tally tag
Check items against tag when returned by customer
Rehang garments and refasten belts, buttons, and zippers
Sew on missing or loose buttons, hooks and loops
Sort and replace tried-on garments in display area
Provide assistance to customers in dressing and undressing
Clean and maintain neat dressing room area
Watch for thefts of clothing

Specific Skill Requirements

Knowledge of dressing room numbers and locations
Ability to correctly count and record items taken to dressing room
Ability to interact tactfully with customers
Knowledge of display area, locations of particular items
Ability to do simple mending (sew on buttons, mend seams)

Relevant DOT Reference

Stock Checker, Apparel 299.667-014

Related Job

Clothing Store Helper (job profile A-4)

JOB PROFILE A-6
Furniture/Appliance Store Helper

General Description

Assists in receipt, display, and delivery of furniture and appliances in a retail store; may also perform housekeeping activities. If delivery of merchandise is a major job activity, see job profile A-15.

Job Activities

Load and unload furniture, appliances, and crates from delivery truck
Open bales, crates, and other containers, using handtools
Transport merchandise to sales area by hand, dolly or handtruck
Perform simple assembly of standard items
Attach price tag to merchandise
Clean surface of furniture and appliances
Assist in minor repairs or refinishing of shipment-damaged merchandise
Spread dust covers
Assist in deliveries to customers' homes
Perform cleaning duties in storage and retail area

Specific Skill Requirements

Ability to use simple hand tools safely
Ability to safely transport large, heavy items by hand truck or dolly
Ability to safely lift and carry heavy loads
Ability to lift and move heavy items with another person
Ability to assemble specific items sold in store
Ability to correctly attach tags with pins or string
Knowledge of storage and retail areas in store
Ability to use special procedures in cleaning furniture and appliances
Knowledge of minor repair and refinishing techniques

Relevant DOT Reference

Laborer, Stores 922.687-058

Related Job

Department Store Helper (job profile A-3)

JOB PROFILE A-7
Lumber and Building Supplies Store Helper

General Description

Assists in loading, unloading, and storing of lumber and building supplies. May be employed in either retail or wholesale lumber business. Work may be performed either outdoors or in the warehouse area. If merchandise delivery is a major job activity, see job profile A-15.

Job Activities

Load and unload merchandise from trucks and railroad cars
Install strapping, bracing, or padding to prevent shifting or damage during transit
Transport merchandise using forklift or stock car
Load lumber onto dollies and pallets, or stack in yard
Sort and order merchandise by weight or length
Help count, weigh, and record units of materials handled or moved
Package or bundle merchandise for customer
Help customer transport merchandise to car
Package for shipment
Deliver merchandise to customer
Assemble crates to contain loose products such as sand or gravel
Assist in building sheds to protect lumber
Keep yard in order

Specific Skill Requirements

Ability to safely handle heavy lumber and building supplies
Ability to operate forklift truck
Knowledge of correct procedures for stacking lumber and storing other merchandise
Ability to use hand saw and hammer
Ability to use tape measure, weight scales
Knowledge of general arrangement of storage area
Knowledge of special nomenclature

Relevant DOT Reference

Material Handler 929.687-030

Related Job

Lumber Handler (Sawmill) 922.687-070

JOB PROFILE A-8
Floral Shop Assistant

General Description

Assists in caring for flowers and plants and in preparing them for display and sale. May also perform housekeeping tasks in shop. If delivery of orders is a major job activity, see job profile A-14.

Job Activities

Load and unload merchandise from delivery trucks
Water plants and cut flowers daily
Prepare flowers for making into corsages and arrangements
Wrap and package flowers and potted plants for delivery
Paint wreaths and sprays
Write and attach tags and cards to arrangements
Assist in making deliveries
Answer telephone and take messages
Clean retail and stockroom areas

Specific Skill Requirements

Ability to handle flowers and plants without damage
Ability to use watering equipment (cans, sprays)
Ability to trim, wire, pin, and wrap flower stems
Ability to use paint correctly and safely
Knowledge of correct storage procedures for flowers and plants
Knowledge of packaging techniques used in shop
Ability to recognize and name common flowers and plants
Caution in using sharp cutting tools

Relevant DOT Reference

Laborer, Stores 922.687-058

Related Jobs

(Helper to) Floral Arranger 142.081-010
(Helper to) Salesperson, Flowers 260.357-026
Horticultural Worker 405.687-014
Flower Picker 405.687-010

JOB PROFILE A-9
Gas Station Attendant

General Description

Provides a variety of routine services for customers in a gas station; may also assist in automobile maintenance and repair (see job profile E-18). Gas station attendants may be responsible for keeping restrooms and service areas clean and orderly. They also may work at stations which service private boats and aircraft.

Job Activities

Pump gas into cars and trucks
Check oil, water, antifreeze, or other fluids; add when necessary
Add air to tires
Clean car windshields
Change tires; help repair tires
Put on or remove tire chains
Wash and wax cars, clean interiors
Receive cash and credit card payments and make change
Clean restrooms and office and replenish supplies
Clean garage and pump area
Store delivered supplies
Move equipment around station
Clear snow and ice
Help with simple repairs, such as changing water hose

Specific Skill Requirements

Ability to recognize different makes and types of automobiles
Ability to operate fuel pump and read meter accurately
Ability to locate and read oil stick and add oil as required
Ability to locate radiator cap and add water as required
Ability to read pressure gauge and add air to tires
Knowledge of cleaning techniques for automobile exteriors and interiors
Ability to handle money and make change
Ability to complete credit card charge slips

Ability to remove and replace tires on car
Ability to put on and remove tire chains
Knowledge of cleaning procedures for restrooms, office, garage, and pump area
Ability to use broom, rake, shovel, mop, hoses, and snow/ice removal equipment
Knowledge of standard stock and storage display procedures
Ability to safely lift, carry, or transport heavy loads
Ability to interact with customers

Relevant DOT Reference

Automobile Service Station Attendant 915.467-010

Related Jobs

Automobile Mechanic Helper (job profile E-18)
Tire Repairer 915.684-010

JOB PROFILE A-10
Fuel Sales Yard Worker

General Description

Assists in activities in receiving, storing and delivering fuels to customers. This employee works outdoors or in a warehouse, in either a wholesale or retail operation. See job profile A-15 if delivery of merchandise is a major job activity.

Job Activities

Load and unload fuels from trucks and railroad cars
Sort and stack fuels in sales yard or warehouse
Weigh amount of fuel to be packaged
Package bulk fuels for sale
Load bags or bundles of fuel into customer's car
Maintain orderly warehouse and yard
Help deliver from truck

Specific Skill Requirements

Familiarity with common fuels sold in yard
Ability to safely handle heavy or bulky materials such as logs, propane containers, bags of coal
Knowledge of fuel storage arrangement and procedures
Ability to use shovel to load coal into bags
Ability to accurately weigh bags or bundles of fuel
Ability to operate forklift truck
Knowledge of special nomenclature
Caution in handling combustible materials

Relevant DOT Reference

Laborer, Stores 922.687-058

Related Job

Lumber and Building Supplies Store Helper (job profile A-7)

JOB PROFILE A-11
Newspaper Carrier

General Description

Delivers newspapers to subscribers on route and collects money owed at specified intervals.

Job Activities

Purchase newspapers from local source
Assemble and fold newspapers
Wrap newspapers in protective cover when required
Deliver newspapers by car, bicycle, or on foot
Keep records of delivery and payments
Collect from subscribers at regular intervals

Specific Skill Requirements

Knowledge of procedures for purchasing newspapers
Ability to assemble, fold, and wrap newspapers

Knowledge of route and subscribers
Ability to use transportation as required
Ability to keep simple records
Understanding of collection dates and procedures
Ability to handle money and make change
Use of safety precautions along delivery route (crossing streets, obeying traffic laws)
Ability to meet time schedules
Ability to interact with customers

Relevant DOT Reference

Newspaper Carrier 292.457-010

Related Jobs

Merchandise Deliverer (job profile A-14)
Driver Helper, Sales Route 292.667-010
Peddler 291.457-018
Vendor 291.457-022

JOB PROFILE A-12
Gift Wrapper

General Description

Gift wrappers box and wrap gift items for retail store customers. They are responsible for preparing attractively wrapped packages and collecting service charges when appropriate.

Job Activities

Wrap gift packages with decorative paper and ribbon
Assemble boxes
Operate bow-making device
Collect gift-wrap charges
Order supplies from stockroom as needed
Maintain an orderly work area
Record simple information on services performed

Specific Skill Requirements

Ability to select appropriate carton, packing material, and wrapping for gifts
Ability to communicate effectively with customers
Ability to collect charges and make change
Ability to keep simple records of work performed

Relevant DOT Reference

Packager, Hand 920.587-018

Related Jobs

Bagger, Laundry 920.687-018
Packer, Agricultural Produce 920.687-134
Candy Packer 920.587-018

JOB PROFILE A-13
Pet Shop Assistant

General Description

Assists in merchandise handling, animal care, and general pet shop cleaning. If delivery is a major job activity, see job profiles A-14 and A-15.

Job Activities

Handle and feed animals, birds, and fish
Disinfect, clean, and prepare cages and fish tanks
Check and adjust temperature and humidity of animal quarters
Load, unload, and transport stock
Mark, stamp, or tag stock
Rack or shelve stock such as feed, cages, animal supplies
Make local deliveries and pickups
Operate cash register and make change
General cleaning of storage and display areas
Assist in treatment of sick animals

Assist in grooming of animals
Repair cages
Direct customers toward products or animals

Specific Skill Requirements

Knowledge of special procedures required in handling animals, birds, and fish
Knowledge of correct kind and amount of feed for pets
Knowledge of special procedures for cleaning and preparing cages and tanks
Knowledge of nomenclature used in animal care
Ability to use cautious handling procedures, both to prevent injury to the animals and to self

Related DOT Reference

Animal Caretaker 410.674-010

Related Jobs

Dog Pound Attendant 410.674-010
Veterinary Hospital Attendant 410.674-010
Animal Keeper 412.674-010
Kennel Attendant 410.674-010

JOB PROFILE A-14
Merchandise Deliverer

General Description

Delivers, or assists in the delivery of, merchandise from a retail store to local customers. The types of stores usually are those in which relatively light packages are to be delivered, such as grocery store, restaurant or fast-food outlet, bakery, pharmacy, or floral shop. Deliveries may be made on foot, by bicycle, by company vehicle, or by public transportation.

The delivery person also may run other errands outside the building or work area.

Job Activities

Wrap or bag purchases
Carry packages
Walk, operate vehicle, or use public transportation to make delivery
Collect money from customer if COD order
Obtain charge-account signature from customer
Make change
Write receipts

Specific Skill Requirements

Knowledge of streets and addresses in the delivery area
Knowledge of public transportation schedules, routes, fares
Ability to operate vehicle (bicycle, car, van, light truck)
Ability to handle money and make change
Ability to ignore distractions while on route to and from delivery site
Use of safety precautions along delivery route (crossing streets, obeying traffic regulations)
Ability to lift and carry heavy loads

Relevant DOT Reference

Deliverer, Merchandise 299.477-010

Related Jobs

Delivery Truck Helper (job profile A-15)
General Office Messenger (job profile B-2)
Deliverer, Outside 230.667-010

JOB PROFILE A-15
Delivery Truck Helper

General Description

Assists in the delivery of bulky merchandise from retail stores to customers. Generally, this is merchandise that requires more than one person in handling or transporting, such as furniture, appliances, lumber, or building supplies.

Job Activities

Transport merchandise to and from delivery truck by hand, handtruck, or dolly
Load and unload merchandise from delivery truck
Pad, stack or secure items in position on truck to prevent damage
Position, stack or set up merchandise at customer's direction

Specific Skill Requirements

Ability to follow directions of customer and/or truck driver
Ability to lift and carry heavy single loads, or to assist another person with heavier merchandise
Observance of safety precautions in crossing streets, or climbing in and out of truck
Knowledge of procedures of stowing merchandise, to prevent damage in shipment

Relevant DOT Reference

Truck-Driver Helper 905.687-010

Related Jobs

Merchandise Deliverer (job profile A-14)
Driver-Helper, Sales Route 292.667-010

Master Profile B: **Office Occupations**

General Description

Jobs in this category involve assisting in routine clerical duties such as simple filing and sorting, stuffing and sealing envelopes, packing, and so on. Some jobs may require operating business machines and simple data processing equipment; some also may involve delivering messages and running errands. Job activities that are frequently found in office occupations include the following: perform messenger service within organization, receive and lay out mail, shelve supplies, collate papers, and operate office machines.

Job settings might include both public and private agencies large enough to require helpers in the performance of clerical tasks—for example, businesses, schools, libraries, and governmental agencies.

Clerical employees can be expected to have considerable contact with other employees and, in organizations generally open to the public, with nonemployees. Hours are regular, with a fairly rigid schedule. The activities probably will not be too varied, but work required should conform to fairly accurate standards, and production will be expected at a rather consistent rate.

Job Profiles (see pages immediately following this master profile.)

B-1 General Office Assistant
B-2 General Office Messenger
B-3 Library Assistant
B-4 Copy Messenger
B-5 Typist
B-6 Computer Keying Operator
B-7 Sorting Machine Operator
B-8 Collator Operator
B-9 Addressing Machine Operator
B-10 Hand Collator
B-11 Duplicating Equipment Operator
B-12 Mail Clerk, General Office
B-13 Postage Meter Operator
B-14 Direct Mail Clerk

Skill Requirements

The following basic, core, and personal/social skills are considered to apply generally to all jobs in the office occupations. In addition to these, each job profile lists specific skill requirements relevant to that particular job.

Basic skills The numbers in parentheses refer to the sequence of the skills listed in the basic skills chart, beginning on page 43, which defines the individual skills and cites applications for each one.

- Read (varies from minimal to considerable, as in typing) (1)
- Write (simple records, copy words and figures) (2)
- Count and record numbers (3)
- Perform simple calculations (4)
- Count money (5)
- Sort by category (6)
- Arrange in order (8)
- Communicate verbally (10)
- Use telephone (11)
- Write simple messages (12)
- Tell time (13)
- Measure (with ruler, weights, liquids) (14)
- Read dials (minimal) (17)
- Manipulate small objects (minimal) (17)
- Tie with string or rope (19)
- Secure with tape (20)

Core skills The numbers in parentheses refer to the sequence of the skills listed in the core skills chart, beginning on page 47, which defines the individual skills and cites applications for each one.

- Fold paper (1)
- Bundle (2)
- Assemble and collate papers (3)
- Fasten (glue, staples, clips, binders) (4)
- Package and wrap for mailing (5)
- Cut paper, cord, tape, etc. (6)
- Lift and carry (7)
- Load and unload (8)
- Stack and shelve office supplies (10)
- Open and unpack supplies (12)
- Stamp and label (13)
- Receive and transmit messages (14)
- Run errands (15)
- Find streets and addresses (16)
- Type (17)
- Use standard office supplies (stapler, staple remover, rubber stamp, paper punch, pencil sharpener) (18)
- Stuff envelopes (19)
- Affix postage (20)
- Use hand tools (minimal) (33)

Personal/social skills Sociability and a neat appearance are particularly important because the jobs in this group require considerable contact with other employees and with the public. Many of the jobs involve delivering or receiving messages or filling requests from co-workers; thus communication skills are very important. In some of the jobs, such as in keypunching or typing, the worker has a great deal of independence with only periodic supervision. In others, such as stuffing envelopes for a mail order service, a high degree of tolerance for repetitive work is necessary.

Other skills required to a major extent are shown in the following profile.

Master Profile: **B: Office Occupations**

	Personal/Social Skill Requirements	Extent Required: Minimal	Extent Required: Moderate	Extent Required: Major
Social Skills	1. *SELF EXPRESSION* - communicate, ask for assistance, question			●
	2. *SOCIABILITY* - interact with other employees or public			●
	3. *WORK INDEPENDENCE* - work without supervision or guidance			●
	4. *APPEARANCE/HYGIENE* - cleanliness, good manners, neatness in appearance			●
	5. *TEAMWORK* - perform in close coordination with other jobs			●
Time Factors	6. *PACE* - perform at a consistent rate of speed			●
	7. *ATTENDANCE* - be reliable in attendance and punctuality			●
	8. *SIMULTANEITY* - perform several activities at near same time		●	
	9. *TIMING* - perform timed, scheduled activities; be aware of time			●
Performance Skills	10. *ACCURACY* - perform within well-defined tolerances			●
	11. *DEXTERITY* - make fine manipulations, coordinated movements		●	
	12. *CHOICES* - select among alternatives, make decisions		●	
	13. *DIRECTION* - follow procedures, instructions or directions			●
	14. *MEMORY* - remember locations, procedures, nomenclatures, etc.			●
	15. *CAUTION* - use care in activities which pose personal hazard		●	
	16. *NEATNESS* - work in a neat, orderly manner		●	
	17. *CONCENTRATION* - attend to task despite environmental distraction		●	
Tolerance	18. *REPETITION* - tolerate repetitive work assignments			●
	19. *PERSEVERANCE* - perform continuously, over normal periods		●	
	20. *STAMINA* - have physical stamina, strength, resist fatigue		●	

JOB PROFILE B-1
General Office Assistant

General Description

Assists in routine clerical work in a variety of office settings, including both public and private agencies. Office assistants may help in performing general clerical duties such as filing, typing, recordkeeping, and reproduction of materials.

Job Activities

Type simple cards and forms
Copy information from one record to another
Receive, sort, and distribute incoming mail
Collect, seal, and stamp outgoing mail
Prepare printed matter for mailing
Address envelopes by hand, typewriter, or addressing machine
Prepare packages for mailing
Initiate, receive, and relay telephone messages
Maintain supply cabinet
Furnish workers with clerical supplies
Copy documents, using office duplicating equipment
Collect and distribute paperwork from one department to another
Sort and file printed matter
Deliver messages and run errands within organization

Specific Skill Requirements

Ability to type on manual or electric typewriter
Knowledge of mail distribution procedures within organization
Knowledge of mail preparation and mailing procedures
Ability to operate specific office equipment as required (duplicating equipment, postage meter, addressing machine)
Knowledge of supply storage areas and procedures
Knowledge of specific office filing system
Ability to recognize forms commonly used in the office
Knowledge of physical facility, special personnel locations, and schedules

Relevant DOT Reference

Clerk, General (Clerical) 209.562-010

Related Jobs

General Office Messenger (job profile B-2)
Duplicating Equipment Operator (job profile B-11)
Mail Clerk, General Office (job profile B-12)
Addressing Clerk 209.587-010
Sorter (Clerical) 209.687-022

JOB PROFILE B-2
General Office Messenger

General Description

Performs messenger and delivery services within the organization and to outside locations. Messengers also may assist in various routine office procedures. Outside deliveries may be made by bicycle, motorcycle, truck, on foot, or by public transportation.

Job Activities

Sort and distribute incoming mail
Prepare outgoing mail
Sort, collate, and prepare paperwork for delivery inside or outside the agency
Deliver messages and materials within organization
Wrap packages for delivery
Make local pickups and deliveries
Obtain signature or receipt for deliveries made
Pay or sign for materials being picked up

Specific Skill Requirements

Knowledge of mail distribution procedures within organization
Knowledge of mail preparation and mailing procedures
Knowledge of physical facility and personnel locations

Ability to operate delivery vehicle (bicycle, motorcycle, company truck, or van)
Knowledge of public transportation schedules, routes, fares
Knowledge of local delivery routes, destinations
Use of safety precautions along delivery route (crossing streets, obeying traffic regulations)
Ability to lift and carry heavy loads
Awareness of time and schedules

Relevant DOT Reference

Office Helper (Clerical) 239.567-010
Messenger, Clerical 239.567-010

Related Jobs

Merchandise Deliverer (job profile A-14)
Mail Clerk, General Office (job profile B-12)
Deliverer, Outside 230.667-010

JOB PROFILE B-3
Library Assistant

General Description

Assists in sorting and shelving library loan materials such as magazines, books, records, and pictures. Library assistants also may perform messenger services, mail handling duties, and assist in book labeling and repair.

Job Activities

Uncrate and store incoming materials
Sort and shelve library loan materials
Stuff envelopes and prepare materials for mailing
Perform messenger services within the organization
Serialize or alphabetize cards
File cards by letter or number
Stamp books with library identification
Paste card holders inside books

Mend torn pages and binding
Answer telephone and refer calls
Duplicate printed materials
Receive and distribute incoming mail
Furnish workers with clerical supplies
Refer patron requests to librarian
Clean stack and work areas

Specific Skill Requirements

Ability to alphabetize or serialize cards and library materials
Knowledge of shelving locations in library
Knowledge of mailing procedures
Ability to operate library duplicating equipment
Knowledge of location and function of departments in library (cataloging, circulation)
Ability to assist in preparing books for circulation (stamp, paste in card holders)
Knowledge of telephone answering procedures in a library
Knowledge of library nomenclature

Relevant DOT Reference

Page (Library) 249.687-014

Related Jobs

General Office Assistant (job profile B-1)
(Helper to) Library Assistant 249.367-046

JOB PROFILE B-4
Copy Messenger

General Description

Performs routine and on-call in-house delivery of copy in a newspaper office. Copy messengers also may assist in other clerical activities.

Job Activities

Deliver copy to various departments
Perform messenger services within office
Furnish workers with clerical supplies
Make local deliveries
Answer telephone and take messages

Specific Skill Requirements

Knowledge of location of departments and personnel
Knowledge of local delivery locations
Ability to use company vehicle or public transportation for deliveries
Use of traffic safety precautions along delivery route
Knowledge of newspaper nomenclature
Awareness of time and schedules

Relevant DOT Reference

Messenger, Copy 239.677-010

Related Job

General Office Messenger (job profile B-2)

JOB PROFILE B-5
Typist

General Description

Types routine forms, cards, or straight copy under direct supervision. The employee also may assist in other general office tasks.

Job Activities

Type from printed or handwritten copy
Type standard cards, forms, and labels
Address and stuff envelopes, and affix correct postage

Answer telephone
File printed materials
Use duplicating equipment to prepare multiple copies

Specific Skill Requirements

Ability to type 35–50 words per minute
Ability to type documents in specified form (block, indented)
Knowledge of mailing procedures
Ability to file by letter or number
Ability to operate specific equipment in office (addressing machine, postage meter, duplicating machine)

Relevant DOT Reference

Typist (Clerical) 203.582-066

Related Jobs

General Office Assistant (job profile B-1)
Computer Keying Operator (job profile B-6)

JOB PROFILE B-6
Computer Keying Operator

General Description

Operates computer keying machine to transcribe data onto punch cards or directly to magnetic tape. The employee may use other equipment, such as a computer card sorter to sort, merge or match punched cards into specified groups.

Job Activities

Operate alphabetic or numeric keying machine
Detect and correct minor machine malfunctions
Report major machine malfunctions for repair
Remove jammed cards
Verify accuracy of data, using verifying machine
Sort or order punched cards as specified

Mark and identify box of punched cards or reel of tape
Use telephone and take messages

Specific Skill Requirements

Ability to type 40–50 words per minute
Ability to operate alphabetic or numeric keying machine (load cards or magnetic tape, select correct keys and switches, verify punched cards or tape, unload cards or tape)
Ability to detect and correct card jams
Ability to recognize faulty feeding, ejecting, duplicating, or punching
Understanding of action to be taken in specific cases of machine malfunction

Relevant DOT Reference

Keypunch Operator (Clerical) 203.582-030
Data-Coder Operator (Clerical, Magnetic Tape Encoder) 203.582-026

Related Jobs

Typist (job profile B-5)
Sorting Machine Operator (job profile B-7)
Data Typist 203.582-022
Verifier Operator 203.582-070

JOB PROFILE B-7
Sorting Machine Operator

General Description

Operates machine that automatically sorts perforated computer cards. If cards are damaged, this employee might be responsible for reproducing them on a keypunch machine.

Job Activities

Operate automatic card sorting machine
Verify accurate operation of the machine

Remove jammed cards to clear machine
Reproduce damaged cards
Report major machine malfunctions for repair
Remove sorted cards from bins in specified order
Place cards in box or bundle for routing or storing; label
Route cards to recipient or storage
Use telephone and take messages

Specific Skill Requirements

Ability to correctly load cards in machine (riffle them to prevent overfeeding)
Ability to select proper switches and controls
Ability to detect and correct card jams
Ability to select appropriate course of action in case of other machine malfunction
Knowledge of card distribution and storage procedures

Relevant DOT Reference

Sorting Machine Operator (Clerical) 208.685-030

Related Jobs

Computer Keying Operator (job profile B-6)
Collator Operator (job profile B-8)

JOB PROFILE B-8
Collator Operator

General Description

Operates collating machine that assembles pages of printed material in numerical sequence. Employee also may be responsible for fastening or binding the completed copies with staples, clips, ring binders or other fastening devices.

Job Activities

Operate automatic collating machine
Remove assembled pages from machine
Examine pages for correct order and insert missing pages
Assemble complete copies of the printed materials, if in sections
Fasten completed copies as directed
Route or shelve finished sections or assembled copies
Use telephone and take messages

Specific Skill Requirements

Ability to accurately order pages by number
Ability to load pages to be assembled in the holding or feeding trays of the collating machine
Ability to adjust controls for paper size
Ability to fasten completed copies (staple, clip, punch, bind)
Knowledge of routing and storage procedures for completed copies
Tolerance for repetitive activities

Relevant DOT Reference

Collator Operator (Clerical) 208.685-010

Related Jobs

Sorting Machine Operator (job profile B-7)
Hand Collator (job profile B-10)
Bindery Worker (job profile E-32)
Inserting Machine Operator 208.685-018

JOB PROFILE B-9
Addressing Machine Operator

General Description

Operates machine to print addresses and code numbers on envelopes, charge statements or other accounting forms, packages, and advertising literature. The addressing machine operator also may make new plates, using a plate embossing machine, when necessary.

Job Activities

Position plate in addressing machine
Load machine with articles to be addressed
Adjust and operate addressing machine
Maintain plate file
Make corrections, additions or changes in plates using plate embossing machine
Type address lists from plate file
Prepare materials for mailing
Use telephone and take messages

Specific Skill Requirements

Ability to adjust ink flow in addressing machine
Ability to adjust paper guides of addressing machine to fit varying sizes of paper, using wrench and pliers
Ability to operate electrically powered or manual plate embossing machine
Ability to type 30–40 words per minute
Knowledge of mailing procedures

Relevant DOT Reference

Addressing Machine Operator 208.582-010

Related Jobs

Embossing Machine Operator II 208.682-010
Microfilm Mounter 208.685-022

JOB PROFILE B-10
Hand Collator

General Description

Orders and assembles printed pages into units, using standard hand-collating equipment such as racks or trays. This worker also may be responsible for binding completed units, using staples, clips, rings or other binders, or by gluing the edges of the assembled sheets.

Job Activities

Sort and stack pages in order for collating
Assemble pages in correct order
Tap or jog pages to align the edges of the pages
Stack finished copies
Fasten or bind completed copies into units
Count out number of units to be routed to different recipients
Store or route completed copies
Use telephone and take messages

Specific Skill Requirements

Ability to sort by size, weight, color or number sequence
Ability to use hand-collating equipment (boxes, racks, trays)
Manual dexterity for handling multiple printed copies
Ability to order by letter or number
Safety precautions in using large stapler or punch
Knowledge of routing or storage procedures for completed copies
Tolerance for repetitive activities

Relevant DOT Reference

Collator (Printing and Publishing) 977.687-010

Related Jobs

Collator Operator (job profile B-8)
Sorter (Clerical) 209.687-022

JOB PROFILE B-11
Duplicating Equipment Operator

General Description

Operates ditto, mimeograph, offset, or instant copying machines to produce copies in volume. An additional job responsibility might be collating and binding the reproduced copies.

Job Activities

Set master copy on machine
Load paper into machine
Add fluid, ink, or toner to machine as indicated
Set control for number of copies
Operate specific duplicating machines to produce volume copies
Stack reproduced sheets by jogging or tapping them to align the edges
Collate and fasten the copies, if required
Record copy production
Store or route copies
Maintain adequate stock of duplicating supplies
Use telephone and take messages
Confer with user or supervisor to determine preference of materials or methods
Reset jammed machine
Report malfunctions for repair

Specific Skill Requirements

Ability to set up and operate specific duplicating equipment
Ability to keep simple production records
Knowledge of copy distribution or storage procedures
Ability to request and maintain adequate supplies
Knowledge of location of equipment and supplies and familiarity with storage and work areas
Safety precautions in handling fluids for the machines
Tolerance for repetitive activities

Relevant DOT Reference

Duplicating Machine Operator (Clerical) II 207.682-014
Offset Duplicating Machine Operator 207.682-018
Photocopying Machine Operator 207.685-014

Related Jobs

Hand Collator (job profile B-10)
Print Shop Worker (job profile E-31)

JOB PROFILE B-12
Mail Clerk, General Office

General Description

Sorts incoming mail for distribution and dispatches outgoing mail. This worker also may be required to wrap packages or prepare other outgoing material for mailing. If delivery or pickup of mail from the post office is one of the job activities, see job profile B-2.

Job Activities

Sort mail according to type and destination
Stamp date and time of receipt on incoming mail
Return undeliverable mail to post office
Open envelopes
Deliver and collect mail in office
Stuff and seal envelopes
Wrap packages for mailing
Weigh mail to determine postage
Use postage meter or stamp mail by hand
Keep records of incoming and outgoing mail
Use telephone and take messages
Pay for stamps or special services purchased at post office; obtain receipt

Specific Skill Requirements

Ability to route printed material to correct location
Ability to operate mailroom equipment
Knowledge of general mail handling procedures
Ability to keep simple records
Awareness of time and schedules

Relevant DOT Reference

Mail Clerk (Clerical) 209.587-026

Related Jobs

General Office Messenger (job profile B-2)
Mail Handler Distribution Clerk (Government Service) 209.687-014

JOB PROFILE B-13
Postage Meter Operator

General Description

Operates machine that seals envelopes and stamps postage on envelopes. Determination of postage may be done by supervisor.

Job Activities

Weigh articles to be mailed and record weights
Determine postage from chart or from postal code book
Set dials as directed by supervisor, to indicate letters and numbers to be printed
Load envelopes or tape into machine
Monitor envelope position while the machine operates
Remove postmarked envelope or tape from machine
Affix the tape to the envelope, if applicable
Fold papers and stuff envelopes for mailing
Use telephone and take messages

Specific Skill Requirements

Ability to read postage scales accurately
Ability to accurately record weights on materials to be mailed
Ability to load, operate, and monitor postage meter
Knowledge of general mail handling procedures

Relevant DOT Reference

Sealing-and-Cancelling Machine Operator (Clerical) 208.685-026

Related Jobs

Folding Machine Operator 208.685-014
Inserting Machine Operator 208.685-018

JOB PROFILE B-14
Direct Mail Clerk

General Description

Assembles and prepares direct mail packets of samples and promotional literature for mailing to prospective customers. This worker also may assist in maintaining records of customer transactions and in preparing shipping orders.

Job Activities

Unpack and shelve samples and other materials to be mailed
Staple or clip together printed material consisting of more than one sheet
Fold printed material and insert into envelopes by hand or machine; seal envelopes
Wrap samples for shipment
Address letters and packages to be mailed
Process letters and packages for mailing (weigh, indicate class of mail on package, affix postage)
Receive and fill written requests for samples and information
Use telephone and record messages
Keep simple records of requests received and items mailed
Serialize shipping slips by numbers, dates, or as directed
File records either numerically or alphabetically, as directed

Specific Skill Requirements

Knowledge of general mail-handling procedures
Ability to fold printed materials and stuff envelopes by hand
Ability to wrap packages according to postal regulations
Ability to operate mail room equipment (folding and stuffing machine, addressing machine, postage meter)
Ability to keep simple records
Familiarity with standard items stocked by company, location of stock

Relevant DOT Reference

Direct Mail Clerk 209.587-018

Related Jobs

Hand Packager 920.587-018
Mailer (Printing and Publishing) 222.587-030

Master Profile C: **Service Occupations**

General Description

Service jobs are performed in institutions, public agencies, hotels, motels, restaurants, resorts, private businesses, in outdoor settings, and private homes. Typical job activities may include: cleaning and washing; providing simple maintenance; gardening and simple landscaping; preparing and serving food; providing simple health care and personal services; and collecting fees for services.

A significant element of the jobs within this section is the amount of contact the worker will have with co-workers and with the general public. The ability to interact with co-workers will be needed on all these jobs. When effective interaction with the public is required, this has been noted in the specific skill requirements section of the individual job profiles.

Because of wide variation among the subgroups of this master profile, separate descriptions and skill requirements are listed for each. In addition to the basic, core, and personal/social skills presented below, each job profile lists specific skill requirements relevant to that particular job.

Job Profiles (See pages immediately following this master profile.)

1. Domestic service

C-1 Day Worker, Housecleaning
C-2 Day Worker, Meal Preparation
C-3 Day Worker, Home Laundry
C-4 Day Worker, Child Care
C-5 Caretaker

2. Food service

C-6 Cooking Assistant
C-7 Steam Table Assistant
C-8 Dining Room Attendant
C-9 Waiter/Waitress
C-10 Kitchen Clean-Up Worker
C-11 Dishwasher
C-12 Hospital Food Service Worker
C-13 Pantry Worker

3. Personal service

C-14 Beauty or Barber Shop Helper
C-15 Health Salon Helper

C-16 Sewing and Alteration Helper
C-17 Baggage Porter
C-18 Laundry Worker

4. Building services

C-19 Custodian
C-20 Rug Cleaner Helper
C-21 Elevator Operator
C-22 Security Guard (Unarmed)
C-23 Building Porter
C-24 Window Washer

5. Recreation and leisure services

C-25 Bellhop
C-26 Hotel/Motel Cleaner
C-27 Room Preparation Worker
C-28 Resort Worker
C-29 Recreation Assistant
C-30 Golf Range Attendant
C-31 Ticket Taker
C-32 Concession Worker

6. Patient services

C-33 Hospital Cleaner
C-34 Patient Service Helper
C-35 Nurse's Aide
C-36 Physical Therapist Aide

7. Public service

C-37 Road Maintenance Worker
C-38 Garbage Collection Helper
C-39 Parking Meter Collector
C-40 Mail Sorter
C-41 Sewage Treatment Worker

8. Groundskeeping

C-42 Park Worker
C-43 Landscaping Worker
C-44 Painting and Maintenance Helper
C-45 Cemetery Worker

9. Other

C-46 Nursery School Aide
C-47 Veterinary Hospital Attendant
C-48 Parking Garage Attendant
C-49 Laboratory Helper

1. Domestic service

Workers in domestic service perform activities in private homes related to food preparation, laundry and general cleaning, and child care. Typical job activities include cleaning, washing dishes, watching children or elderly members of the family, washing and ironing clothes, and limited outdoor work.

Domestic service almost always involves close contact with at least one individual—the employer—and often with other members of the family, especially the children. A work day will include a wide variety of activities to be performed according to specific directions. Most of the activities are physical and may involve hazards to both the employee and the materials used in the work being done.

Basic skills
Sort by category (6)*
Locate by number, word, or symbol (9)
Communicate verbally (10)
Use telephone (11)
Tell time (13)
Measure weight, volume (14)
Combine liquid and dry ingredients (16)

Core skills
Fold (1)*
Mix and blend (22)
Use heat and heating units (23)
Perform indoor cleaning (24)
Make beds (25)
Dress and undress another person (26)
Set and clear tables (27)
Use common kitchen utensils (28)
Perform kitchen clean-up (29)
Handle dangerous substances (30)
Hand stitch (31)
Iron (32)

Personal/social skills
See Requirements Profile C-1 on page 136. Particularly important are interacting with other people, caution in using hazardous substances, and physical stamina.

*The numbers in parentheses refer to the sequence of the skills listed in the basic skills chart (page 43) and the core skills chart (page 47), which define the individual skills and cite applications for each one.

2. *Food service*

Jobs in food service involve food preparation, service, and cleanup in public dining areas such as restaurants. Representative job activities are: gathering ingredients and equipment; lifting and carrying trays; setting up and replenishing food, dishes or silver; cleaning up breakage or spills; and scraping and washing dishes and other cooking implements.

Most employees in this job group will have considerable contact with other employees and often with patients or customers. Variety may be lacking and the demand for continuous physical activity may be high. Work areas generally are large and complex. There may be many distracting activities in the work area.

Basic skills

- Read (recipes) (1)
- Write (2)
- Count and record numbers (3)
- Perform simple calculations, adding/subtracting (4)
- Count money/make change (5)
- Sort (6)
- Locate by number, word or symbol (9)
- Communicate verbally (10)
- Tell time (13)
- Measure (14)

Core skills

- Lift and carry (7)
- Load and unload (8)
- Transport (9)
- Receive and transmit messages (14)
- Use cash register (21)
- Use heating units (23)
- Set and clear tables (27)
- Use common kitchen utensils (28)
- Perform kitchen clean-up (29)
- Handle dangerous substances (30)

Personal/social skills

See Requirements Profile C-2. Interacting with others, physical strength, stamina, and ability to work under pressure are particularly important. Good hygiene is a critical requirement in food handling jobs.

3. *Personal service*

Workers provide services in individual self-care in such places as barber or beauty shops, in jobs having to do with fashion, and so on. Typical activities are: washing hair, cleaning equipment, making simple clothing alterations, and washing clothing.

These employees will have considerable contact with the public and fellow employees. However, the need for high verbal abilities generally is not great. Appearance is quite important.

Basic skills

- Read (minimal) (1)
- Write (minimal) (2)
- Locate by number, word or symbol (9)

Core skills

- Fold (1)
- Bundle (2)
- Load and unload (8)
- Stamp or label (13)

Personal/social skills

See Requirements Profile C-3. Skills of major importance are: interacting with others;

Basic skills

Communicate verbally (10)
Use telephone (11)
Write simple messages (12)
Tell time (13)

Core skills

Receive and transmit messages (14)
Perform indoor cleaning (24)
Handle dangerous substances (30)
Hand stitch (31)
Iron (32)

Personal/social skills

appearance and hygiene; and physical stamina, e.g., standing for long periods while working.

4. *Building services*

Building-services workers are responsible for cleaning and maintenance. Frequently found job activities are cleaning and dusting, vacuuming or scrubbing floors, washing windows and walls, making simple repairs, operating elevators, and moving furniture or boxes.

Employees in this job group often will be working alone, in large, generally complex work areas. The work is mostly routine, sometimes strenuous; some of the job activities require observance of special safety measures.

Basic skills

Sort by category (6)
Locate by number, word or symbol (9)
Communicate verbally (10)
Tell time (13)
Tie with string or rope (19)
Secure with tape (20)

Core skills

Package and wrap (5)
Lift and carry (7)
Load and unload (8)
Transport (9)
Stack and shelve (10)
Pack or crate (11)
Perform indoor cleaning (24)
Handle dangerous substances (30)
Use hand tools (33)
Dig and shovel (34)
Use garden tools (35)

Personal/social skills

See Requirements Profile C-4. The most critical personal skills for these jobs are physical stamina and ability to work without supervision.

5. *Recreation and leisure services*

Jobs in recreation and leisure services involve assisting guests in resorts or recreational facilities by discharging such tasks as carrying luggage, cleaning rooms, helping with recreational activities, preparing food, running errands, servicing cars, and performing light outdoor cleaning or maintenance.

Employees will be working both indoors and outdoors. The range of skills required is very broad, since the jobs encompass activities related to food, personal, and building services.

Basic skills	*Core skills*	*Personal/social skills*
Read (1)	Lift and carry (7)	See Requirements Profile C-5. Of major importance are physical strength and stamina, willingness to work in a variety of weather conditions, and ability to interact with the public.
Write (2)	Load and unload (8)	
Count and record numbers (3)	Transport (9)	
Perform simple calculations (4)	Receive and transmit messages (14)	
Count money/make change (5)	Use cash register (21)	
Sort (6)	Mix and blend (22)	
Locate by number, word or symbol (9)	Perform indoor cleaning (24)	
Communicate verbally (10)	Handle dangerous substances (30)	
Use telephone (11)	Use hand tools (33)	
Write simple messages (12)	Use garden tools (35)	
Tell time (13)		
Measure (14)		
Tie with string or rope (19)		
Secure with tape (20)		

6. *Patient services*

Workers in this job group assist with care of patients in hospitals or nursing homes, and perform cleaning tasks. Job activities may include cleaning rooms and equipment, making beds, moving and transporting patients, dressing and undressing patients, helping patients shave or wash hair, preparing and serving food, feeding patients, and assisting in patient treatment. Generally these employees work with relatively little supervision. Contact with patients, visitors, and other employees is frequent. Since the moving, cleaning, and lifting activities occur frequently, physical requirements will be substantial. The work areas are usually large and complex.

Basic skills	*Core skills*	*Personal/social skills*
Read (1)	Fold (1)	See Requirements Profile C-6. A special personal skill for many jobs in this group is the ability to accept working around ill, injured or dying patients.
Write (2)	Lift and carry (7)	
Count (3)	Load and unload (8)	
Perform simple calculations (4)	Transport (9)	
Locate by number, word or symbol (9)	Stack and shelve (10)	
Communicate verbally (10)	Stamp or label (13)	
Use telephone (11)	Receive or transmit messages (14)	
Write simple messages (12)	Perform indoor cleaning (24)	
	Make beds (25)	

Basic skills	*Core skills*
Tell time (13) Measure (14) Read meters (15) Combine liquids and/ or dry materials (16) Manipulate small objects (17)	Dress and undress another person (26) Handle dangerous substances (30)

7. *Public service*

Workers assist in services to the public such as trash collection, street cleaning, or mail sorting. Digging, sweeping, lifting and carrying, painting, and sorting mail and coins are typical activities.

The work generally involves strenuous and continuous physical movements with little variety, although painting and maintenance require special procedures such as spray painting and setting up of outdoor equipment. Mail sorting involves more clerical skills.

Basic skills	*Core skills*	*Personal/social skills*
Read (1) Arrange in order (8) Locate by number, word or symbol (9) Communicate verbally (10) Tell time (13)	Lift and carry (7) Load and unload (8) Transport (9) Use hand tools (33) Dig and shovel (34) Use garden tools (35)	See Requirements Profile C-7. The major requirement is physical stamina. Also important are willingness to work in a variety of weather conditions, and wearing clothing appropriate for the job.

8. *Groundskeeping*

Workers are concerned with the planting and maintenance of parks, yards, lawns, or gardens. Typical activities include digging, weeding, simple repair, sweeping, planting, mowing, and raking.

These employees will be working outdoors and most likely in large areas or several different locations. Much physical activity is involved, and there must be some familiarity with simple hand tools. Special safety procedures must be observed near hazardous power equipment.

Basic skills	*Core skills*	*Personal/social skills*
Locate or identify by number, word or symbol (9) Communicate verbally (minimal) (10) Tell time (13)	Lift and carry (7) Load and unload (8) Transport (9) Use hand tools (33) Dig and shovel (34) Use garden tools (35)	See Requirements Profile C-8. Physical strength and stamina are important.

Master Profile: **C-1. Service Occupations (Domestic Service)**

	Personal/Social Skill Requirements	Extent Required		
		Minimal	Moderate	Major
Social Skills	1. *SELF EXPRESSION* - communicate, ask for assistance, question			●
	2. *SOCIABILITY* - interact with other employees or public			●
	3. *WORK INDEPENDENCE* - work without supervision or guidance		●	
	4. *APPEARANCE/HYGIENE* - cleanliness, good manners, neatness in appearance			●
	5. *TEAMWORK* - perform in close coordination with other jobs	●		
Time Factors	6. *PACE* - perform at a consistent rate of speed	●		
	7. *ATTENDANCE* - be reliable in attendance and punctuality		●	
	8. *SIMULTANEITY* - perform several activities at near same time	●		
	9. *TIMING* - perform timed, scheduled activities; be aware of time		●	
Performance Skills	10. *ACCURACY* - perform within well-defined tolerances		●	
	11. *DEXTERITY* - make fine manipulations, coordinated movements		●	
	12. *CHOICES* - select among alternatives, make decisions		●	
	13. *DIRECTION* - follow procedures, instructions or directions			●
	14. *MEMORY* - remember locations, procedures, nomenclatures, etc.			●
	15. *CAUTION* - use care in activities which pose personal hazard			●
	16. *NEATNESS* - work in a neat, orderly manner		●	
	17. *CONCENTRATION* - attend to task despite environmental distraction		●	
Tolerance	18. *REPETITION* - tolerate repetitive work assignments	●		
	19. *PERSEVERANCE* - perform continuously, over normal periods	●		
	20. *STAMINA* - have physical stamina, strength, resist fatigue			●

Master Profile: **C-2. Service Occupations (Food Service)**

Personal/Social Skill Requirements		Extent Required: Minimal	Extent Required: Moderate	Extent Required: Major
Social Skills	1. *SELF EXPRESSION* - communicate, ask for assistance, question		●	
	2. *SOCIABILITY* - interact with other employees or public			●
	3. *WORK INDEPENDENCE* - work without supervision or guidance			●
	4. *APPEARANCE/HYGIENE* - cleanliness, good manners, neatness in appearance			●
	5. *TEAMWORK* - perform in close coordination with other jobs		●	
Time Factors	6. *PACE* - perform at a consistent rate of speed		●	
	7. *ATTENDANCE* - be reliable in attendance and punctuality		●	
	8. *SIMULTANEITY* - perform several activities at near same time		●	
	9. *TIMING* - perform timed, scheduled activities; be aware of time		●	
Performance Skills	10. *ACCURACY* - perform within well-defined tolerances		●	
	11. *DEXTERITY* - make fine manipulations, coordinated movements		●	
	12. *CHOICES* - select among alternatives, make decisions		●	
	13. *DIRECTION* - follow procedures, instructions or directions		●	
	14. *MEMORY* - remember locations, procedures, nomenclatures, etc.			●
	15. *CAUTION* - use care in activities which pose personal hazard			●
	16. *NEATNESS* - work in a neat, orderly manner		●	
	17. *CONCENTRATION* - attend to task despite environmental distraction		●	
Tolerance	18. *REPETITION* - tolerate repetitive work assignments	●		
	19. *PERSEVERANCE* - perform continuously, over normal periods	●		
	20. *STAMINA* - have physical stamina, strength, resist fatigue			●

Master Profile: **C-3. Service Occupations (Personal Service)**

Personal/Social Skill Requirements		Extent Required: Minimal	Moderate	Major
Social Skills	1. *SELF EXPRESSION* - communicate, ask for assistance, question			●
	2. *SOCIABILITY* - interact with other employees or public			●
	3. *WORK INDEPENDENCE* - work without supervision or guidance		●	
	4. *APPEARANCE/HYGIENE* - cleanliness, good manners, neatness in appearance			●
	5. *TEAMWORK* - perform in close coordination with other jobs			●
Time Factors	6. *PACE* - perform at a consistent rate of speed		●	
	7. *ATTENDANCE* - be reliable in attendance and punctuality		●	
	8. *SIMULTANEITY* - perform several activities at near same time		●	
	9. *TIMING* - perform timed, scheduled activities; be aware of time		●	
Performance Skills	10. *ACCURACY* - perform within well-defined tolerances		●	
	11. *DEXTERITY* - make fine manipulations, coordinated movements		●	
	12. *CHOICES* - select among alternatives, make decisions		●	
	13. DIRECTION - follow procedures, instructions or directions		●	
	14. *MEMORY* - remember locations, procedures, nomenclatures, etc.		●	
	15. *CAUTION* - use care in activities which pose personal hazard		●	
	16. *NEATNESS* - work in a neat, orderly manner		●	
	17. *CONCENTRATION* - attend to task despite environmental distraction		●	
Tolerance	18. *REPETITION* - tolerate repetitive work assignments	●		
	19. *PERSEVERANCE* - perform continuously, over normal periods	●		
	20. *STAMINA* - have physical stamina, strength, resist fatigue			●

Master Profile: **C-4. Service Occupations (Building Services)**

	Personal/Social Skill Requirements	Extent Required: Minimal	Extent Required: Moderate	Extent Required: Major
Social Skills	1. *SELF EXPRESSION* - communicate, ask for assistance, question		●	
	2. *SOCIABILITY* - interact with other employees or public		●	
	3. *WORK INDEPENDENCE* - work without supervision or guidance			●
	4. *APPEARANCE/HYGIENE* - cleanliness, good manners, neatness in appearance		●	
	5. *TEAMWORK* - perform in close coordination with other jobs	●		
Time Factors	6. *PACE* - perform at a consistent rate of speed	●		
	7. *ATTENDANCE* - be reliable in attendance and punctuality			●
	8. *SIMULTANEITY* - perform several activities at near same time	●		
	9. *TIMING* - perform timed, scheduled activities; be aware of time		●	
Performance Skills	10. *ACCURACY* - perform within well-defined tolerances		●	
	11. *DEXTERITY* - make fine manipulations, coordinated movements		●	
	12. *CHOICES* - select among alternatives, make decisions		●	
	13. *DIRECTION* - follow procedures, instructions or directions		●	
	14. *MEMORY* - remember locations, procedures, nomenclatures, etc.			●
	15. *CAUTION* - use care in activities which pose personal hazard		●	
	16. *NEATNESS* - work in a neat, orderly manner		●	
	17. *CONCENTRATION* - attend to task despite environmental distraction		●	
Tolerance	18. *REPETITION* - tolerate repetitive work assignments			●
	19. *PERSEVERANCE* - perform continuously, over normal periods	●		
	20. *STAMINA* - have physical stamina, strength, resist fatigue			●

Master Profile: **C-5. Service Occupations (Recreation and Leisure Services)**

	Personal/Social Skill Requirements	Extent Required: Minimal	Extent Required: Moderate	Extent Required: Major
Social Skills	1. *SELF EXPRESSION* - communicate, ask for assistance, question			●
	2. *SOCIABILITY* - interact with other employees or public			●
	3. *WORK INDEPENDENCE* - work without supervision or guidance		●	
	4. *APPEARANCE/HYGIENE* - cleanliness, good manners, neatness in appearance			●
	5. *TEAMWORK* - perform in close coordination with other jobs			●
Time Factors	6. *PACE* - perform at a consistent rate of speed		●	
	7. *ATTENDANCE* - be reliable in attendance and punctuality		●	
	8. *SIMULTANEITY* - perform several activities at near same time	●		
	9. *TIMING* - perform timed, scheduled activities; be aware of time		●	
Performance Skills	10. *ACCURACY* - perform within well-defined tolerances		●	
	11. *DEXTERITY* - make fine manipulations, coordinated movements		●	
	12. *CHOICES* - select among alternatives, make decisions		●	
	13. *DIRECTION* - follow procedures, instructions or directions		●	
	14. *MEMORY* - remember locations, procedures, nomenclatures, etc.		●	
	15. *CAUTION* - use care in activities which pose personal hazard		●	
	16. *NEATNESS* - work in a neat, orderly manner		●	
	17. *CONCENTRATION* - attend to task despite environmental distraction		●	
Tolerance	18. *REPETITION* - tolerate repetitive work assignments	●		
	19. *PERSEVERANCE* - perform continuously, over normal periods	●		
	20. *STAMINA* - have physical stamina, strength, resist fatigue			●

Master Profile: **C-6. Service Occupations (Patient Services)**

	Personal/Social Skill Requirements	**Extent Required** Minimal	Moderate	Major
Social Skills	1. *SELF EXPRESSION* - communicate ask for assistance, question			●
	2. *SOCIABILITY* - interact with other employees or public			●
	3. *WORK INDEPENDENCE* - work without supervision or guidance		●	
	4. *APPEARANCE/HYGIENE* - cleanliness, good manners, neatness in appearance			●
	5. *TEAMWORK* - perform in close coordination with other jobs			●
Time Factors	6. *PACE* - perform at a consistent rate of speed		●	
	7. *ATTENDANCE* - be reliable in attendance and punctuality			●
	8. *SIMULTANEITY* - perform several activities at near same time	●		
	9. *TIMING* - perform timed, scheduled activities; be aware of time		●	
Performance Skills	10. *ACCURACY* - perform within well-defined tolerances		●	
	11. *DEXTERITY* - make fine manipulations, coordinated movements		●	
	12. *CHOICES* - select among alternatives, make decisions		●	
	13. *DIRECTION* - follow procedures, instructions or directions		●	
	14. *MEMORY* - remember locations, procedures, nomenclatures, etc.			●
	15. *CAUTION* - use care in activities which pose personal hazard			●
	16. *NEATNESS* - work in a neat, orderly manner		●	
	17. *CONCENTRATION* - attend to task despite environmental distraction		●	
Tolerance	18. *REPETITION* - tolerate repetitive work assignments		●	
	19. *PERSEVERANCE* - perform continously, over normal periods		●	
	20. *STAMINA* - have physical stamina, strength, resist fatigue			●

Master Profile: **C-7. Service Occupations (Public Service)**

Personal/Social Skill Requirements		Minimal	Moderate	Major
Social Skills	1. *SELF EXPRESSION* - communicate, ask for assistance, question		●	
	2. *SOCIABILITY* - interact with other employees or public		●	
	3. *WORK INDEPENDENCE* - work without supervision or guidance			●
	4. *APPEARANCE/HYGIENE* - cleanliness, good manners, neatness in appearance		●	
	5. *TEAMWORK* - perform in close coordination with other jobs			●
Time Factors	6. *PACE* - perform at a consistent rate of speed			●
	7. *ATTENDANCE* - be reliable in attendance and punctuality		●	
	8. *SIMULTANEITY* - perform several activities at near same time	●		
	9. *TIMING* - perform timed, scheduled activities; be aware of time		●	
Performance Skills	10. *ACCURACY* - perform within well-defined tolerances		●	
	11. *DEXTERITY* - make fine manipulations, coordinated movements		●	
	12. *CHOICES* - select among alternatives, make decisions		●	
	13. *DIRECTION* - follow procedures, instructions or directions		●	
	14. *MEMORY* - remember locations, procedures, nomenclatures, etc.		●	
	15. *CAUTION* - use care in activities which pose personal hazard			●
	16. *NEATNESS* - work in a neat, orderly manner		●	
	17. *CONCENTRATION* - attend to task despite environmental distraction		●	
Tolerance	18. *REPETITION* - tolerate repetitive work assignments		●	
	19. *PERSEVERANCE* - perform continuously, over normal periods		●	
	20. *STAMINA* - have physical stamina, strength, resist fatigue			●

(Extent Required: Minimal / Moderate / Major)

Master Profile: **C-8. Service Occupations (Groundskeeping)**

	Personal/Social Skill Requirements	Extent Required: Minimal	Extent Required: Moderate	Extent Required: Major
Social Skills	1. *SELF EXPRESSION* - communicate, ask for assistance, question	●		
	2. *SOCIABILITY* - interact with other employees or public	●		
	3. *WORK INDEPENDENCE* - work without supervision or guidance		●	
	4. *APPEARANCE/HYGIENE* - cleanliness, good manners, neatness in appearance		●	
	5. *TEAMWORK* - perform in close coordination with other jobs		●	
Time Factors	6. *PACE* - perform at a consistent rate of speed		●	
	7. *ATTENDANCE* - be reliable in attendance and punctuality		●	
	8. *SIMULTANEITY* - perform several activities at near same time	●		
	9. *TIMING* - perform timed, scheduled activities; be aware of time		●	
Performance Skills	10. *ACCURACY* - perform within well-defined tolerances		●	
	11. *DEXTERITY* - make fine manipulations, coordinated movements		●	
	12. *CHOICES* - select among alternatives, make decisions	●		
	13. *DIRECTION* - follow procedures, instructions or directions		●	
	14. *MEMORY* - remember locations, procedures, nomenclatures, etc.		●	
	15. *CAUTION* - use care in activities which pose personal hazard			●
	16. *NEATNESS* - work in a neat, orderly manner		●	
	17. *CONCENTRATION* - attend to task despite environmental distraction		●	
Tolerance	18. *REPETITION* - tolerate repetitive work assignments		●	
	19. *PERSEVERANCE* - perform continuously, over normal periods	●		
	20. *STAMINA* - have physical stamina, strength, resist fatigue			●

JOB PROFILE C-1
Day Worker, Housecleaning

General Description

Helps with or assumes major responsibility for housecleaning tasks. Supervision is generally provided.

Job Activities

Sweep, vacuum, or dust
Wash windows, walls, and wallpaper
Clean floors, walks, steps
Wax or polish floors
Beat or clean rugs
Clean bathroom fixtures
Clean kitchen and laundry appliances
Operate washer, dryer, dishwasher, garbage disposal
Defrost and clean refrigerator
Clean kitchen cabinets
Empty vacuum cleaner bag, replace belt
Assemble vacuum cleaner attachments
Polish furniture, woodwork
Change or make beds
Lift or move furniture, boxes
Dispose of trash
Use telephone, receive messages

Specific Skill Requirements

Ability to properly use cleaning equipment and supplies
Knowledge of hazards of use of cleaning equipment and supplies
Ability to safely move furniture and heavy objects
Ability to carefully handle personal and household items
Knowledge of proper bed making/changing
Knowledge of locations of equipment, supplies, and work areas
Knowledge of individual procedures
Ability to interact well with family members
Physical strength; ability to tolerate being on feet for long periods and to perform strenuous activities

Relevant DOT Reference

Day Worker (Domestic Service) 301.687-014

Related Jobs

Day Worker, Home Laundry (job profile C-3)
House Worker, General 301.474-010

JOB PROFILE C-2
Day Worker, Meal Preparation

General Description

Helps with preparation, serving and clean up of home meals, under supervision.

Job Activities

Prepare vegetables, fruits for cooking or eating
Cook or prepare simple foods; prepare beverages
Serve food on dishes, table
Set table informally
Clear table
Wash and dry dishes, pans, and silver (hand)
Wash dishes, pans, and silver (machine)
Sort and shelve dishes, pans, and silver
Clean kitchen appliances
Feed children
Feed pets
Use telephone, receive messages

Specific Skill Requirements

Ability to safely use and clean kitchen utensils and appliances
Ability to clean, cut, and prepare foods for cooking
Ability to cook/prepare simple foods for eating
Ability to store food properly

Knowledge and observance of safe kitchen procedures
Ability to adapt to individual household customs and patterns
Ability to interact well with family members
Knowledge of table setting arrangements
Knowledge of location of equipment and work areas
Awareness of time and schedules

Relevant DOT Reference

House Worker, General 301.474-010

Related Jobs

Cooking Assistant (job profile C-6)
Kitchen Helper 318.687-010

JOB PROFILE C-3
Day Worker, Home Laundry

General Description

Helps with or takes major responsibility for laundering and finishing of clothing in a private home.

Job Activities

Sort laundry before washing
Wash laundry by machine and/or by hand
Operate clothes dryer; clean lint screen
Fold or hang clothes and laundry
Press or iron clothes
Mend or repair clothes
Use telephone, receive messages

Specific Skill Requirements

Knowledge of types and uses of laundry products
Ability to properly use laundry equipment and supplies
Knowledge and observance of safe procedures in the use of laundry equipment and supplies, hot water, or hot irons

Use of proper hand-laundering methods
Use of simple techniques for mending and repairing clothes
Ability to adapt to individual laundering preferences of employers
Ability to interact well with family members

Relevant DOT Reference

Laundry Worker (Launderer, Domestic Service) 302.685-010

Related Jobs

Laundry Worker (job profile C-18)
Ironer 302.687-010

JOB PROFILE C-4
Day Worker, Child Care

General Description

Takes responsibility for one or more young children for part of day in private home, with or without parent present.

Job Activities

Supervise indoor and outdoor play
Play with/read to children
Take children on walks or outings
Bathe children
Dress or undress children
Prepare food for children
Sterilize bottles or other equipment
Clean up after feeding children
Clean children's rooms
Use telephone, receive messages

Specific Skill Requirements

Knowledge of specific household procedures
Ability to supervise and interact well with children

Ability to implement a variety of children's recreational activities
Using caution in protecting children from hazards
Ability to recognize emergency situations and obtain help
Ability to prepare simple foods/formulas
Willingness to adapt to patterns/regulations of individual households
Knowledge of location of household items
Ability to clean children's rooms and kitchen after children's meals
Knowledge of proper methods for lifting or carrying small children and infants

Relevant DOT Reference

Child Monitor 301.677-010

Related Jobs

Recreation Assistant (job profile C-29)
Nursery School Aide (job profile C-46)

JOB PROFILE C-5
Caretaker

General Description

Helps with heavy housework and outdoor work around the home. Supervision is generally available.

Job Activities

Wash windows, walls, and wallpaper
Clean floors, walks, steps
Polish and wax floors
Beat or clean rugs
Lift or move furniture, boxes
Make simple house repairs
Paint furniture or surfaces
Wash or wax automobile
Mow lawn, trim lawn, bushes, hedges; prune trees
Weed lawn, gardens; mulch; spread fertilizer

Water lawns
Sweep/rake paths and open areas
Dig or spade garden beds
Dispose of garden cuttings, leaves, and trash
Clean rain gutters
Change screen windows; calk windows and doors
Groom, feed and/or exercise pets

Specific Skill Requirements

Proper use of cleaning equipment and supplies
Proper use of hand and power garden equipment
Proper use of basic home repair tools
Ability to use basic painting techniques and equipment
Ability to safely move furniture and heavy objects
Knowledge and observance of safety procedures when lifting, climbing, reaching, cutting, or mowing
Ability to work with care around personal and household items, and with garden plants
Ability to work well with pets
Physical strength, ability to perform strenuous activities
Willingness to work in a variety of weather conditions

Relevant Dot Reference

Caretaker 301.687-010

Related Jobs

Park Worker (job profile C-42)
Painting and Maintenance Helper (job profile C-44)
Groundskeeper, Industrial-Commercial 406.684-014

JOB PROFILE C-6
Cooking Assistant

General Description

Assists in the preparation and cooking of foods in large quantities in public dining rooms or institutions.

Job Activities

Gather ingredients, equipment; open containers
Measure and combine ingredients for simple recipes
Watch, stir cooking food; may use timer or clock
Package and store food for later cooking
Clean and cut meats, fish, and poultry for cooking
Wash, peel, slice vegetables, fruits for cooking or salads
Prepare simple foods: coffee, eggs, sandwiches, hamburgers
Package and wrap food for carry-outs
Sort and shelve canned and packaged foods
Lift and carry tray with food, dishes
Store or shelve dishes, cooking utensils, silver
Mop floors, clean up breakage and spills
Clean work areas and utensils used

Specific Skill Requirements

Ability to read and follow simple recipes and prepare foods properly
Ability to handle food in a safe, neat, and sanitary manner
Ability to accurately measure ingredients and portions
Ability to handle safely hot food and equipment, and sharp utensils
Caution in handling perishable food
Knowledge of techniques of handling large quantities of food
Knowledge of proper uses of kitchen equipment
Knowledge of basic clean-up procedures
Knowledge of specific kitchen routines and procedures
Physical strength; ability to tolerate standing for long periods
Ability to work in close cooperation with other employees

Relevant DOT Reference

Cook Helper 317.687-010

Related Jobs

Steam Table Assistant (job profile C-7)
Pantry Worker (job profile C-13)

JOB PROFILE C-7
Steam Table Assistant

General Description

Serves or assists in serving at steam table in cafeteria or in the kitchen of some restaurants. May assist in other kitchen activities.

Job Activities

Set up or replenish counter food, dishes, silver
Carve meat for serving (easy-to-carve meats)
Portion out food to plates
Serve food—dining room, counter
Replenish beverages, rolls, serve relishes
Take orders; answer questions from customers
Make sandwiches
Wrap foods for carry-out
Watch, stir cooking food; may use timer or clock
Clean work tables, meat blocks, counter
Mop floors, clean up breakage and spills

Specific Skill Requirements

Ability to handle food and utensils in a safe, neat, and sanitary manner
Knowledge and observance of safe procedures when near heat or using sharp utensils
Ability to adapt to established kitchen and serving area routines
Ability to make a variety of sandwiches to order
Proper methods for packaging of carry-out foods
Ability to use cleaning equipment and supplies
Ability to interact well with a variety of people

Relevant DOT Reference

Cafeteria Attendant (Hotel and Restaurant) 311.677-010
Counter Attendant 311.677-014

Related Jobs

Waiter/Waitress (job profile C-9)
Raw Shellfish Preparer 311.674-014

JOB PROFILE C-8
Dining Room Attendant

General Description

Assists in setting up dining room; busses dishes; may assist in serving food.

Job Activities

Set tables (partially or completely)
Replenish beverages, rolls, relishes for patrons
Replenish table supplies: salt, napkins, other supplies
Clear dishes from table, cart, tray
Lift and carry tray with food, dishes
Set up or replenish counter food, dishes, silver
Assemble menu cards or folders
Mop floors; clean up breakage, spills
Wash, dust, polish furniture, fixtures, and counter equipment
Sweep or vacuum floors, rugs, drapes
Remove garbage from serving stations

Specific Skill Requirements

Ability to handle food and utensils in a safe, neat, and sanitary manner
Ability to arrange table settings and replenish table supplies
Ability to handle hot food and equipment, and sharp utensils
Ability to adapt to established kitchen and dining room routines
Ability to interact well with a variety of people
Knowledge of locations, traffic patterns, specific procedures

Relevant DOT Reference

Dining Room Attendant 311.677-018

Related Job

Hospital Food Service Worker (job profile C-12)

JOB PROFILE C-9
Waiter/Waitress

General Description

Performs or assists in activities in waiting on tables or counter; may also assist in food preparation and in clean-up.

Job Activities

Set tables, rearrange tables for large groups
Assemble menu cards or folders
Conduct guests to table; answer patrons' questions
Take orders
Prepare simple foods, beverages, sandwiches
Portion out food to plates
Lift and carry tray with food, dishes
Replenish table supplies—salt, napkins, other supplies
Set up or replenish counter food, dishes, silver
Clear dishes from table, cart, tray
Wrap foods for carry-out
Add up bill
Count money, use cash register, fill out credit card charge slips
Wash, dust, polish furniture, fixtures, and counter equipment
Mop floors, clean up breakage and spills

Specific Skill Requirements

Ability to handle food and utensils in a safe, neat, and sanitary manner
Knowledge and observance of safe procedures when near heat or using sharp utensils
Ability to adapt to established kitchen and serving area routines
Ability to make a variety of sandwiches to order
Proper methods for packaging carry-out foods
Ability to use cleaning equipment and supplies
Ability to interact well with a variety of people
Knowledge of proper food service methods
Ability to prepare simple foods and beverages

Ability to total bills, make change, operate cash register, fill out credit card charge slips
Knowledge of establishment policy for patron seating
Ability to tolerate being on feet for long periods
Ability to work under pressure

Relevant DOT Reference

Waiter/Waitress (Hotel and Restaurant) 311.477-030

Related Job

Steam Table Assistant (job profile C-7)

JOB PROFILE C-10
Kitchen Clean-Up Worker

General Description

Performs clean-up activities of kitchen, dining room, steam table and fountain. Job settings might include restaurants, hospitals, and other eating establishments.

Job Activities

Clean work tables, meat blocks, counter, and counter equipment
Clean stove, refrigerator
Wash windows and walls
Mop floors, clean up breakage and spills
Sweep or vacuum floors, rugs, drapes
Scrub, wash floors by hand or machine
Wash, dust, polish furniture and fixtures
Scrape dishes, trays, pans
Clean garbage cans
Dispose of trash

Specific Skill Requirements

Proper use of cleaning equipment and supplies
Knowledge of hazards of kitchen appliances, cleaning equipment and supplies

Ability to handle breakable objects with care
Ability to safely move furniture and heavy objects
Ability to work steadily for extended periods, usually in standing position
Ability to tolerate repetitive activities

Relevant DOT Reference

Kitchen Helper 318.687-010

Related Jobs

Dining Room Attendant (job profile C-8)
Dishwasher (job profile C-11)

JOB PROFILE C-11
Dishwasher

General Description

Performs activities in cleaning and shelving of dishes and utensils in restaurants, cafeterias, hospitals, other eating establishments.

Job Activities

Clear dishes from table, cart, tray
Scrape dishes, trays, pans
Load and unload automatic dishwasher
Wash dishes, silver, pans by hand
Store or shelve dishes, cooking utensils, silver
Polish, burnish silver, wrap silver
Set up or replenish counter, dishes, silver
Lift and carry tray with food, dishes
Mop floors; clean up breakage and spills
Clean garbage cans

Specific Skill Requirements

Ability to wash dishes, pans, utensils by hand or using automatic dishwasher
Ability to handle breakable items with care

Knowledge of hazards of heat, sharp objects, and cleaning agents
Ability to use simple clean-up equipment and supplies
Ability to handle dishes and utensils in a safe, neat, and sanitary manner
Ability to work steadily for extended periods, usually in standing position
Ability to tolerate repetitive activities

Relevant DOT Reference

Kitchen Helper 318.687-010

Related Jobs

Dining Room Attendant (job profile C-8)
Kitchen Clean-up Worker (job profile C-10)

JOB PROFILE C-12
Hospital Food Service Worker

General Description

Assists in preparing and delivering food trays to hospital patients. Collects and returns trays to the hospital kitchen and assists in kitchen clean-up and waste disposal.

Job Activities

Pick up menu cards
Prepare fruits, juices, and salads
Prepare and wrap sandwiches
Slice butter and place pats on cardboard
Prepare trays with standard items—silver, napkins, other supplies
Place trays in conveyor or cart
Transport trays to serving units
Serve trays to patients
Pick up soiled trays and return to carts
Return carts to kitchen area
Remove waste from dishes and trays
Place dishes and trays in dishwasher
Unload dishwasher

Store dishes and trays
Collect and carry waste to designated area

Specific Skill Requirements

Proper preparation of specific foods—fruits, juices, salads, sandwiches
Correct use of wrappers and food containers
Knowledge of standard tray set-up
Ability to dispose of waste properly and safely
Knowledge of location of dishes, trays, equipment
Knowledge of hospital routines and regulations
Ability to tolerate long period of working in standing position
Caution in lifting and serving hot foods
Ability to interact well with patients

Relevant DOT Reference

Food-Service Worker, Hospital 355.677-010

Related Jobs

Steam Table Assistant (job profile C-7)
Dishwasher (job profile C-11)
Nourishment Worker 355.677-010

JOB PROFILE C-13
Pantry Worker

General Description

Prepare salads, appetizers, sandwich fillings and other cold dishes for serving.

Job Activities

Wash, peel, and slice vegetables and fruits
Carve and slice meats and cheese
Gather ingredients and equipment; open cans
Measure ingredients

Mix ingredients
Portion and arrange food on serving dishes
Give food to waiters
Lift and carry food or dish trays
Clean work areas and utensils used
Sort and shelve canned and packaged foods

Specific Skill Requirements

Ability to handle food in a safe, neat, and sanitary manner
Knowledge of proper uses of kitchen equipment
Ability to read and follow recipes and prepare foods properly
Ability to accurately measure ingredients and portions
Ability to handle safely hot foods, equipment, and sharp utensils
Knowledge of basic clean-up procedures
Knowledge of specific kitchen routines and procedures
Ability to tolerate working in standing position for long periods
Ability to work within time schedule and with time pressures

Relevant DOT Reference

Pantry Goods Maker 317.684-014

Related Jobs

Steam Table Assistant (job profile C-7)
Salad Maker 317.384-010

JOB PROFILE C-14
Beauty or Barber Shop Helper

General Description

Assists primarily in cleaning activities and supply maintenance and distribution; may also perform services such as shoe shining.

Job Activities

Sweep, vacuum, dust, and mop shop
Clean operator stations

Dispose of trash
Wash and sterilize combs, brushes, and other equipment
Maintain and stock supply cabinet and individual stations
Mix and package shampoos, rinses, and waving solutions
Brush clothing
Clean, shine shoes
Use telephone, receive messages

Specific Skill Requirements

Knowledge of supplies and equipment used in shop
Ability to properly use cleaning equipment and supplies
Ability to clean and shine shoes
Ability to follow directions for mixing hairdressing solutions
Knowledge of proper equipment sterilization methods
Ability to interact well with the public

Relevant DOT Reference

Personal Service Supply Clerk 339.687-010

Related Jobs

Health Salon Helper (job profile C-15)
Hot Room Attendant 335.677-014
Shoe Shiner 366.677-010

JOB PROFILE C-15
Health Salon Helper

General Description

Assists in operating reducing, steam, and cold bath equipment; also helps to keep rooms and equipment clean.

Job Activities

Clean floors, tiled surfaces, fixtures
Clean, polish exercise equipment

Tend locker room, washroom
Sweep, vacuum, dust
Remove trash
Operate equipment for exercising
Give massage, rub
Tend special bath (Turkish, Russian)
Furnish towels for shower baths
Supply drinking water
Brush clothing
Use telephone, receive messages

Specific Skill Requirements

Ability to properly use cleaning equipment and supplies
Ability to safely and properly operate exercising equipment
Ability to interact well with a variety of people
Knowledge of massage, rub, and special bath techniques
Knowledge of salon routines and procedures
Ability to tolerate working in standing position for long periods

Relevant DOT Reference

Reducing Salon Attendant 359.567-010

Related Jobs

Beauty or Barber Shop Helper (job profile C-14)
Hot Room Attendant 335.677-014

JOB PROFILE C-16
Sewing and Alteration Helper

General Description

Assists custom sewer in the alteration and repair of clothing, linens, or draperies. A sewing and alteration helper may work in a clothing or department store, laundry or dry cleaner, or hotel or hospital linen room.

Job Activities

Assist in measuring customers; marking garments for alterations
Baste or pin fabric parts for final sewing
Sew fabric parts together by hand or machine
Press fabrics with hand iron
Fit garments to customers
Replace worn collars, pockets, cuffs
Patch or darn tears
Sew on buttons and trim

Specific Skill Requirements

Ability to hand stitch—basting, hemming, tacking, buttons
Ability to operate power sewing machine
Ability to position and join fabrics as specified
Use hand iron
Knowledge and observance of hazards in use of scissors, needles, sewing machines
Ability to interact well with a variety of people
Ability to use hands in a close, well-coordinated manner
Ability to distinguish between different colors, cloths, and button styles

Relevant DOT Reference

Mender 787.682-030

Related Jobs

Sewing Machine Operator (job profile F-22)
Sewer, Hand 782.684-058

JOB PROFILE C-17
Baggage Porter

General Description

Carries or transports baggage, packages, and other personal effects of people entering and leaving transportation terminals (airline, railroad, bus, steamship).

Job Activities

Move baggage, packages, crates, trunks, by handtruck, dolly, or pushcart
Assist passengers in locating proper ticket window or other services
Summon taxicabs upon request
Answer simple questions from the public
Assist handicapped persons

Specific Skill Requirements

Ability to interact well with the public
Ability to safely and carefully move heavy items
Knowledge of proper use of handtruck, dolly, pushcart
Knowledge of locations within and near the terminal
Physical strength and the ability to perform strenuous activities over extended periods
Good grooming and manners; neat and clean appearance

Relevant DOT Reference

Porter 357.677-010

Related Job

Building Porter (job profile C-23)

JOB PROFILE C-18
Laundry Worker

General Description

Performs activities in the washing, sterilizing, blocking, folding, and packaging of laundry for private employer or in an institutional setting. May assist customers in self-service laundry.

Job Activities

Operate washer and dryer
Operate special cleaning equipment

Measure and record garment dimensions
Pin garment to steam table
Apply steam to garment
Shrink or stretch garment by hand to original size
Sort clothing
Fold laundry, clothing
Bundle, tie, and label laundry packages
Receive and give receipt for clothing
Mark or tag clothing
Locate clothing from receipt
Simple maintenance and repair of equipment

Specific Skill Requirements

Ability to properly use washers, dryers, and special cleaning equipment
Knowledge of hazards of laundry/cleaning equipment, cleaning agents, solvents, and steam
Knowledge of laundry procedures and routines, including blocking
Ability to perform simple equipment maintenance and repair
Ability to use simple building cleaning equipment, supplies
Ability to receive, mark, locate, and return laundry according to receipt names or numbers
Ability to interact well with co-workers and the public
Ability to move heavy laundry bundles safely
Ability to handle laundry with care, respect
Ability to sort laundry according to type, color, material
Awareness of time, schedules, deadlines
Knowledge of locations

Relevant DOT Reference

Laundry Laborer 361.687-018

Related Job

Dry-Cleaner Helper 362.686-010

JOB PROFILE C-19
Custodian

General Description

Performs cleaning and minor maintenance activities; often works at night with little or no supervision.

Job Activities

Sweep, vacuum, dust, mop, and shampoo rugs or carpets
Empty trash containers, ashtrays
Clean lavatory fixtures
Replenish lavatory supplies
Polish metalwork
Clean windows, walls, wallpaper
Move furniture, boxes, other large objects
Replace light bulbs using ladder, scaffolding
Dispose of trash
Sort, shelve supplies
Raise, lower, fold, and store flag
Mow lawn, trim hedges
Make simple repairs
Hang drapes, curtains
Shovel snow
Operate self-leveling or nonself-leveling elevator
Check for fire, leakage, other irregularities (minimal)
Monitor boiler (minimal)
Read and set thermostat (minimal)
Maintain heating system and air conditioning system (minimal)

Specific Skill Requirements

Observance of safety precautions in the use of cleaning supplies and tools and in the maintenance and operation of equipment
Knowledge of simple maintenance and operating procedures for boiler, heating and air conditioning equipment, electrical, and plumbing systems
Ability to move furniture and heavy objects in a safe, careful manner
Knowledge of cleaning and maintenance routines and procedures
Ability to recognize when help is needed in repairs or emergencies

Ability to use tools to make simple repairs
Ability to operate elevators and escalators
Physical strength; ability to perform strenuous outdoor tasks such as shoveling snow
Knowledge of location of supplies and of facility layout

Relevant DOT Reference

Janitor 382.664-010

Related Jobs

Building Porter (job profile C-23)
House Cleaner 323.687-018

JOB PROFILE C-20
Rug Cleaner Helper

General Description

Assists in cleaning rugs and carpets in a plant or in the customer's home. The helper may work with equipment or perform manual tasks only.

Job Activities

In customer's home
Move furniture to prepare for cleaning
Vaccum rug to remove dirt
Operate shampooing machine
Vaccum rug to remove cleaning solution
Operate pile-lifter over dried rugs
Spray rugs to mothproof

In plant
Place rugs in position for various machine processing (vacuuming, cleaning, drying, pile-lifting)
Roll and tie rugs
Assist in pickup from and delivery to customer's home
Move rugs between processing areas and into storage

Specific Skill Requirements

Ability to move furniture and heavy rugs safely
Ability to properly use rug cleaning equipment and chemicals in home or plant
Ability to correctly roll and tie rugs
Knowledge of hazards of rug cleaning equipment and chemicals

Relevant DOT Reference

Rug Cleaner Helper 362.686-014

Related Job

Furniture Cleaner 362.684-022

JOB PROFILE C-21
Elevator Operator

General Description

Operates elevator in building, either for people or freight. May work in buildings used by the public or in industrial settings.

Job Activities

Operate self-leveling elevator
Operate nonself-leveling elevator
Supply information to passengers
Load and unload freight
Move furniture, boxes, other large objects
Check identification after hours or in security building
Tend door

Specific Skill Requirements

Ability to operate self-leveling and nonself-leveling elevators safely
Ability to safely and carefully move furniture and heavy objects by hand or using appropriate equipment
Ability to interact well with a variety of people
Ability to assist the handicapped with care and respect

Relevant DOT Reference

Elevator Operator 388.663-010

Related Job

Building Porter (job profile C-23)

JOB PROFILE C-22
Security Guard (Unarmed)

General Description

Stands guard or patrols buildings and/or plant premises to detect fire, illegal intrusions, or other irregularities; may also do cleaning and minor maintenance. Often works at night, with little or no supervision.

Job Activities

Check for fire, leakage, or other irregularities
Check doors, windows for security
Check identification of visitors
Register at watch stations
Sound alarm in case of fires, burglary
Monitor boiler
Read and set thermostat
Receive freight deliveries
Operate elevator
Sweep, vacuum, dust, mop
Empty trash containers, ashtrays
Move furniture, boxes, other large objects
Replace light bulbs, using ladder, scaffolding
Sort, shelve supplies

Specific Skill Requirements

Ability to recognize when to summon help for emergencies or intrusions
Ability to operate simple fire-fighting equipment
Ability to use public address and emergency alarm systems
Knowledge of safe operating procedures for building utilities

Knowledge of utility shutdown procedures during emergencies
Knowledge of proper and safe use of cleaning equipment and supplies
Ability to safely and carefully move furniture and heavy objects
Ability to operate elevators and escalators
Ability to adhere to schedules
Ability to work without supervision

Relevant DOT References

Guard 372.667-034

Related Job

Custodian (job profile C-19)

JOB PROFILE C-23
Building Porter

General Description

Assists in light cleaning and attendant duties in office buildings, retail stores, hotels, and other commercial or public buildings. May assist building occupants by carrying packages, delivering mail, or performing other indoor or outdoor services.

Job Activities

Move furniture, boxes; carry baggage, packages
Sweep, dust, vacuum, mop
Replenish lavatory supplies
Empty trash containers, ashtrays
Sort, shelve supplies
Tend washroom
Tend door
Operate elevator
Assist handicapped persons
Summon taxicabs upon request
Answer simple questions from the public
Shovel snow

Perform light grounds maintenance
Set up tables and chairs

Specific Skill Requirements

Ability to safely and properly use cleaning equipment and supplies
Ability to safely and carefully move furniture, packages, and heavy objects
Knowledge of cleaning and maintenance routines and procedures
Ability to relate well to a variety of people
Physical strength; ability to tolerate standing for long periods

Relevant DOT Reference

Cleaner, Commercial or Institutional 381.687-014

Related Jobs

Baggage Porter (job profile C-17)
Custodian (job profile C-19)

JOB PROFILE C-24
Window Washer

General Description

Cleans exterior windows on ground floor of building; may clean interior windows and other glass.

Job Activities

Collect and replenish cleaning equipment and supplies
Carry cleaning equipment to windows
Wash windows using soapy water or cleaner
Rinse windows with hose
Dry windows with squeegee
Clean sponges and other equipment after use
Store cleaning equipment after use

Specific Skill Requirements

Ability to safely and properly use cleaning equipment, ladders, and supplies
Ability to work safely around glass
Ability to do thorough cleaning work
Ability to remember location of equipment and assigned work areas
Ability to tolerate working in tiring positions, such as keeping the head back and arms up in washing high windows

Relevant DOT Reference

Window Cleaner 389.687-014

Related Jobs

Custodian (job profile C-19)
Housecleaner 323.687-018
Cleaner, Commercial or Industrial 381.678-014

JOB PROFILE C-25
Bellhop

General Description

Carries baggage to and from room; helps guests to become settled in rooms; runs errands.

Job Activities

Carry baggage or packages
Locate room in building
Inspect room to see that it is in order and properly supplied
Settle guest in room; explain room features
Help pack or unpack clothes
Supply information to guests
Run errands, deliver messages, and provide room service in building
Summon taxicab for guests
Operate elevator

Tend door
Tend checkroom

Specific Skill Requirements

Ability to carry baggage in a safe, careful manner
Ability to treat guests' personal belongings with care and respect
Knowledge of services and facilities available to guests
Knowledge of applicable routines and procedures
Ability to operate elevators safely
Knowledge of facility layout
Physical strength; ability to lift and carry heavy baggage for extended periods of time
Ability to interact well with the public

Relevant DOT Reference

Bellhop 324.677-010

Related Jobs

Baggage Porter (job profile C-17)
Building Porter (job profile C-23)

JOB PROFILE C-26
Hotel/Motel Cleaner

General Description

A cleaner in a hotel or motel performs general cleaning duties in guest rooms, hallways and lobbies, and service areas.

Job Activities

Sweep, vacuum, dust, mop
Clean furniture and room fixtures
Clean bathrooms
Replenish soap, towels, glasses, tissues, matches, and so on
Wash walls, woodwork, and windows
Sort, fold, and carry linens

Make or change beds
Empty ashtrays and trash baskets
Wax and polish floors
Shampoo carpets

Specific Skill Requirements

Ability to properly use cleaning equipment and supplies
Knowledge of hazards of using cleaning equipment and supplies
Ability to safely move furniture and heavy objects
Knowledge of locations of equipment, supplies and work areas
Knowledge of proper bed-making/changing techniques
Ability to interact well with the public
Ability to treat guests' personal belongings with care, respect
Ability to adapt to routines and procedures

Relevant DOT Reference

Housecleaner 323.687-018

Related Jobs

Day Worker, Housecleaning (job profile C-1)
Hospital Cleaner (job profile C-33)

JOB PROFILE C-27
Room Preparation Worker

General Description

Performs or assists in daily activities required to prepare rooms for guests.

Job Activities

Sweep, vacuum, dust, mop
Clean bathroom fixtures
Clean furniture
Replenish guest room supplies and linen
Change or make beds
Empty trash containers, ashtrays

Sort, count, record, or issue linens
Fold linens
Move furniture, boxes
Hang drapes, curtains
Clean up spills and breakage
Fill water pitchers

Specific Skill Requirements

Ability to properly use cleaning equipment and supplies
Knowledge of hazards of using cleaning equipment and supplies
Ability to safely move furniture and heavy objects
Ability to handle guests' personal items with care and respect
Knowledge of proper bed-making/changing
Knowledge of locations of equipment, supplies, and work areas
Knowledge of guest facility's routines and procedures

Relevant DOT Reference

Housecleaner 323.687-018

Related Jobs

Day Worker, Housecleaning (job profile C-1)
Houseworker, General 301.474-010

JOB PROFILE C-28
Resort Worker

General Description

A resort worker performs general cleaning and maintenance tasks in a resort, campground, or other recreational setting. May also be responsible for providing guests with information concerning services and facilities and for assisting with registration, reservations, and the collection of fees.

Job Activities

Sweep, vacuum, dust, mop
Clean furniture, bathroom, and kitchen fixtures
Replenish guest room supplies and linen

Dispose of trash
Change bed linen
Maintain outdoor recreational areas
Mow grass, prune shrubs
Maintain recreational equipment and distribute to guests
Register guests
Collect fees
Provide information regarding services and facilities
Service cars with gasoline, oil, water

Specific Skill Requirements

Ability to properly use cleaning equipment and supplies
Knowledge of hazards of using cleaning equipment and supplies
Knowledge of general grounds and building maintenance techniques
Knowledge of simple recordkeeping procedures
Ability to handle money and make change
Knowledge of basic car servicing procedures
Ability to interact well with a variety of people
Ability to safely move furniture and heavy objects
Physical strength; ability to perform strenuous activities, such as mowing lawns or handling trash barrels
Willingness to work in a variety of weather conditions

Relevant DOT Reference

Attendant, Lodging Facilities 329.467-010

Related Jobs

Day Worker, Housecleaning (job profile C-1)
Hotel/Motel Cleaner (job profile C-26)

JOB PROFILE C-29
Recreation Assistant

General Description

Assists recreation leader in conducting recreation activities with assigned groups in public department, voluntary agency, or other recreational facility (private club, day camp).

Job Activities

Assist with activities such as arts and crafts
Watch participants in sports and games
Assist with hikes, camping trips, and so on
Aid in protecting participants from activity hazards
Perform general cleaning if indoors
Lead informal group work as instructed by recreation leader

Specific Skill Requirements

Ability to interact well with a variety of people
Knowledge of basic rules and equipment for indoor and outdoor games
Knowledge and observance of hazards inherent in recreational activities
Knowledge of recreational agency's routines and procedures
Ability to decide when to seek help in emergencies or injuries
Ability to observe and assist others in their recreational activities
Knowledge of basic cleaning methods and equipment
Knowledge of locations of equipment and recreational areas

Relevant DOT Reference

Playroom Attendant 359.677-026

Related Jobs

Nursery School Aide (job profile C-46)
Campground Attendant 329.683-010
Children's Institution Attendant 359.677-010

JOB PROFILE C-30
Golf Range Attendant

General Description

Collects, cleans and replaces equipment at golf driving range.

Job Activities

Sweep, vacuum, mop, rake indoor and outdoor areas
Find and pick up balls by hand
Assist with trailer that automatically picks up balls
Wash balls
Clean and buff golf club heads
Replace balls and clubs in rack
Find and return lost equipment to clubhouse
Prepare buckets of balls for later use
Perform simple maintenance on range equipment

Specific Skill Requirements

Ability to clean and prepare balls and clubs for rental
Knowledge of simple maintenance procedures for range equipment
Knowledge of proper use of basic cleaning equipment, supplies
Knowledge of proper use of basic maintenance tools
Knowledge of range routines and procedures
Knowledge of locations of work areas, equipment, supplies

Relevant DOT Reference

Golf Range Attendant 341.683-010

Related Job

Caddie 341.677-010

JOB PROFILE C-31
Ticket Taker

General Description

Collects admission tickets and passes from patrons at entertainment events or at amusement parks; assists patrons entering amusement rides.

Job Activities

Verify tickets
Stamp or tear tickets to cancel
Refuse admission if no ticket
Distribute programs to patrons
Direct patrons to their seats; assist handicapped persons
Hand out door checks for returning patrons
Count and record number of tickets

Specific Skill Requirements

Ability to interact well with the public
Knowledge of locations and nomenclature
Knowledge of establishment's routines and procedures
Ability to recognize appropriate tickets, passes
Knowledge of safe methods for assisting persons on and off rides
Willingness to work outdoors (amusement parks)
Ability to tolerate repetitive activities
Ability to work without constant supervision
Awareness of time schedules

Relevant DOT Reference

Ticket Taker (Amusement and Recreation) 344.667-010

Related Job

Ride Attendant (Amusement and Recreation) 342.677-010

JOB PROFILE C-32
Concession Worker

General Description

Assists in preparing refreshments and selling them to patrons from concession booth at theaters, sporting events, fairs. May also do general cleaning.

Job Activities

Take orders from customers for food, beverages
Prepare simple foods (hot dogs, popcorn)
Prepare beverages for later sale (mix syrups, juices)
Fill drink cups
Watch or stir cooking foods
Wrap food for carry-out
Total charges
Use cash register, make change
Perform general cleaning of equipment, seating and service areas
Mop floors; clean up breakage, spills

Specific Skill Requirements

Ability to interact well with co-workers and the public
Ability to prepare simple hot and cold foods, beverages
Knowledge of food packaging methods for carry-outs
Knowledge of neat, sanitary methods for handling foods
Ability to use cash register, make change
Knowledge of locations of supplies, equipment, work areas
Knowledge of basic cleaning procedures
Ability to properly use cleaning equipment and supplies
Ability to remember prices and items available for sale
Ability to work quickly and accurately under time pressure

Relevant DOT Reference

Canteen Operator 311.674-010

Related Job

Waiter/Waitress, Takeout 311.477-038

JOB PROFILE C-33
Hospital Cleaner

General Description

A hospital cleaner performs general cleaning tasks in a hospital or clinic. Additional responsibilities may include distributing linens, disinfecting equipment, and assembling packages of cleaning supplies for specialized hospital units.

Job Activities

Assemble cleaning supply packets for use in specialized settings
Disinfect equipment
Sweep, vacuum, dust, mop
Clean furniture and room fixtures
Wash walls, windows, woodwork
Clean bathrooms
Strip, disinfect, and make beds
Clean specialized areas (x-ray, lab, pharmacy)
Replenish soap, towels, and tissue
Collect and dispose of trash, contaminated materials
Sort, fold, and carry linens

Specific Skill Requirements

Ability to properly use cleaning equipment, supplies, and disinfectant
Knowledge of hazards of using cleaning equipment and supplies
Ability to safely move furniture and heavy objects
Knowledge of locations of equipment, supplies, and work areas
Knowledge of proper bed-making/changing techniques
Knowledge of proper handling techniques for contaminated materials
Ability to interact well with co-workers and patients
Ability to adapt to routines and procedures
Ability to work around ill, injured, or terminal patients

Relevant DOT Reference

Hospital Cleaner 323.687-010

Related Jobs

Day Worker, Housecleaning (job profile C-1)
Hotel/Motel Cleaner (job profile C-26)

JOB PROFILE C-34
Patient Service Helper

General Description

Assists in activities which help keep patients comfortable and may relieve nursing staff of simpler duties.

Job Activities

Locate room in building
Settle patient in room (heat, supplies, lights, storage)
Move beds; operate wheelchairs and gurneys
Lift or help patients move
Help pack or unpack clothes
Dress or undress patients
Carry and serve room trays
Feed and bathe patients
Help patients shave, fix hair, and perform other grooming activities
Empty bedpans and urinals
Change or make beds
Fold, sort, count, record, or issue linens
Fill water pitchers
Mop floor, clean up spills and breakage
Clean with disinfectant
Operate elevator
Run errands, deliver in building
Collect necessary medical equipment
Make up surgical packs; make bandages

Specific Skill Requirements

Ability to properly use simple cleaning equipment, supplies, and disinfectants
Knowledge of hazards of cleaning supplies and disinfectants
Knowledge of safe patient handling and bathing procedures
Ability to safely move furniture and heavy objects
Ability to coordinate efforts with other employees
Knowledge of proper use of hospital furniture and basic equipment
Knowledge of locations of supplies, equipment, and hospital services

Knowledge of proper bed-making/changing
Knowledge of sanitary methods of handling food, waste, medical equipment, and infectious materials
Ability to interact well with patients
Ability to work with sick, injured, and dying persons
Physical strength; ability to use proper body mechanics in moving and lifting patients, to prevent self-injury and lessen fatigue

Relevant DOT Reference

Orderly 355.674-018

Related Job

Nurse's Aide (job profile C-35)

JOB PROFILE C-35
Nurse's Aide

General Description

A nurse's aide assists medical and nursing staff in the care and treatment of patients in long-term or convalescent hospital settings. Duties range from general care, such as bathing and feeding patients, to more specialized activities, such as taking temperatures and administering simple treatments.

Job Activities

Assist patients in bathing, shaving, oral hygiene
Assist patients in turning or getting in and out of bed
Assist patients in toileting
Serve and collect food trays; feed patients when necessary
Prepare and serve between-meal nourishments
Observe and report on patient comfort
Take and record temperature
Give alcohol rub or massage
Count and record pulse and respiration
Collect urine and stool specimens
Apply icebags, heating pads, and hot water bottles
Provide general skin care

Transport patients within hospital using gurneys, wheelchairs
Change soiled linen and clothes

Specific Skill Requirements

Ability to assist patients with various hygiene activities
Knowledge of safe patient handling procedures
Ability to perform simple procedures such as taking temperatures, collecting specimens
Ability to perform simple treatments
Knowledge of sanitary techniques for handling food, waste, medical equipment, and infectious materials
Knowledge of bed making/changing
Knowledge of locations of supplies, equipment, and hospital services
Ability to operate basic hospital furniture and equipment
Ability to interact well with patients
Ability to work with sick, injured, and dying persons
Physical strength; ability to use proper body mechanics in moving and lifting patients, to prevent self-injury and lessen fatigue

Relevant DOT Reference

Nurse's Aide 355.674-014

Related Jobs

Patient Service Helper (job profile C-34)
Physical Therapist Aide (job profile C-36)

JOB PROFILE C-36
Physical Therapist Aide

General Description

Assists physical therapist in setting up and conducting patient treatment. Also responsible for cleaning and maintaining equipment and treatment area.

Job Activities

Assist patients in dressing, undressing, and moving about
Assist patients in self-care activities
Transport patients by wheelchair or stretcher
Set up equipment
Observe and report on patients' comfort
Assist in patient treatment
Clean and maintain equipment

Specific Skill Requirements

Ability to assist with various hygiene activities
Use of proper patient-handling techniques
Knowledge of setup, use, and maintenance of equipment
Ability to carefully observe patients and equipment
Ability to interact well with patients
Knowledge of treatments and procedures
Knowledge of locations of supplies, equipment, and hospital services
Ability to adapt to routines and procedures
Physical strength; ability to use proper body mechanics in moving and lifting patients, to prevent self-injury and lessen fatigue

Relevant DOT Reference

Physical Therapy Aide 355.354-010

Related Jobs

Patient Service Helper (job profile C-34)
Nurse's Aide (job profile C-35)

JOB PROFILE C-37
Road Maintenance Worker

General Description

Assists in street and highway maintenance, repair, cleaning, snow removal and marking; may also assist in installation and maintenance of fences and landscaping.

Job Activities

Dig with pick and shovel
Assist in paving operations
Assist in operating street-cleaning equipment
Assist in operating mowing equipment
Assist in operating snow removal equipment
Assist in operating salt or cinder equipment
Assist in operating road-lining equipment
Sweep roads or walks by hand
Repair signs, fences
Collect trash along roadside
Operate sprinklers or other irrigation equipment
Plant and maintain roadside landscaping
Assist in cleaning and maintaining tools and equipment

Specific Skill Requirements

Knowledge of the safe and proper use of simple hand tools
Knowledge of the hazards of working with various types of power equipment
Ability to properly use a variety of power-operated equipment
Knowledge of simple landscaping installation and maintenance techniques
Knowledge of safe methods for moving heavy objects
Knowledge of basic cleaning and maintenance methods for equipment
Physical strength; ability to perform strenuous physical activity such as digging and shoveling

Relevant DOT Reference

Laborer, Road 869.687-026
Laborer, Landscape 408.687-014

Related Job

Road Construction Helper (job profile E-8)

JOB PROFILE C-38
Garbage Collection Helper

General Description

Assists in activities related to trash and garbage collection.

Job Activities

Pick up trash or garbage and transport to truck
Dump refuse from containers onto trucks
Assist with collection truck operation
Sweep roads or walks by hand
Assist in cleaning and maintaining containers and trucks

Specific Skill Requirements

Knowledge of proper methods for lifting and carrying heavy loads
Knowledge of hazards of working in street traffic
Knowledge of hazards of using powered garbage collection equipment
Ability to properly use simple clean-up tools (shovel, broom, rake)
Knowledge of simple cleaning and maintenance procedures for trucks and their equipment
Knowledge of locations of trash containers on various routes
Physical strength; ability to perform strenuous physical activity such as handling heavy trash cans

Relevant DOT Reference

Garbage Collector 909.687-010

Related Job

Laborer, General (Motor Freight Transportation) 909.687-014

JOB PROFILE C-39
Parking Meter Collector

General Description

Collects money from coin boxes of parking meters, following established route. May assist parking meter painter or installer.

Job Activities

Open and close coin box with key
Make simple repairs to meter (for example, unjam mechanism)
Place collection device under opening to receive coins
Check for needed repairs or adjustments; record in book and submit to supervisor
Install parking meter on stand (minimal)
Paint parking meter (minimal)

Specific Skill Requirements

Ability to properly use coin collection device
Knowledge of proper operation of meter
Knowledge of simple repair techniques (for example, unjamming)
Ability to recognize when complex repairs are needed
Ability to record type and location of needed repairs
Knowledge of meter installation procedures and tools
Knowledge of proper use of tools and supplies for painting meters
Knowlege of meter locations and collection routes
Tolerance of repetitive activities

Relevant DOT Reference

Coin Machine Collector 292.687-010

Related Job

Telephone Coin Box Collector 292.687-010

JOB PROFILE C-40
Mail Sorter

General Description

Sorts and processes mail in post office.

Job Activities

Sort mail into pigeonholes
Transfer mail into mail sacks
Feed letters into cancelling machine
Hand cancel mail
Deliver messages within building
Move sacks and bins of mail within building
Write simple messages

Specific Skill Requirements

Knowledge of patterns of pigeonholes and mail sacks for sorting
Knowledge of locations within building
Ability to safely move heavy objects, bins, dollies
Ability to safely operate mail cancelling machine
Knowledge of post office procedures and regulations
Ability to work at a rapid, consistent pace
Tolerance of repetitive activities

Relevant DOT Reference

Mail Handler, Distribution Clerk (Government service) 209.687-014

Related Job

Sorter, Clerical 209.687-022

JOB PROFILE C-41
Sewage Treatment Worker

General Description

Performs a variety of tasks in a sewage disposal plant to facilitate the flow and treatment of sewage.

Job Activities

Clean filter screens
Scrub processing tanks and walkways
Clean catch basins
Lubricate equipment
Monitor gauges and warning lights
Open and close gates and valves when indicated
Load precipitates for removal
Collect samples of refuse for testing

Specific Skill Requirements

Ability to properly clean sewage treatment facilities and equipment
Knowledge of safe use of specialized chemicals and detergents
Knowledge of simple equipment maintenance procedures
Ability to read gauges and dials
Ability to operate gates and valves (manual and electric types)
Knowledge of plant layout
Knowledge of plant routines and procedures
Ability to recognize need for adjustments and repairs

Relevant DOT Reference

Sewage Disposal Worker 955.687-010

Related Jobs

Sewage Plant Attendant 955.585-010
Water Filter Cleaner 954.587-010

JOB PROFILE C-42
Park Worker

General Description

Assists in keeping municipal parks and building grounds clean; helps in caring for landscaping, park cabins, play areas and recreation equipment. May also work in a private recreational setting.

Job Activities

Dig with pick and shovel
Assist with mowing equipment
Pick up trash or garbage
Weed and care for gardens, other plantings
Cut wood, using hand or power saws
Repair and maintain signs, fireplaces, tables, fences
Assemble or set up outdoor equipment, shelters
Lift or carry furniture, equipment, supplies
Sweep roads or walks by hand
Plant trees, shrubs, flowers
Roll lawn, track, field, court
Rake leaves, sand, gravel, cinders
Mark off playing area, field, court
Clean swimming pool, water, surrounding areas
Service pool filtration systems

Specific Skill Requirements

Ability to safely use and maintain simple hand and power tools
Ability to properly use painting equipment and supplies
Ability to safely use simple cleaning equipment and supplies
Knowledge of safe methods for moving furniture and heavy objects
Knowledge of simple gardening and landscaping techniques
Willingness to work in a variety of weather conditions
Knowledge of basic pool maintenance procedures
Ability to recognize the existence of emergencies or the need for repairs
Knowledge of locations of equipment and work areas
Knowledge of simple building maintenance and repair procedures

Knowledge of proper mixing and use of concrete
Physical strength; ability to perform strenuous physical activities
Ability to work without constant supervision

Relevant DOT Reference

Groundskeeping, Parks and Grounds 406.687-010

Related Jobs

Caretaker (job profile C-5)
Groundskeeper, Industrial-Commercial 406.684-014

JOB PROFILE C-43
Landscaping Worker

General Description

Assists in general activities in contracted landscaping, usually in newly developed areas.

Job Activities

Plant by hand
Weed by hand
Spread mulch and fertilizer
Use common garden and building tools
Load, unload, transport
Use power garden and building tools
Prune trees and shrubs
Use garden sprayer
Use tree sprayer
Install sprinkler systems
Assist in constructing retaining walls, dividers, benches, other structures
Install outdoor lighting fixtures

Specific Skill Requirements

Ability to properly use and maintain common garden and building tools (hand, power)

Knowledge of hazards of using hand and power tools, equipment, and garden chemicals
Knowledge of basic gardening and landscaping techniques
Knowledge of basic construction techniques for using wood, concrete, rock
Knowledge of assembly techniques for sprinkler piping
Ability to safely move small trees and other heavy objects and materials
Physical strength; ability to perform strenuous physical activities such as digging and pruning

Relevant DOT Reference

Groundskeeper 406.684-014

Related Jobs

Caretaker (job profile C-5)
Park Worker (job profile C-42)

JOB PROFILE C-44
Painting and Maintenance Helper

General Description

Helps in painting and minor repair activities on signs, buildings and equipment, and recreational equipment. May be employed by a public or private concern.

Job Activities

Remove old paint using mechanical and/or chemical means
Prepare surfaces with brush or sandpaper, plaster or putty
Prepare paints for application
Place and remove drop cloths to protect areas near painting
Paint with spray-gun equipment or by hand
Repair signs, fireplaces, tables, fences; make minor repairs to buildings and equipment
Assemble and set up outdoor equipment, shelters

Specific Skill Requirements

Ability to properly use and maintain both hand and power painting equipment, and different paint types
Ability to properly use and maintain basic hand and power building tools
Knowledge of hazards of using hand and power tools and equipment, solvents, and flammable liquids
Ability to safely move heavy objects
Knowledge of proper procedures for mixing paints, other finishes
Knowledge of proper mixing and use of concrete
Knowledge of basic repair techniques for common building and equipment situations
Physical strength; ability to tolerate working in tiring positions, such as in painting high areas

Relevant DOT Reference

Painter, Rough (Construction) 741.687-018

Related Jobs

Park Worker (job profile C-42)
Painter, Brush (any industry) 740.684-022
Painter Helper (Construction Worker II) 869.687-026

JOB PROFILE C-45
Cemetery Worker

General Description

Prepares graves and maintains cemetery grounds. The worker may also set up sites for burial services.

Job Activities

Dig graves
Line graves with preformed concrete slabs
Position casket-lowering device on grave

Erect canopy and arrange chairs for burial services
Assist with simple carpentry and concrete work
Mow grass
Plant and prune flowers and shrubs
Rake leaves and other debris
Dispose of trash
Fill in graves; install memorial markers

Specific Skill Requirements

Ability to excavate with pick and shovel
Knowledge of correct arrangement of burial site and equipment
Application of simple carpentry techniques (use of hammer, saw)
Ability to properly use mower, rake, clippers, and other garden tools
Knowledge of basic gardening techniques
Ability to safely move heavy objects
Ability to maintain and make simple repairs to gardening and burial equipment
Physical strength; ability to perform strenuous activities such as digging and shoveling
Willingness to work in a variety of weather conditions

Relevant DOT Reference

Cemetery Worker 406.684-010

Related Jobs

Groundskeeper (Industrial-Commercial) 406.684-014
Groundskeeper (Parks and Grounds) 406.687-010

JOB PROFILE C-46
Nursery School Aide

General Description

Assists teacher in providing activities and supervision for preschool children.

Job Activities

Help children put on and remove coats
Serve meals or snacks
Play games, indoor and outdoor, with children
Participate in art, music, and learning activities with children
General cleaning
Collect and put away play, art, music equipment
Enforce discipline
Help children with toileting

Specific Skill Requirements

Ability to coordinate work with other employees
Knowledge and observance of hazards to children
Knowledge of basic rules and equipment for indoor and outdoor games for children
Knowledge of simple arts and crafts techniques and equipment
Ability to use simple cleaning equipment and supplies
Ability to enforce simple rules
Knowledge of locations of equipment and supplies
Ability to determine when to seek help in emergency
Ability to handle food in a neat, sanitary manner
Ability to interact well with young children and adults
Ability to observe routines and procedures

Relevant DOT Reference

Nursery School Attendant 359.677-018

Related Jobs

Recreation Assistant (job profile C-29)
Children's Institution Attendant 359.677-010
Playroom Attendant 359.677-026

JOB PROFILE C-47
Veterinary Hospital Attendant

General Description

Assists in activities occurring in veterinary hospitals such as caring for and cleaning after the animals. May also be responsible for general cleaning of the hospital.

Job Activities

Handle, groom, and feed animals
Disinfect and clean cages
Generally clean work and reception areas
Store medical supplies, feed
Prepare instruments, supplies for use by veterinarian
Measure feed portions, provide water
Assist veterinarian in hospital or on out-calls

Specific Skill Requirements

Ability to interact well with large and small animals
Ability to interact well with co-workers
Knowledge of equipment and procedures for handling, grooming, and feeding animals
Use of caution in handling animals, to prevent self-injury and harm to the animals
Knowledge of locations of supplies, equipment, and work areas
Ability to lift and move heavy animals and objects safely
Knowledge of safe and proper use of cleaning and sterilizing equipment, disinfectants, other supplies
Knowledge of hospital routines and procedures, nomenclature
Physical strength
Willingness to work with sick, injured, or dying animals

Relevant DOT Reference

Veterinary Hospital Attendant (Animal Caretaker) 410.674-010

Related Jobs

Pet Shop Assistant (job profile A-13)
General Farm Worker (job profile D-1)
Poultry Farm/Hatchery Worker (job profile D-3)
Dairy Farm Worker (job profile D-4)

JOB PROFILE C-48
Parking Garage Attendant

General Description

Helps in garages and parking lots operated by either public or private employers.

Job Activities

Issue parking lot ticket
Identify cars having permit parking sticker
Record time customer enters parking lot by hand or machine
Collect parking tag from customer
Compute parking charge
Operate cash register, count money
Drive customer's car between lot entrance and parking space
Check and adjust fluid and air levels on cars receiving maintenance service
Patrol area to prevent thefts, vandalism
Clear snow; sweep
Use telephone

Specific Skill Requirements

Ability to identify cars by model, style and color
Ability to drive a variety of automatic and manual shift cars
Ability to properly use time-stamping machine
Ability to compute charges according to length of stay or other standard
Ability to operate cash register, make change
Ability to recognize the need to summon help in emergencies

Ability to interact well with co-workers and the public
Ability to properly use simple tools (broom, shovel)
Knowledge of facility layout
Ability to exercise care and respect in driving cars

Relevant DOT Reference

Parking-Lot Attendant (Auto. Ser.) 915.473-010

Related Jobs

Transportation Fleet Maintenance Helper (job profile E-15)
Industrial Garage Attendant (job profile E-16)

JOB PROFILE C-49
Laboratory Helper

General Description

Cleans laboratory equipment and performs other simple tasks. This worker also may pick up samples and other materials needed by the laboratory or deliver laboratory products to clients. If pickup and delivery are part of the job, see job profile A-14.

Job Activities

Wash equipment with solvents, brushes, and rags
Rinse equipment
Dry equipment, using rags, hot-air dryer, or acetone bath
Sterilize glassware and instruments using autoclave
Store equipment
Clean walls, tables, floor, and other parts of laboratory
Mix together components of cleaning solutions
Measure liquid and dry quantities
Fill tubes and bottles with prepared solutions
Label tubes and bottles
Transport supplies and equipment in-house between work and cleaning areas

Tend distilled water still
Store delivered supplies
Pick up samples, other materials for the laboratory
Deliver laboratory products to clients

Specific Skill Requirements

Knowledge of tools, equipment, chemicals, and techniques used in cleaning lab equipment.
Knowledge of proper storage and transportation techniques for lab equipment and supplies
Knowledge of tools, chemicals, and techniques for cleaning work areas
Ability to accurately mix dry and/or liquid components to create specific lab solutions
Ability to carefully fill, seal, and label containers with prepared solutions
Ability to monitor operation of distilled water still
Ability to safely lift, carry, and move heavy objects, using handtruck and cart
Knowledge of the hazards of cleaning equipment, tools, chemicals, glassware, and of laboratory settings in general
Knowledge of locations of tools, equipment, supplies, and storage and in-house work areas
Knowledge of streets and addresses in delivery area
Ability to use public transportation or company vehicle to make pickups and deliveries

Relevant DOT Reference

Cleaner, Laboratory Equipment 381.687-022

Related Job

Laboratory-Sample Carrier (any industry) 922.687-054

Master Profile D: **Agriculture/Fishing/Forestry**

General Description

These jobs are performed around farms, orchards, nurseries, and hatcheries, involving operations related to the commercial production of fish, poultry, livestock, fruits, vegetables, nuts, timber, and nursery plants and flowers. Typical job activities include: loading, unloading, and transporting; cleaning up barns, buildings, and yards; horticultural activities such as planting, weeding, cultivating, and harvesting; feeding, watering, and handling a variety of poultry, fish, or livestock; performing simple repairs; and setting and checking fish nets or traps. Employment opportunities might be seasonal; some opportunities, such as nursery or greenhouse jobs, may be more numerous during holiday seasons.

Most agricultural, fishing, or forestry workers will be doing strenuous physical labor, often outdoors. A variety of weather conditions may prevail, and the jobs may entail performing wet and dirty tasks. Since the work areas are generally large, many of the activities may be performed with little supervision, even in isolation. In the case of fishing jobs, the work area may be quite complex, such as a wharf, so employees will need to know the area well.

Employees are exposed to many hazards from animals, knives, saws, heavy machinery, chemicals, and poisons. Activities around boats and water involve special dangers.

Job Profiles (See pages immediately following this master profile.)

- D-1 General Farm Worker
- D-2 Vegetable Farm Worker
- D-3 Poultry Farm/Hatchery Worker
- D-4 Dairy Farm Worker
- D-5 Ranch Hand
- D-6 Orchard/Vineyard Worker
- D-7 Forestry Worker
- D-8 Nursery/Greenhouse Worker
- D-9 Logging Operations Worker
- D-10 Fishing Boat Deckhand
- D-11 Fish Hatchery Worker

Skill Requirements

The following basic, core, and personal/social skills are considered to apply generally to all the jobs in the agricultural/fishing/forestry occupations. In addition to these, each job profile lists specific skill requirements relevant to that particular job.

Basic Skills The numbers in parentheses refer to the sequence of the skills listed in the basic skills chart beginning on page 43, which defines the individual skills and cites applications for each one.

- Read (labels on feed mix, etc.) (1)
- Write (simple records) (2)
- Count and record numbers (3)
- Perform simple calculations (4)
- Sort by category (6)
- Arrange in order (8)
- Locate and collect supplies and materials (9)
- Communicate verbally (10)
- Tell time (13)
- Measure (linear, weight, volume) (14)
- Read dials, gauges, meters (minimal) (15)
- Combine liquids and/or dry materials (16)
- Tie with string or rope (17)

Core skills The numbers in parentheses refer to the sequence of the skills listed in the core skills chart, beginning on page 47, which defines the individual skills and cites applications for each one.

- Fold (cloths used to cover crops) (1)
- Bundle (tree boughs, agricultural products) (2)
- Cut (twine, produce) (6)
- Lift and carry (heavy loads and equipment) (7)
- Load and unload (supplies and produce) (8)
- Transport (feed, animals, supplies) (9)
- Stack and shelve (farm supplies) (10)
- Pack and crate (produce) (11)
- Open and unpack (12)
- Handle dangerous substances (insecticides, disinfectants) (30)
- Use hand tools (carpentry, maintenance of equipment) (33)
- Dig and shovel (34)
- Use garden tools (35)
- Handle live animals and fish (36)

Personal/social skills Since many of the jobs in this job group require that the worker be relatively isolated from other workers for long periods of time, ability to work with minimum supervision is particularly important. Clothing appropriate to the job activities and weather conditions should be worn. Caution is imperative because of the many hazards to which the worker is exposed. Physical stamina also is critical, as most of the jobs require handling of heavy loads and continuous work at strenuous activities.

A special personal requirement for these occupations is the acceptance by the worker of tasks that involve killing or handling of dead poultry, fish, livestock, or other animals.

The extent of other personal/social skills required in agricultural and related jobs is shown in the following profile.

Master Profile: **D: Agriculture/Fishing/Forestry**

Personal/Social Skill Requirements		Extent Required: Minimal	Extent Required: Moderate	Extent Required: Major
Social Skills	1. *SELF EXPRESSION* - communicate, ask for assistance, question		●	
	2. *SOCIABILITY* - interact with other employees or public		●	
	3. *WORK INDEPENDENCE* - work without supervision or guidance			●
	4. *APPEARANCE/HYGIENE* - cleanliness, good manners, neatness in appearance		●	
	5. *TEAMWORK* - perform in close coordination with other jobs		●	
Time Factors	6. *PACE* - perform at a consistent rate of speed	●		
	7. *ATTENDANCE* - be reliable in attendance and punctuality		●	
	8. *SIMULTANEITY* - perform several activities at near same time		●	
	9. *TIMING* - perform timed, scheduled activities; be aware of time		●	
Performance Skills	10. *ACCURACY* - perform within well-defined tolerances		●	
	11. *DEXTERITY* - make fine manipulations, coordinated movements			●
	12. *CHOICES* - select among alternatives, make decisions		●	
	13. *DIRECTION* - follow procedures, instructions or directions			●
	14. *MEMORY* - remember locations, procedures, nomenclatures, etc.			●
	15. *CAUTION* - use care in activities which pose personal hazard			●
	16. *NEATNESS* - work in a neat, orderly manner		●	
	17. *CONCENTRATION* - attend to task despite environmental distraction		●	
Tolerance	18. *REPETITION* - tolerate repetitive work assignments		●	
	19. *PERSEVERANCE* - perform continuously, over normal periods	●		
	20. *STAMINA* - have physical stamina, strength, resist fatigue			●

JOB PROFILE D-1
General Farm Worker

General Description

Assists in performing a wide variety of tasks in the operation of multipurpose farms (produce, grains, and livestock). Tasks usually are performed outdoors, in a variety of weather conditions.

Job Activities

Plant and seed by hand or from power farm equipment
Weed and cultivate by hand or with power farm equipment
Spread mulch, apply fertilizer
Thin young plants
Spray to control pests and disease
Open and close irrigation lines
Harvest produce, fruits and grains by hand or from power farm equipment
Feed and water stock, pets, horses (perform other hostling tasks)
Clean up barns, building, yards, pens
Handle eggs (gather, wash, sort, crate)
Operate milking machine; clean and sterilize machine
Assist with farm equipment
Load, unload, transport supplies, farm products
Perform simple carpentry and painting (buildings and fences)
Perform simple maintenance/repairs on tools and farm equipment

Specific Skill Requirements

Ability to safely use garden/carpentry tools (hand/power)
Ability to properly and safely operate basic farm equipment (milker, egg sorter, plows, and harvesting equipment)
Knowledge of proper use and hazards of disinfectants, fertilizers, poisons, flammable liquids, and other chemicals
Knowledge of basic carpentry and maintenance/repair techniques
Knowledge of safe methods for lifting and moving heavy objects
Knowledge of cleaning procedures for work areas and farm equipment
Ability to work with care and safety with large and small animals
Ability to handle produce and livestock in a sanitary manner
Knowledge of locations of work areas and equipment

Physical strength; ability to perform strenuous activities over extended periods

Relevant DOT References

Farmworker, General I 412.683-010
Farmworker, General II 421.687-010

Related Jobs

Vegetable Farm Worker (job profile D-2)
Poultry Farm/Hatchery Worker (job profile D-3)
Dairy Farm Worker (job profile D-4)
Ranch Hand (job profile D-5)
Orchard/Vineyard Worker (job profile D-6)
Farmworker, Field Crop II 404.687-010
Harvest Worker, Field Crop 404.687-014

JOB PROFILE D-2
Vegetable Farm Worker

General Description

Assists in general farm work on vegetable truck farm, usually working outdoors, in a variety of weather conditions. Employment opportunities may be seasonal.

Job Activities

Plant and seed by hand or from power farm equipment
Weed and cultivate by hand and with power farm equipment
Spread mulch
Thin young plants
Transplant seedlings
Set bean poles and other poles and string with twine
Lay and connect portable irrigation equipment; operate fixed irrigation lines
Spray to control pests and disease
Cover plants with treated cloth or paper to protect from weather
Harvest vegetables by hand or from power farm equipment

Pitch crops into viner or shelling machine
Sort vegetables
Pack or crate vegetables
Load, unload, transport
Attach farm implements such as plow or planter to tractor
Operate or assist with farm equipment
Perform simple maintenance/repair on tools and farm equipment
Clean up barns, buildings, yards
Perform simple carpentry and painting (buildings/fences)

Specific Skill Requirements

Ability to safely use garden/carpentry tools (hand/power)
Ability to assist in operating basic farm equipment (tractor, plows, planting and harvesting equipment)
Knowledge of hazards of fertilizers, poisons, and flammable liquids
Knowledge of basic carpentry and maintenance/repair techniques
Knowledge of safe methods for lifting and moving heavy objects
Knowledge of cleaning procedures for work area and farm equipment
Knowledge of basic farm procedures and routines
Ability to sort produce according to assigned quality standards
Ability to handle and crate produce in a careful, sanitary manner
Knowledge of locations of work areas and equipment
Physical strength; ability to perform strenuous activities over extended periods

Relevant DOT Reference

Farmworker, Vegetable II 402.687-010

Related Jobs

General Farm Worker (job profile D-1)
Orchard/Vineyard Worker (job profile D-6)
Harvest Worker, Vegetable 402.687-014

JOB PROFILE D-3
Poultry Farm/Hatchery Worker

General Description

Assists in the care of poultry; performs other general poultry farm activities. This employee may assist in brooder care of chicks and preparation of chicks for shipment or delivery. Work is performed both indoors and outdoors.

Job Activities

Unpack chicks from shipping crates and place in brooder house
Operate incubator
Spray poultry areas with disinfectants and disease control agents
Remove weak, ill, or dead poultry from flocks
Clean and fill feeders and watering containers
Monitor illumination and ventilation systems
Handle eggs (gather, wash, sort, crate)
Assist in selecting, killing, dressing and packing poultry for shipment
Assist in maintaining records (receiving, shipping, feeding, breeding, egg production)
Clean droppings and waste from floor; spread wood shavings
Clean up barns, buildings, yards, incubators, brooder houses
Perform simple carpentry and painting (buildings/fences)
Perform simple maintenance/repairs on tools and hatchery equipment

Specific Skill Requirements

Ability to safely use basic garden/carpentry tools (hand/power)
Knowledge of basic poultry farm procedures and routines
Knowledge of hazards of tools, equipment, disinfectants, poisons and related chemicals
Ability to operate basic poultry farm equipment (egg sorter, incubator, and so on)
Knowledge of simple carpentry and maintenance/repair techniques
Knowledge of safe methods of lifting and moving heavy objects such as sacks of feed
Ability to handle poultry and eggs in a careful, sanitary manner
Knowledge of cleaning procedures for farm areas and equipment

Knowledge of locations of work areas and equipment
Ability to keep simple records on numbers of poultry and eggs processed

Relevant DOT Reference

Farmworker, Poultry 411.584-010

Related Jobs

Dairy Farm Worker (job profile D-4)
Poultry Farm Laborer 411.687-018

JOB PROFILE D-4
Dairy Farm Worker

General Description

Assists in care of animals; assists in farm work on farms essentially concerned with milk production. Work involves both indoor and outdoor activities, in a variety of weather conditions. This worker also may assist in growing and storing feed crops.

Job Activities

Drive cows between stalls and pastures
Milk by machine or by hand
Feed and water stock by hand or using automated equipment
Weigh, load, mix and distribute feed
Cleanse and sterilize milking equipment
Clean up barns, buildings, yards, pens; place straw in stalls
Wash cows, spray with disinfectants, insect repellants
Assist in inoculating and castrating animals
Apply dehorning paste
Groom horses, perform other hostling activities
Load animals onto trucks for shipment
Assist in planting, cultivating, harvesting, and storing of hay and grains
Perform simple carpentry and painting (buildings/fences)
Perform simple maintenance/repairs on tools and farm equipment

Specific Skill Requirements

Ability to use milking machine
Knowledge of proper cleaning, sterilizing and basic maintenance of milking and dairy equipment
Knowledge of dairy farm routines and procedures
Knowledge of cleaning procedures for work areas
Knowledge of proper use and hazards of hand and power tools, disinfectants, poisons, and related chemicals
Awareness of personal hazards in working with livestock
Ability to handle dairy products and equipment in a neat, sanitary manner
Ability to safely operate basic powered farm equipment (tractor, truck)
Knowledge of safe methods for lifting and moving heavy objects
Knowledge of locations of work areas and equipment
Physical strength; ability to perform strenuous activities over extended periods

Relevant DOT Reference

Dairy Farm Worker 410.684-010

Related Jobs

General Farm Worker (job profile D-1)
Poultry Farm/Hatchery Worker (job profile D-3)
Milking Machine Operator 410.685-010
Sheepherder 410.687-022

JOB PROFILE D-5
Ranch Hand

General Description

Assists in care of stock and general farm work on ranch. The type of farm might be a beef, hog, sheep, or goat ranch. Work is performed both indoors and outdoors in a variety of weather conditions. This worker may assist in the growing and storing of feed.

Job Activities

Move stock from one pasture to another
Mix feed and additives
Feed and water stock
Clean up barns, buildings, yards, pens
Assist in marking stock with identification (brands, ear clips, rings)
Spray and otherwise treat stock for disease control
Assist in planting, cultivating, harvesting, and storing hay and grains
Lay and connect portable irrigation equipment; open and close fixed lines
Milk by hand or machine
Cleanse and sterilize milking equipment
Apply dehorning paste
Wash, groom, clip, dock, shear, or trim livestock
Apply medication to cuts and bruises
Assist in inoculating and castrating livestock
Check fences, feed and water troughs, outbuildings for repairs
Perform simple carpentry and painting (buildings/fences)
Perform simple maintenance/repairs on tools and ranch equipment
Hitch and unhitch farm equipment to tractor or horse
Saddle and ride horse; care for horse and riding equipment

Specific Skill Requirements

Knowledge of basic ranch and farm procedures and routines
Ability to properly and safely operate basic farm equipment (milking machine, tractor, truck)
Ability to safely use basic garden/carpentry tools (hand/power)
Knowledge of basic carpentry and maintenance/repair techniques
Knowledge of basic cleaning procedures for work areas, and farm and riding equipment
Knowledge of basic techniques for handling, saddling, and riding horses
Knowledge of safe methods for lifting and moving heavy objects
Awareness of personal hazards in working with livestock
Knowledge of hazards and proper use of disinfectants, poisons, and related chemicals
Knowledge of locations of work areas and equipment
Physical strength; ability to perform strenuous activities for extended periods

Relevant DOT Reference

Farm Worker, Livestock 410.664-010

Related Jobs

General Farm Worker (job profile D-1)
Dairy Farm Worker (job profile D-4)
Cowpuncher 410.674-014
Stable Attendant 410.674-022

JOB PROFILE D-6
Orchard/Vineyard Worker

General Description

Assists in planting, cultivating, and harvesting in fruit, nut, or sugar maple orchards, and in grape vineyards. This worker also may assist in processing and preparation of products for shipment. Employment opportunities may be seasonal.

Job Activities

Plant by hand
Weed and cultivate in orchards or vineyards using hand and power equipment
Treat trees or vines with fertilizers and pesticides
Thin seedlings; remove blossoms or thin young fruit
Assist in grafting trees and vines
Lay and connect portable irrigation equipment; open and close fixed lines
Prune trees or vines, dispose of cuttings
Assist in operating frost control equipment (smudge pots, wind machines)
Harvest orchard or vineyard products by hand or machine
Clear fields of brush and roots; dispose of waste
Sort orchard or vineyard products according to assigned standards
Dry and process grapes for marketing
Pack and crate products for shipment; load and unload trucks
Perform simple carpentry and painting (buildings/fences)
Perform simple maintenance/repairs on tools and equipment
Clean up barns, buildings, yards
Assist in processing sap into maple syrup
Assist in operating farm equipment, hitching and unhitching equipment from tractor

Specific Skill Requirements

Knowledge of basic techniques of pruning, grafting, fertilizing, irrigating, and disease control treatment for trees and vines
Ability to safely use simple garden/carpentry tools (hand/power)
Knowledge of basic maintenance/repair techniques for tools and equipment
Knowledge of hazards of disease control chemicals
Knowledge of proper and sanitary methods for harvesting, processing and packaging fruits, nuts, maple tree sap, or grapes
Ability to safely operate simple farm equipment (tractor, truck)
Ability to safely lift and move heavy objects
Knowledge of locations of work areas and equipment
Physical strength; ability to perform strenuous activities for extended periods

Relevant DOT Reference

Farm Worker, Fruit 403.687-010

Related Jobs

General Farm Worker (job profile D-1)
Vegetable Farm Worker (job profile D-2)
Harvest Worker, Fruit 403.678-018
Orchard Pruner 408.684-018

JOB PROFILE D-7
Forestry Worker

General Description

Assists in the planting and cultivation of forests in commercial and recreational settings. This worker also may assist in maintenance of forest facilities, in fire prevention and in forest survey. Employment opportunities may be seasonal.

Job Activities

Clear underbrush
Pile and burn underbrush

Dig firebreaks, irrigation canals
Plant seedlings
Clean, pick up seedlings
Weed and cultivate around seedlings
Spread mulch
Mix and apply fertilizers, pesticides
Cut out diseased trees; prune young trees to foster desirable growth
Assist in operation of forestry equipment (trucks, tractors, plows)
Perform simple carpentry (construction/maintenance of outbuildings, fences)
Perform simple maintenance/repair on forestry tools and equipment
Replenish firewood supplies for campsites
Assist in maintenance of campsites
Assist forest survey crew (carry equipment, set stakes)

Specific Skill Requirements

Ability to recognize plants
Knowledge of proper use of carpentry and forestry hand tools, sprayers
Knowledge of hazards of hand tools, forestry equipment, insecticides, animals and fire
Knowledge of basic techniques for cleaning underbrush, fire control, and irrigation
Knowledge of basic techniques for planting and cultivating seedlings
Ability to properly mix fertilizers, insecticides, and apply with sprayers
Ability to safely lift and move heavy objects
Ability to assist with operation of forestry equipment (trucks, tractors, plows)
Ability to recognize danger from wild animals, fires
Physical strength; ability to perform strenuous activities over extended periods

Relevant DOT Reference

Forest Worker 452.687-010

Related Jobs

Logging Operations Worker (job profile D-9)
Christmas Tree Farm Worker 451.687-010
Tree Planter 452.687-018
Seedling Sorter 451.687-022

JOB PROFILE D-8
Nursery/Greenhouse Worker

General Description

Assists in horticultural activities, such as planting, cultivating, and harvesting trees, shrubs, and ornamental flowering plants. Work may be performed both indoors (greenhouse) and outdoors, in a variety of weather conditions. Employment opportunities might be seasonal or holiday-related.

Job Activities

Mix soils, transport to work areas
Prepare plant beds
Plant seeds, seedlings, or bulbs by hand
Thin young plants
Weed by hand
Prune plants of limbs, leaves, flowers
Pick out and discard dead/defective plants
Transplant plants, trees, sod
Spread mulch
Water plants by hand, with sprinkler, or irrigation systems
Prepare and apply fertilizers and insecticides
Trap pests such as gophers and mice
Harvest cut flowers, pack plants for sale or shipment
Wrap tree roots in burlap
Move trees, shrubs in containers by wheelbarrow or hand truck
Clean work areas, buildings, yards
Assist in maintenance of buildings, equipment
Assist in trapping or killing pests that threaten plants

Specific Skill Requirements

Ability to identify plants
Knowledge of basic nursery/greenhouse routines and procedures, methods of plant care
Knowledge of basic techniques for mixing soils, planting, weeding, thinning, pruning, transplanting, watering, harvesting
Knowledge of proper methods of mixing and applying fertilizers, insecticides
Knowledge of hazards of fertilizers, poisons, garden tools and equipment

Ability to properly use common garden tools, sprayers, sprinkler systems
Ability to recognize defective plants according to specified standards
Knowledge of proper plant handling and preparation for shipment
Ability to safely and carefully lift and move heavy objects
Physical strength; ability to perform strenuous activities over extended periods

Relevant DOT Reference

Horticultural Worker II 405.687-014

Related Jobs

Flower Picker 405.687-010
Orchid Transplanter 405.687-018
Landscape Laborer 408.687-014
Tree Surgeon Helper 408.687-018

JOB PROFILE D-9
Logging Operations Worker

General Description

Assists in tasks relating to the cutting and transporting of timber, and reforestation of harvested areas. Employment opportunities may be seasonal.

Job Activities

Assist in logging-road construction
Clean underbrush and growth along roads and right-of-way
Assist in marking trees for cut
Assist in felling trees and removing their limbs
Assist in moving logs to waterway or onto trucks
Pile and burn brush and slash
Dig ditches, firebreaks
Prepare harvested areas for reforestation
Plant and cultivate seedlings for reforestation of harvested areas
Feed mulcher
Assist in disease control operations
Assist with chain saw, crane operation, tractor operation

Specific Skill Requirements

Ability to identify trees
Knowledge of proper use of hand tools (saws, axes, brush hook, shovels) and chain saw
Knowledge of hazards of hand tools, chain saw, flammable liquids, poisons, logging equipment
Knowledge of basic techniques for clearing underbrush, road construction, fire control
Knowledge of proper techniques for preparing cleared land for reforestation
Knowledge of basic techniques for planting and cultivating seedlings
Ability to properly mix insecticides and apply with sprayer
Ability to safely lift and move heavy objects
Ability to assist in the operation of major logging equipment (tractors, trucks, bulldozers)
Physical strength; ability to perform strenuous activities for extended periods
Willingness to work in a variety of weather conditions

Relevant DOT Reference

Laborer, Brush Clearing 459.687-010

Related Jobs

Forestry Worker (job profile D-7)
Pulp Mill Worker (job profile F-27)
Logger, All-round 454.684-018
Tree Cutter 454.684-026

JOB PROFILE D-10
Fishing Boat Deckhand

General Description

Assists in tasks related to the general housekeeping of a fishing boat, for the obtaining of sea or lake products and delivery to a central port. This worker also may assist with activities involved in setting traps and nets and harvesting the fish.

Job Activities

Load equipment and supplies on vessel
Assist in rowing boat or skiff to tow and position nets
Set traps (fish or shellfish)
Watch and check traps
Set nets
Empty traps, nets
Fold or store nets
Shovel or rake fish and shellfish
Sort fish
Place catch in containers, preserve with salt or ice, and store
Assist in counting, weighing, or weigh-counting fish
Wash and hang sponges
Clean decks and fishing equipment
Clean and make simple repairs to fishing and boat equipment (decking, fittings, traps, nets, lines)
Assist with major boat maintenance (scraping barnacles, painting, refitting)

Specific Skill Requirements

Knowledge of techniques for specific kinds of fishing (fish or shellfish)
Ability to make simple repairs to traps, nets, lines
Knowledge of proper general cleaning methods for deckings, fittings, and so on
Ability to do simple painting, scraping, sanding
Ability to properly use simple hand and power tools, cleaning equipment
Knowledge of hazards of hand and power tools, flammable liquids, boat equipment, and working near water
Ability to safely lift and move heavy objects
Ability to recognize and sort different types of fish, shellfish
Knowledge of locations of work areas, equipment, boat procedures
Ability to keep simple records of catch
Ability to swim
Ability to work closely with co-workers, in a team effort
Physical strength; ability to perform strenuous activities for extended periods

Relevant DOT Reference

Deckhand, Fishing Vessel 449.667-010

Related Jobs

Fish Hatchery Worker (job profile D-11)
Fisher, Net 441.684-010
Laborer, Aquatic Life 446.687-014

JOB PROFILE D-11
Fish Hatchery Worker

General Description

Assists in tasks occurring around fish hatcheries; care and cultivation of fish, equipment. This employee also may assist in simple maintenance of buildings and grounds. (See job profile C-42.)

Job Activities

Assist culturist in collecting, fertilizing, incubating eggs
Feed fish in hatchery
Add medication to food as directed
Tend water valves
Monitor water temperature gauges
Sort fish
Drain and clean reservoirs, tanks, and troughs; refill them
Assist in transferring fish to streams and ponds
Clean work areas
Perform simple carpentry on buildings
Perform simple repairs to hatchery equipment
Maintain grounds

Specific Skill Requirements

Knowledge of basic techniques for collecting, fertilizing, and incubation of eggs
Knowledge of feed and water temperature requirements for various fish
Ability to properly operate hatchery equipment (tanks, temperature controls)
Ability to handle fish and eggs in a careful, sanitary manner
Knowledge of basic cleaning techniques for work areas, equipment

Safety precautions in using cleaning chemicals
Ability to properly use basic hand and power tools, cleaning equipment
Knowledge of basic carpentry and repair/maintenance techniques
Ability to safely lift and move heavy objects
Ability to recognize and sort various kinds of fish

Relevant DOT Reference

Fish Hatchery Worker 446.684-010

Related Jobs

Fishing Boat Deckhand (job profile D-10)
Laborer, Aquatic Life 446.687-014

Master Profile E: **Skilled Trades**

General Description

Jobs in this group are concerned primarily with assisting skilled workers in major industries. Many of the jobs emphasize the position of helper or assistant; for example, job profile E-2 defines plasterer helper, not plasterer. Job activities listed in the job profiles describe activities to be performed by a helper, and not those activities performed by the skilled worker. However, the helper may perform higher-level tasks under the supervision of the skilled worker.

The jobs are clustered in general employment areas. However, some of the more specific jobs such as carpet layer's assistant or painter's helper may be appropriate to job group F as well (Processing and Manufacturing). In general, jobs relating to industries hiring skilled workers are found in E, while F contains jobs relating more to unskilled workers or factory production. However, it is entirely possible that some of the jobs presented in E also could be listed in F.

This category is divided into three major divisions: construction, maintenance and repair, and printing. Some of the job activities common to all of these divisions are: gather, move, and clean tools and equipment; sort, stack, and move materials and boxes; use common hand and power tools; clean up work areas; and prepare materials for use by craftsperson or skilled worker. The work requires substantial physical strength and stamina, and may be performed inside or outdoors. Many of the jobs expose the worker to dirty materials such as dust, grease, ink, paint, or a variety of construction materials. Contacts with the public will be minimal, but coordination with co-workers frequently is required.

Because of the variation among the subgroups of this master profile, separate descriptions and skill requirements are presented for each subgroup. In addition to the basic, core and personal/social skills given below, each job profile lists specific skill requirements relevant to that particular job.

Job Profiles (See pages immediately following this master profile.)

1. Construction

E-1 Building Construction Helper
E-2 Plasterer Helper
E-3 Dry-Wall Helper

E-4 Painter Helper
E-5 Carpet Layer Helper
E-6 New Building Cleaner
E-7 Brick Cleaner
E-8 Road Construction Helper
E-9 Asphalt Raker
E-10 Flagger
E-11 Form-Builder Helper
E-12 Surveyor's Helper
E-13 Paint Striping Machine Helper

2. Maintenance and repair

E-14 Automobile-Body Repairer Helper
E-15 Transportation Fleet Maintenance Helper
E-16 Industrial Garage Attendant
E-17 Automobile Painter Helper
E-18 Automobile Mechanic Helper
E-19 New Car Preparation Helper
E-20 Used Car Lot Porter
E-21 Engine Mechanic Helper (Aircraft, Diesel, Marine)
E-22 Electric Appliance Repair Helper
E-23 Small Engine Repair Helper (Gasoline Engines)
E-24 Heating and Air-Conditioning Service Helper
E-25 Swimming Pool Service Helper
E-26 Upholstery Shop Helper
E-27 Furniture Refinishing Helper
E-28 Shoe Repair Helper
E-29 Meter Repair Helper

3. Printing

E-30 Newspaper Production Worker
E-31 Print Shop Worker
E-32 Bindery Worker

Skill Requirements

1. Construction Construction jobs require strenuous labor such as digging, shoveling, hammering, and lifting or holding construction materials. Some of the jobs are performed indoors, some outdoors. Adverse weather conditions may prevail for the road construction helper and flagger, who might have to assist in emergency repairs during storms.

Basic skills

Fasten (4)*

Locate and collect supplies, materials (9)

Communicate verbally (ask and answer questions, express observation) (10)

Tell time (13)

Measure length, weight, volume (14)

Combine liquids/dry materials (16)

Core skills

Lift and carry (7)*

Load and unload (8)

Transport (hand truck, cart, wheelbarrow) (9)

Perform indoor cleaning (24)

Handle dangerous substances (30)

Dig and shovel (34)

Use garden tools (35)

Personal/social skills

See Requirements Profile for E-1 on page 222. Particularly important are physical stamina and attentiveness to the task despite environmental distraction.

2. **Maintenance and repair** While most of the job activities involve assembling and providing supplies for the craftsperson, or cleaning the work area, the helper may be required to assist the skilled worker in performing complex tasks such as automobile engine repair. Most of the work will be performed indoors in rather complex and potentially dangerous areas.

Basic skills

Read (basic) (1)

Sort by category (5)

Locate and collect supplies, materials (9)

Communicate verbally (ask and answer questions, express observations) (10)

Tell time (13)

Measure length, weight, volume (14)

Read dials, gauges, meters (15)

Manipulate small objects (17)

Core skills

Lift and carry (7)

Load and unload (8)

Transport (handtruck, cart) (9)

Stack and shelve (10)

Pack or crate (11)

Perform indoor cleaning (24)

Handle dangerous substances (30)

Use hand tools (33)

Personal/social skills

See Requirements Profile E-2, page 223. Teamwork is especially important since most of the jobs are of a supportive nature. Also critical is caution in working with engines, automobiles and trucks, and toxic substances such as paint and cleaning chemicals.

---

*The numbers in the parentheses refer to the sequence of the skills listed in the basic skills chart (page 43) and the core skills chart (page 47), which define the individual skills and cite applications for each one.

3. **Printing** Job activities involve cleaning equipment, gathering and stacking papers, packaging or wrapping for shipment, and monitoring automatic equipment. Work is indoors and in quite complex areas, containing potentially dangerous equipment.

Basic skills
- Read (1)
- Write (simple messages, records) (2)
- Count and record numbers (3)
- Perform simple calculations (add and subtract) (4)
- Sort by category (5)
- Arrange in order (alphabetize) (8)
- Locate and collect supplies, materials (9)
- Communicate verbally (ask and answer questions, express observations) (10)

Core skills
- Bundle (2)
- Package and wrap (5)
- Lift and carry (7)
- Load and unload (8)
- Transport (handtruck, cart) (9)
- Stack and shelve (10)
- Pack or crate (11)
- Stamp and label (13)
- Perform indoor cleaning (24)
- Handle dangerous substances (30)

Personal/social skills

See Requirements Profile E-3, page 224. Following directions, memory, and tolerance for repetitive work are especially important.

Master Profile: **E-1. Skilled Trades (Construction)**

	Personal/Social Skill Requirements	Extent Required		
		Minimal	Moderate	Major
Social Skills	1. *SELF EXPRESSION* - communicate, ask for assistance, question		●	
	2. *SOCIABILITY* - interact with other employees or public		●	
	3. *WORK INDEPENDENCE* - work without supervision or guidance		●	
	4. *APPEARANCE/HYGIENE* - cleanliness, good manners, neatness in appearance		●	
	5. *TEAMWORK* - perform in close coordination with other jobs			●
Time Factors	6. *PACE* - perform at a consistent rate of speed		●	
	7. *ATTENDANCE* - be reliable in attendance and punctuality			●
	8. *SIMULTANEITY* - perform several activities at near same time		●	
	9. *TIMING* - perform timed, scheduled activities; be aware of time		●	
Performance Skills	10. *ACCURACY* - perform within well-defined tolerances		●	
	11. *DEXTERITY* - make fine manipulations, coordinated movements		●	
	12. *CHOICES* - select among alternatives, make decisions			●
	13. *DIRECTION* - follow procedures, instructions or directions			●
	14. *MEMORY* - remember locations, procedures, nomenclatures, etc.			●
	15. *CAUTION* - use care in activities which pose personal hazard			●
	16. *NEATNESS* - work in a neat, orderly manner		●	
	17. *CONCENTRATION* - attend to task despite environmental distraction			●
Tolerance	18. *REPETITION* - tolerate repetitive work assignments		●	
	19. *PERSEVERANCE* - perform continuously, over normal periods		●	
	20. *STAMINA* - have physical stamina, strength, resist fatigue			●

Master Profile: **E-2. Skilled Trades (Maintenance/Repair)**

Personal/Social Skill Requirements		Extent Required: Minimal	Extent Required: Moderate	Extent Required: Major
Social Skills	1. *SELF EXPRESSION* - communicate, ask for assistance, question		●	
	2. *SOCIABILITY* - interact with other employees or public		●	
	3. *WORK INDEPENDENCE* - work without supervision or guidance		●	
	4. *APPEARANCE/HYGIENE* - cleanliness, good manners, neatness in appearance		●	
	5. *TEAMWORK* - perform in close coordination with other jobs			●
Time Factors	6. *PACE* - perform at a consistent rate of speed			●
	7. *ATTENDANCE* - be reliable in attendance and punctuality			●
	8. *SIMULTANEITY* - perform several activities at near same time			●
	9. *TIMING* - perform timed, scheduled activities; be aware of time		●	
Performance Skills	10. *ACCURACY* - perform within well-defined tolerances			●
	11. *DEXTERITY* - make fine manipulations, coordinated movements			●
	12. *CHOICES* - select among alternatives, make decisions		●	
	13. *DIRECTION* - follow procedures, instructions or directions			●
	14. *MEMORY* - remember locations, procedures, nomenclatures, etc.		●	
	15. *CAUTION* - use care in activities which pose personal hazard			●
	16. *NEATNESS* - work in a neat, orderly manner		●	
	17. *CONCENTRATION* - attend to task despite environmental distraction		●	
Tolerance	18. *REPETITION* - tolerate repetitive work assignments		●	
	19. *PERSEVERANCE* - perform continuously, over normal periods		●	
	20. *STAMINA* - have physical stamina, strength, resist fatigue		●	

Master Profile: **E-3. Skilled Trades (Printing)**

	Personal/Social Skill Requirements	Extent Required: Minimal	Extent Required: Moderate	Extent Required: Major
Social Skills	1. *SELF EXPRESSION* - communicate, ask for assistance, question		●	
	2. *SOCIABILITY* - interact with other employees or public		●	
	3. *WORK INDEPENDENCE* - work without supervision or guidance		●	
	4. *APPEARANCE/HYGIENE* - cleanliness, good manners, neatness in appearance		●	
	5. *TEAMWORK* - perform in close coordination with other jobs			●
Time Factors	6. *PACE* - perform at a consistent rate of speed			●
	7. *ATTENDANCE* - be reliable in attendance and punctuality			●
	8. *SIMULTANEITY* - perform several activities at near same time			●
	9. *TIMING* - perform timed, scheduled activities; be aware of time		●	
Performance Skills	10. *ACCURACY* - perform within well-defined tolerances		●	
	11. *DEXTERITY* - make fine manipulations, coordinated movements		●	
	12. *CHOICES* - select among alternatives, make decisions		●	
	13. *DIRECTION* - follow procedures, instructions or directions			●
	14. *MEMORY* - remember locations, procedures, nomenclatures, etc.			●
	15. *CAUTION* - use care in activities which pose personal hazard		●	
	16. *NEATNESS* - work in a neat, orderly manner		●	
	17. *CONCENTRATION* - attend to task despite environmental distraction		●	
Tolerance	18. *REPETITION* - tolerate repetitive work assignments			●
	19. *PERSEVERANCE* - perform continuously, over normal periods		●	
	20. *STAMINA* - have physical stamina, strength, resist fatigue		●	

JOB PROFILE E-1
Building Construction Helper

General Description

Assists carpenters or other members of crew in building construction. Work is mostly performed outdoors. This worker may be required to transfer from one task to another as the construction progresses. Employment opportunities may be seasonal in regions with cold climate.

Job Activities

Gather and carry tools and building materials between storage and work areas
Unload and store materials
Clear and clean work areas; stack up scrap lumber
Dismantle, clean and store wood and metal forms
Clean and sort bricks
Shovel cement, sand, gravel
Tend cement mixer
Mix mortar or plaster
Assist in assembling scaffolding and guy wires
Scrape and wash windows
Paint by hand
Assist with simple carpentry tasks
Dig shallow holes and trenches
String wire
Use hoist to move tools, equipment, and materials to upper floors
Perform simple maintenance on construction equipment, for example, grease and oil

Specific Skill Requirements

Ability to use basic hand and power tools
Ability to use basic clean-up tools (rake, shovel, broom, vacuum, hose)
Ability to use wheelbarrow, handtruck, and dolly
Ability to clean, assemble, and dismantle wood and metal forms
Ability to perform simple carpentry as directed
Knowledge of basic rough painting techniques

Ability to clean and wash windows
Ability to load, unload, and correctly store construction materials
Ability to safely lift, carry, and transport heavy objects
Ability to use power or manual hoist
Knowledge of common hazards of construction settings
Ability to work in close coordination with other members of crew
Physical strength; ability to perform strenuous tasks over extended periods

Relevant DOT Reference

Laborer, Carpentry 869.664-014

Related Jobs

Pump Tender, Cement Based Materials 849.665-010
(Helper to) Carpenter II 860.681-010
Sider 860.684-014

JOB PROFILE E-2
Plasterer Helper

General Description

Assists journey-level plasterer in the preparation and application of plaster and similar materials to interior walls and ceilings. Also performs general cleanup tasks.

Job Activities

Gather and move plaster, materials between storage and work areas
Gather and move tools between storage and work areas
Mix concrete, plaster, mortar manually or with power mixer
Shovel plaster onto mortarboard for plasterer
Hand tools to plasterer
Clean tools, equipment, work areas
Use common tools (shovel, rake, broom, mop, vacuum)
Use hoist to move buckets of plaster, tools, and so on, to upper floors
Shovel cement, sand, gravel

Unload and store delivered materials
Assemble, dismantle scaffolding
Assist in operating plaster-spraying machine

Specific Skill Requirements

Knowledge of basic routines, procedures, tools and materials for plastering
Knowledge of cleaning techniques for tools and equipment
Knowledge of cleaning tools and techniques for work areas
Ability to prepare plaster, other materials for plasterer
Ability to use wheelbarrow, handtruck, dolly, and manual and power hoists
Ability to assemble and dismantle scaffolding
Knowledge of operation of plaster-spraying machine
Ability to safely lift, carry, and transport heavy objects
Knowledge of hazards of hand and power tools, equipment, flammables, plastering materials, and of construction settings in general
Knowledge of locations of tools and equipment, materials, and work areas
Knowledge of proper storage techniques for materials, tools, equipment
Ability to work in close coordination with other members of crew
Physical strength; ability to perform strenuous tasks over extended periods

Relevant DOT Reference

Plasterer Helper (Construction) 869.687-026

Related Jobs

Dry-wall Helper (job profile E-3)
Bricklayer Helper 869.687-026

JOB PROFILE E-3
Dry-Wall Helper

General Description

Assists journey-level dry-wall applicator with the preparation and installation of wallboard to interior ceilings and walls of buildings.

Job Activities

Gather and move tools and supplies between storage and work areas
Move wallboard sheets to work area, using handtruck or manually
Assist in measuring and cutting wallboard to appropriate dimensions
Assist in fitting and nailing wallboard to walls, ceilings
Prepare sealing compound, by hand or using electric mixer
Assist with sealing, taping, sanding, and other surface finishing
Clean and maintain work tools
Clean work areas; remove scraps, dust

Specific Skill Requirements

Knowledge of use of basic tools and supplies for dry-wall preparation/installation
Ability to safely lift and move heavy objects manually and by handtruck
Knowledge of techniques for measuring, cutting, and installing wallboard
Knowledge of basic techniques for sealing, taping, sanding, and other surface finishing
Ability to recognize different kinds of wallboard material
Ability to prepare sealing compound, by hand or using electric mixer
Knowledge of cleaning and maintenance techniques for dry-wall tools
Ability to clean work areas of scraps, dust
Ability to use rake, broom, shovel, industrial vacuum, wheelbarrow, handtruck
Knowledge of procedures and routines characteristic of specific job setting
Knowledge of hazards of tools, supplies, and job settings
Ability to work in close coordination with other members of crew
Physical strength; ability to perform strenuous activities over extended periods

Relevant DOT Reference

Construction Worker I 869.664-014

Related Job

Plasterer Helper (job profile E-2)

JOB PROFILE E-4
Painter Helper

General Description

Assists painter in preparation of materials, of painting surfaces, and of work site. Also performs general cleanup tasks. May work indoors and/or outdoors, in a wide variety of settings. Employment opportunities may be seasonal in cold climates.

Job Activities

Gather and move tools, equipment, and materials between storage and work areas
Mix or stir paint
Place drop cloths over exposed items and surfaces
Wash surfaces to prepare for painting
Apply paint remover to remove old paint
Remove loose paint, using scraper, steel wool, wire brush, chipping hammer, blowtorch
Sand surfaces, manually or with power sander
Fill cracks and holes with putty, using spatula and related tools
Assemble, dismantle scaffolding
Use manual or power hoist to transport tools, paint up to scaffolding
Clean up brushes, equipment
Clean work area using mop, broom, vacuum
Clean spattered paint off windows, other surfaces
Move furniture; remove wall hangings, fixtures, wall plates, and so on to prepare painting site; replace when painting is completed
Assist in operating paint-spraying machine

Specific Skill Requirements

Ability to use tools, materials for filling cracks, holes, and so on
Ability to use tools, chemicals, solvents for removing old paint
Ability to use cleanup and window washing tools
Ability to safely lift and move furniture and other heavy objects
Knowledge of proper placement of drop cloths
Ability to assemble and dismantle scaffolding

Ability to use manual or power hoist
Knowledge of proper cleaning techniques for tools and equipment
Knowledge of hazards of hand and power tools and equipment, flammables, solvents, and work settings in general
Knowledge of locations of tools, equipment, materials, and work areas
Knowledge of basic routines and procedures of painting (both general and peculiar to specialized work settings)
Knowledge of basic operation of spray-painting machine
Physical strength; ability to perform strenuous activities over extended periods

Relevant DOT Reference

Painter Helper 869.687-026

Related Jobs

Dry-Wall Helper (job profile E-3)
Bricklayer Helper 869.687-026

JOB PROFILE E-5
Carpet Layer Helper

General Description

Helps measure, cut, and lay floor padding and carpet on the floors of residential, commercial, and industrial buildings. If delivery or transporting of carpeting is part of the job, see job profile A-15.

Job Activities

Move carpet, padding from warehouse to truck and from truck to work area
Gather and move tools, supplies between truck and work area
Use measuring devices to measure room, padding, and carpet
Lay out padding and carpet on the floor
Assist carpet layer in cutting, stretching, fastening, and seaming padding and carpet
Move furniture
Use roller to obscure seam markings

Remove scraps from work site
Clean room and work area
Assist in the delivery of carpeting to the installation site

Specific Skill Requirements

Knowledge of tools, materials to measure, cut, and lay padding and carpet
Knowledge of proper techniques for measuring, cutting, and laying padding and carpet
Ability to safely lift and move furniture, heavy objects
Ability to use carpet dolly
Knowledge of locations of tools, materials, and work areas
Knowledge of hazards of sharp cutting tools, materials, and new construction work settings
Ability to use basic cleanup tools (broom, vacuum)
Physical strength; ability to perform strenuous activities over extended periods

Relevant DOT Reference

Carpet-Layer Helper 864.687-010

Related Jobs

(Helper to) Linoleum-Tile Floor Layer 864.481-010
(Helper to) Carpet or Linoleum Cutter 929.381-010

JOB PROFILE E-6
New Building Cleaner

General Description

Responsible for removing any construction materials (for example, sawhorses, boards) from new building. Cleans building and prepares it for occupants.

Job Activities

Remove tools or other equipment
Pick up scrap lumber and other materials

Pile or stack up boards
Separate salvageable and unsalvageable materials
Load equipment, materials onto truck
Vacuum carpets and drapes
Mop/scrub floors
Clean counters, cabinets, walls
Wash windows

Specific Skill Requirements

Knowledge of construction tools, equipment, and materials
Ability to properly use cleaning tools and equipment
Ability to properly use window washing equipment
Knowledge of cleanup routines and procedures
Ability to separate, as directed, salvageable and unsalvageable materials
Ability to safely lift and move heavy objects
Ability to use wheelbarrow, hand truck, dolly
Knowledge of the hazards of tools, equipment, cleaning agents, flammables, and construction settings in general
Knowledge of locations of tools, equipment, materials, and work areas
Knowledge of basic cleaning techniques for tools and equipment
Physical strength; ability to perform strenuous tasks over extended periods

Relevant DOT Reference

Cleaner, Commercial or Institutional 381.687-014

Related Jobs

Caretaker (job profile C-5)
Building Porter (job profile C-23)
Cleaner, Industrial 381.687-018
Cleaner, Manufactured Buildings 869.687-018
Building Cleaner (Construction Worker I) 869.687-026
Project Crew Worker 891.687-018

JOB PROFILE E-7
Brick Cleaner

General Description

Cleans mortar from used bricks and stacks them in piles. Work may be performed on new building sites, at building demolition sites, or in salvage yards. Since most of the work occurs outdoors, employment opportunities may be seasonal in some climates.

Job Activities

Clean mortar from used bricks, using hammer and chisels
Sort bricks according to size and quality
Stack bricks
Bind bricks into bundles, using strapping machine
Carry bricks
Load and unload onto cart or wheelbarrow
Push or move cart or wheelbarrow
Clean tools
Clean work area, using rake, shovel, and broom

Specific Skill Requirements

Ability to use hammer, chisels, strapping machine, rake, shovel, and broom
Knowledge of techniques for removing mortar from bricks
Ability to sort bricks according to specified size and quality standards
Ability to stack bricks into bundles for strapping
Ability to bind bundles using strapping machine
Ability to safely lift and carry heavy objects
Ability to safely stack bricks, bundles onto cart, wheelbarrow
Ability to use wheelbarrow and cart
Knowledge of cleaning techniques for tools, equipment, and work areas
Knowledge of hazards of tools, chipping mortar, handling bricks, and of the work area in general
Knowledge of locations of tools and work areas
Ability to tolerate repetitious tasks
Physical strength; ability to perform strenuous activities over extended periods

Relevant DOT Reference

Brick Cleaner (Construction Worker II) 869.687-026

Related Jobs

Bricklayer Helper 861.687-010
Building Cleaner, Brick or Stone 869.687-026

JOB PROFILE E-8
Road Construction Helper

General Description

Assists in activities related to preparation of roadbed and laying of highway. May also help in traffic control during construction activities. Employment opportunities may be seasonal in some climates.

Job Activities

Use common hand tools
Load and unload construction materials
Gather and move tools, supplies between storage and work areas
Rake, sweep
Pick up scrap lumber
Pile or stack up boards
Pile or stack up stone
Signal (flag) traffic
Clean and store tools and equipment
Perform simple carpentry
Build, clean, and dismantle concrete forms
String wire
Shovel concrete, sand, gravel
Mix concrete, using power concrete mixer
Perform simple maintenance (grease, oil) on construction machinery/equipment
Paint by hand

Specific Skill Requirements

Ability to use common construction hand tools, wheelbarrow, concrete mixer
Ability to safely lift, carry, and transport heavy objects
Knowledge of basic road construction routines and procedures
Knowledge of cleaning and maintenance techniques for tools and equipment
Knowledge of simple carpentry techniques
Ability to mix concrete ingredients in correct proportions
Ability to do rough painting by hand
Knowledge of basic traffic control techniques
Ability to clean and dismantle concrete forms
Ability to separate salvageable and unsalvageable construction materials, as directed
Knowledge of hazards of tools, equipment, flammables, solvents, working in traffic, and of road construction work in general
Knowledge of locations of tools, equipment, supplies, and work areas
Willingness to work, on occasion, in adverse weather
Physical strength; ability to perform strenuous activities over extended periods

Relevant DOT Reference

Laborer, Road Construction (Construction Worker II) 869.687-026

Related Jobs

Road Maintenance Worker (job profile C-37)
Building Construction Helper (job profile E-1)
Asphalt Raker (job profile E-9)

JOB PROFILE E-9
Asphalt Raker

General Description

Follows hot-mix paving machine or spreader and rakes asphalt paving materials evenly over road surface. May assist in paving new areas or in repairing old pavements. Employment opportunities may be seasonal in some climates.

Job Activities

Use common tools, including broom, rake, shovel, wheelbarrow, tamper (manual or power)
Clean tools, equipment, and work areas
Rake asphalt dumped by truck
Even seams in surface
Signal for additional asphalt to fill low spots
Remove excess material to reduce high spots
Smooth paved surface, using tamper
Gather and move tools and equipment between storage and work areas
Assist in traffic control

Specific Skill Requirements

Ability to use common road construction tools and equipment
Knowledge of techniques for cleaning tools, equipment, and work areas
Knowledge of basic road construction routines and procedures
Knowledge of techniques for leveling and firming asphalt
Knowledge of basic traffic control techniques
Ability to safely lift, carry, or transport heavy objects
Knowledge of hazards of tools, equipment, flammables, hot oil and asphalt, working in traffic, and of road construction work in general
Knowledge of locations of tools, equipment, supplies, and work areas
Ability to work in close coordination with other members of crew
Physical strength; ability to perform strenuous activities over extended periods

Relevant DOT Reference

Asphalt Raker 869.687-026

Related Jobs

Road Construction Helper (job profile E-8)
Laborer, Bituminous Paving 869.687-026

JOB PROFILE E-10
Flagger

General Description

Directs traffic when construction blocks normal traffic. This job may be performed on road construction sites; it is also applicable to road maintenance and highway paint striping. Employment opportunities may be seasonal in some climates. It may be necessary to work in inclement weather during emergency road repairs.

Job Activities

Erect and dismantle traffic control signs, pylons and barricades
Hold flag or sign
Give directions to cars
Signal to other workers
Use walkie-talkie to coordinate traffic flow with other flaggers
Load and unload equipment, material
Assist with general construction activity

Specific Skill Requirements

Knowledge of traffic control techniques
Knowledge of proper use of traffic control signs, pylons and barricades
Ability to use simple walkie-talkie
Ability to recognize when to stop, start traffic flow
Ability to coordinate traffic control efforts with other flaggers
Knowledge of hazards of working in traffic and of road construction work in general
Ability to safely lift, carry, or move heavy objects
Ability to assist with general construction activity, as directed
Willingness to work in adverse weather when necessary
Ability to work in close coordination with other crew members
Ability to make decisions and use own judgment in directing traffic

Relevant DOT Reference

Flagger 372.667-022

Related Job

School Crossing Guard 371.567-010

JOB PROFILE E-11
Form-Builder Helper

General Description

Assists form-builder to construct forms for molding concrete structures. Work is performed outdoors, therefore employment opportunities may be seasonal in some climates.

Job Activities

Gather and move tools, equipment between storage and work areas, using hoist if necessary
Load and unload materials
Select materials for use; move from storage to work areas
Measure lumber
Saw lumber, using hand and power saws
Arrange boards in position for assembly
Hammer together boards
Erect and dismantle scaffolding
Place forms into position
Fasten forms together
Fasten building paper to forms
Dig shallow holes and trenches
Drive stakes
Shovel sand, gravel, dirt
Pick up scrap lumber and materials
Separate salvageable and unsalvageable materials
Pile or stack up boards
Clean and store tools and equipment

Specific Skill Requirements

Ability to use wheelbarrow, ladder; assist with hoist
Ability to use common hand tools, power saws
Ability to safely lift, carry, and transport heavy objects

Ability to perform simple carpentry
Knowledge of techniques for assembly and disassembly of scaffolding
Knowledge of concrete-form construction and assembly techniques
Knowledge of basic cleaning and maintenance techniques for tools/equipment
Knowledge of cleanup routines and procedures for work areas
Ability to separate, as directed, salvageable from unsalvageable materials
Ability to load, unload, and neatly arrange construction materials
Knowledge of hazards of hand and power tools and equipment, flammables, and of construction settings in general
Ability to work in close coordination with other crew members
Physical strength; ability to perform strenuous activities over extended periods

Relevant DOT Reference

Form-Builder Helper (Construction Worker I) 869.664-014

Related Jobs

Exterminator Helper 383.687-010
Laborer, Carpentry 869.664-014

JOB PROFILE E-12
Surveyor's Helper

General Description

Performs a variety of duties to assist in surveying land. May also clear and remove brush. Workers in this job may perform a single function and be designated as brush clearer, staker, or chain helper.

Job Activities

Carry stakes
Hold rods and stakes at designated points
Drive stakes into ground
Cut and clear brush
Use measuring device to measure distance between survey points
Mark measurement points with identifying mark

Call out readings on instruments
Write down readings in notebook
Clean and store tools and equipment
Gather and move tools, equipment and supplies between truck and work areas

Specific Skill Requirements

Knowledge of basic surveying routines and procedures
Knowledge of proper use of surveying tools, equipment, and supplies
Ability to use brush hook, knife and axe for clearing brush
Knowledge of techniques for cutting and clearing brush
Ability to read and record measurements accurately
Ability to work in close cooperation with other crew members
Ability to safely lift and carry heavy objects
Knowledge of hazards of tools, equipment, and of work setting in general
Knowledge of locations of tools, equipment, supplies, and work areas

Relevant DOT Reference

Surveyor Helper 869.567-010

Related Job

Signaler 869.667-014

JOB PROFILE E-13
Paint Striping Machine Helper

General Description

Assists operator of paint-striping machine in marking streets, runways, parking lots, and hard-surfaced recreational areas. May also assist with spray painting traffic control markings on streets and parking lots. May act as flagger to control traffic flow through work area. (See job profile E-10.)

Job Activities

Assist in measuring and marking lines for striping
Gather and move tools, equipment, and supplies between truck and work areas
Stir paint, pour into sprayer tank
Assist machine operator with sprayer adjustments
Touch up paint by hand, if necessary
Move and position stencils for painting traffic control markings
Set out and pick up pylons and signs warning motorists of work in progress
Direct traffic through work area
Dismantle and clean tools and equipment
Sweep and/or wash areas to be painted
Assist in basic maintenance/repair of tools and equipment

Specific Skill Requirements

Knowledge of use of tools, equipment, and supplies used in painting road surfaces
Knowledge of basic routines and procedures for painting stripes and traffic control markings
Knowledge of basic traffic control, using signs, pylons, and flags
Ability to safely lift and move heavy objects, manually and by handtruck
Ability to dismantle and clean tools and simple equipment
Ability to properly use rake, broom, shovel, wheelbarrow
Knowledge of locations of equipment, supplies in storage areas and on truck
Knowledge of hazards of hand and power tools and equipment, flammables, and working in traffic
Ability to work in close coordination with other crew members
Ability to make decisions and use own judgment in directing traffic

Relevant DOT Reference

Paint-Stripping-Machine Operator (Construction Worker I) 869.664-014

Related Job

Spray Painter Helper 741.687-014

JOB PROFILE E-14
Automobile-Body Repairer Helper

General Description

Assists automobile-body repairer in repairing damaged body and body parts of automobiles.

Job Activities

Gather and move tools, equipment, and materials between storage and work areas
Clean, perform simple maintenance on, and store tools and equipment
Clean work areas
Remove trim, accessories, and other parts to gain access to damaged areas
Replace parts after completion of repairs
Hammer out dents and straighten bent metal
Smooth surfaces by filling depressions
File, grind, and sand surfaces
Assist in priming and painting surfaces
Wax or polish finished surfaces
Move equipment around shop
Store delivered supplies and materials

Specific Skill Requirements

Ability to use simple hand and power tools and equipment for auto-body repair
Knowledge of basic techniques of auto-body repair
Knowledge of basic routines and procedures of an auto-body repair shop
Knowledge of proper storage of tools and equipment
Ability to clean and perform simple maintenance upon tools and equipment
Knowledge of techniques for removing dents, straightening metal parts, and puttying in dents
Knowledge of techniques for filing, grinding, and sanding metal surfaces
Knowledge of techniques for priming, painting, and waxing/polishing surfaces
Ability to clean work areas and dispose of scrap materials
Ability to safely lift, carry, and move heavy objects and equipment
Ability to use hand truck and dolly

Ability to properly store delivered supplies and materials
Knowledge of hazards of hand and power tools and equipment, flammables, solvents, and of repair shop settings in general
Knowledge of locations of tools, equipment, materials, and work areas
Willingness to work in a setting having consistently high levels of noise and dust

Relevant DOT Reference

Automobile-Body-Repairer Helper 807.687-010

Related Jobs

Automobile Painter Helper (job profile E-17)
Streetcar-Repairer Helper 807.687-014

JOB PROFILE E-15
Transportation Fleet Maintenance Helper

General Description

Helps in the service and repair of a fleet of motor vehicles, such as cars, buses, trucks. Employment opportunities also may exist in servicing railroad cars or streetcars.

Job Activities

Clean interior and exterior of vehicles; wax or polish vehicle
Perform routine maintenance of vehicles (check oil, water, tire pressure)
Pump gas
Change and repair tires
Put on and remove tire chains
Assist in lubrication
Assist in minor repairs
Keep records of services performed
Clean and perform simple maintenance on tools and equipment
Clean work areas; clear snow
Drive vehicles between storage, service, and pickup areas
Gather and move supplies and equipment within work area

Specific Skill Requirements

Knowledge of proper tools, supplies, and techniques for washing and waxing/polishing vehicles
Knowledge of proper tools, supplies, and techniques for cleaning automobile interiors
Kowledge of proper tools, supplies, and techniques used in general mechanical and body maintenance and repair
Ability to recognize damaged or missing parts, faulty systems, and damaged paint
Knowledge of techniques for checking vehicle air and fluid levels, and replenishing if necessary
Ability to safely pump gasoline
Ability to drive automatic and manual-shift vehicles
Knowledge of basic routines and procedures of a fleet garage
Knowledge of proper storage of tools and equipment
Ability to use common hand and power tools, hand truck, dolly
Ability to safely lift, carry, and move heavy objects and equipment
Ability to keep simple records and compute mileage
Physical strength; ability to perform strenuous activities over extended periods

Relevant DOT Reference

Garage Servicer, Industrial 915.687-014

Related Jobs

Gas Station Attendant (job profile A-9)
Parking Garage Attendant (job profile C-48)
Cleaner, Any Industry (II) 919.687-014

JOB PROFILE E-16
Industrial Garage Attendant

General Description

Assists in servicing vehicles in public or private motor pools. May also wash cars and be responsible for driving them to and from parking spaces.

Job Activities

Drive vehicles between parking areas and maintenance or pickup/return areas
Check vehicle air and fluid levels, adjust as needed
Perform other basic maintenance tasks (change tires, wash, lube)
Assist garage mechanic with servicing
Make simple notations regarding services performed, mileage, dates
Use telephone
Perform general clean-up of garage areas
Clean vehicles, interior and exterior; wax or polish vehicles

Specific Skill Requirements

Ability to drive a variety of automatic and manual shift vehicles with care and safety
Ability to properly perform simple maintenance and cleaning procedures on vehicles
Knowledge of hazards of vehicles, flammable liquids, and service equipment
Ability to keep simple records
Knowledge of locations of vehicles, maintenance areas, and equipment
Ability to interact well with co-workers
Ability to recognize the need to summon help in emergencies
Ability to properly use simple garage and cleaning tools
Willingness to work under varied weather conditions, temperatures, and in noisy environment

Relevant DOT Reference

Garage Servicer, Industrial 915.687-014

Related Jobs

Parking Garage Attendant (job profile C-48)
Transportation Fleet Maintenance Helper (job profile E-15)
Gas and Oil Servicer 915.587-010
Car Wash Attendant 915.667-010

JOB PROFILE E-17
Automobile Painter Helper

General Description

Assists in painting all or parts of automobiles. Employment opportunities may exist in car painting establishments, used car lots, or trailer and recreational vehicle rental/sales firms.

Job Activities

Gather and move tools, equipment, and materials between storage and work areas
Remove and replace body trim not being painted
Remove paint with liquid remover and scraper
Sand by hand or using power sander
Smooth surfaces by filling depressions
Mask areas of automobile with tape and paper to protect from paint
Mix paint
Position heat lamps to dry paint
Wax/polish the automobile
Store delivered supplies and materials
Clean and perform simple maintenance on tools and equipment
Clean work areas
Use a spray gun to apply paint
Paint with a hand brush

Specific Skill Requirements

Ability to use basic tools, equipment, and materials for auto-body painting
Knowledge of basic techniques of auto-body painting
Knowledge of proper storage of tools and equipment
Ability to clean and perform simple maintenance upon tools and equipment
Knowledge of techniques for removing and replacing parts of autos
Knowledge of techniques for removing old paint, filling depressions, and sanding surfaces
Knowledge of techniques for masking auto parts not being painted
Knowledge of techniques for priming, painting, and waxing/polishing surfaces
Ability to mix paints to attain specified colors

Ability to safely lift, carry and move heavy objects and equipment
Ability to use hand truck and dolly
Knowledge of hazards of hand and power tools and equipment, flammables, solvents, and of paint shop settings in general
Knowledge of locations of tools, equipment, materials and work areas
Willingness to work in a setting having high levels of dust and exposure to paint and solvent vapors
Ability to work neatly and in orderly manner to prevent marring of new paint

Relevant DOT Reference

Automobile Painter Helper 845.684-014

Related Jobs

Automobile-Body Repairer Helper (job profile E-14)
Railroad Car Scrubber 845.684-010

JOB PROFILE E-18
Automobile Mechanic Helper

General Description

Assists mechanic in repair of cars, buses, trucks or other vehicles. Repairs may include the engine and accessories, power trains, suspension systems, brake systems and other automotive mechanical parts.

Job Activities

Obtain parts from stock
Gather and move tools, equipment and supplies between storage and work areas
Use hand tools and simple power tools and equipment
Help remove, disassemble, and assemble units (for example, engine or engine parts)
Assist in repair and replacement of parts and routine maintenance work, tune-up, and so on
Hand tools to mechanic
Clean parts using prescribed solvents and compressed air dryer

Assist in lubricating vehicle
Move equipment around shop
Clean, perform simple maintenance on, and store tools and equipment
Clean work areas
Wash vehicle and clean interior
Store delivered supplies and parts
Operate car lift
Perform state inspection (where applicable)

Specific Skill Requirements

Ability to use basic hand and power tools and equipment for mechanical repairs
Knowledge of basic techniques for removal and disassembly of mechanical units
Knowledge of basic routines and procedures of an automobile repair shop
Ability to clean, perform simple maintenance on, and store tools and equipment
Knowledge of techniques for making repairs/performing routine maintenance
Knowledge of techniques for cleaning mechanical parts using solvents and compressed air dryer
Knowledge of techniques used in lubricating automobiles
Ability to safely lift, carry, and move heavy objects and equipment
Ability to use hand truck, dolly and engine hoist
Ability to properly store delivered supplies and parts
Ability to clean work areas
Knowledge of hazards of hand and power tools and equipment, flammables, solvents, and of automobile repair shops settings in general
Knowledge of locations of tools, equipment, supplies, parts, and work areas
Ability to work in close coordination with mechanic

Relevant DOT Reference

Automobile Mechanic Helper 620.684-014

Related Jobs

Engine Mechanic Helper (Aircraft, Diesel, Marine) (job profile E-21)
(Helper to) Brake Repairer 620.281-026
(Helper to) Tune-up Mechanic 620.281-066
Motorcycle Subassembly Repairer 620.684-026

JOB PROFILE E-19
New Car Preparation Helper

General Description

Assists in servicing new automobiles after delivery to dealer in preparation for sale. This is limited to cleaning and inspection for visible damage to the cars and does not include mechanical repairs.

Job Activities

Inspect for obvious damage and missing parts or accessories
Inspect for chips or scratches in paint
Start engine and activate power equipment to detect faulty systems
Report findings to supervisor
Wash car to remove protective coating; wax/polish
Clean interior, remove stickers
Install hubcaps, bumper guards, equipment removed before shipment
Apply undercoating
Perform minor touch-up painting
Drive cars between work areas and sales lot
Store delivered supplies and parts
Clean and maintain tools and equipment; clean work areas

Specific Skill Requirements

Knowledge of proper tools, supplies, and techniques for washing, waxing, and polishing automobiles
Knowledge of tools, supplies, and techniques for cleaning/preparing interiors
Ability to recognize damaged or missing parts, faulty systems, damaged paint
Ability to clean and perform simple maintenance upon tools and equipment
Ability to clean work areas
Ability to drive automatic and manual-shift automobiles
Knowledge of basic routines and procedures of new automobile preparation
Knowledge of proper storage of tools and equipment
Ability to safely lift, carry, and move heavy objects and equipment

Knowledge of hazards of common hand and power tools and equipment, flammables, solvents, and of automobile shop settings in general
Knowledge of locations of tools, equipment, supplies, parts, and work areas
Ability to properly store delivered parts and supplies

Relevant DOT Reference

(Helper to) New Car Get-Ready Mechanic 806.361-026

Related Jobs

Used Car Lot Porter (job profile E-20)
Used Car Renovator 620.684-034

JOB PROFILE E-20
Used Car Lot Porter

General Description

Cleans and services used cars at used car lot. This worker also might assist a mechanic in minor maintenance or repairs prior to sale, for example, in lubrication, tune-up, brake adjustment, or mechanical repairs.

Job Activities

Wash car
Wax/polish car
Perform touch-up painting
Clean car interior, using brushes, rags, vacuum, cleaning solutions
Clean car engine, using solvents and/or steam cleaner
Repair and change tires
Clean and maintain car lot, office, and work areas
Make minor repairs to interior trim or upholstery
Replace windshield wiper blades, light bulbs
Change car battery, spark plugs
Assist mechanic with lubrication, brake adjustment, and other maintenance or repairs

Specific Skill Requirements

Knowledge of proper tools, supplies, and techniques for washing, waxing, and polishing automobiles, and for cleaning or repairing interiors
Knowledge of proper tools, supplies and techniques for cleaning automobile engines
Knowledge of tools, supplies and techniques used in basic automobile servicing (for example, lube, tune-up)
Ability to repair and change tires, windshield wiper blades, batteries, and light bulbs
Ability to clean and maintain lot, office, and work areas
Knowledge of hazards of common hand and power tools and equipment, steam cleaner, flammables, solvents, and car lot/repair shop settings in general
Knowledge of locations of tools, equipment, supplies, and work areas
Ability to recognize automobiles by make and type
Ability to work without constant supervision

Relevant DOT Reference

Used Car Lot Porter 915.687-022

Related Jobs

Automobile Mechanic Helper (job profile E-18)
New Car Preparation Helper (job profile E-19)
Used Car Renovator 620.684-034

JOB PROFILE E-21
Engine Mechanic Helper (Aircraft, Diesel, Marine)

General Description

Assists engine mechanic by performing tasks involved in the servicing, repairing, and overhauling of aircraft, diesel, or motorboat engines. The helper's participation in actual servicing of aircraft engines may be limited, due to strict licensing requirements for aircraft mechanics.

Job Activities

Use simple hand and power tools, hand truck, dolly, hoist
Gather and move tools, equipment, and supplies between storage and work areas
Hand tools to mechanic
Assist in taking engines apart
Assist in lubricating engine
Clean engine parts, using solvents and compressed air dryer
Obtain parts from stock
Assist in engine reassembly
Fill gas tanks and oil reserves
Clean, perform simple maintenance on, and store tools and equipment
Clean working area
Store delivered supplies and parts

Specific Skill Requirements

Knowledge of nomenclature relevant to aircraft, marine, or diesel engines
Ability to use simple hand and power tools and equipment, hand truck, dolly, hoist
Knowledge of basic repair and maintenance techniques used for engines
Ability to make relatively fine mechanical adjustments
Ability to clean engine parts, using brushes, solvents, tools, and compressed air dryer
Ability to safely fill gas, oil, and other fluid tanks
Ability to clean and perform simple maintenance upon tools and equipment
Knowledge of proper storage of tools and equipment
Ability to safely lift, carry, and move heavy objects and equipment
Knowledge of hazards of hand and power tools and equipment, flammables, solvents, and of repair shop settings in general
Knowledge of locations of tools, equipment, supplies, parts, and work areas
Ability to work in close coordination with mechanic

Relevant DOT Reference

Motorboat Mechanic Helper 623.684-010
Diesel Mechanic Helper (any industry) 625.684-010

Related Jobs

Automobile Mechanic Helper (job profile E-18)
Pump Servicer Helper 630.684-022
Elevator Repairer Helper 825.684-014

JOB PROFILE E-22
Electric Appliance Repair Helper

General Description

Assists electrical-appliance servicer in installing, servicing, and repairing of electrical appliances in customers' homes or in commercial and industrial installations. Some of the job activities may be performed in the repair shop.

Job Activities

Connect appliance to outlet
Uncrate new appliance, attach accessories
Carry or cart appliances around store/repair shop and assist in delivery to customer
Assist servicer with testing, repairing, and replacing parts
Store delivered products and parts at store/shop
Clean parts, using wire brush, buffer, and solvents
Clean and store tools, equipment
Clean working area

Specific Skill Requirements

Knowledge of nomenclature relevant to electric appliances
Ability to use simple hand tools and equipment, hand truck
Knowledge of tools, equipment, and simple techniques used in installation, service, and repair of electric appliances
Knowledge of basic routines and procedures of an electric appliance store/repair shop
Ability to use appliance and regular hand trucks

Ability to safely lift, carry, and move heavy objects
Knowledge of techniques for careful uncrating of new appliances
Knowledge of proper storage techniques for delivered products and parts
Knowledge of proper tools and techniques for cleaning parts
Knowledge of techniques for cleaning and storing tools and equipment
Knowledge of tools and techniques for cleaning work areas
Knowledge of hazards of tools, equipment, flammables, solvents, repair shop settings, and electricity in general
Knowledge of locations of tools, equipment, storage, and work areas
Ability to work in close cooperation with servicer

Relevant DOT Reference

(Helper to) Electrical Appliance Servicer 827.261-014

Related Jobs

Small Engine Repair Helper (job profile E-23)
(Helper to) Household Appliance Installer 827.661-010
Appliance Assembler, Line 827.684-010
Electrician Helper 829.684-022

JOB PROFILE E-23
Small Engine Repair Helper (Gasoline Engines)

General Description

Assists small engine mechanic to repair and overhaul small engines (power garden equipment and small motor vehicles such as snowmobiles). May work at customer's home or business, or in repair shop.

Job Activities

Assist mechanic to remove and disassemble engines
Clean parts, using wire brush, buffer, and solvents
Assist mechanic with adjusting, repairing, or replacing engine parts
Assist mechanic in replacing engines on machine
Change tires
Fill fuel tank

Clean and store tools, equipment
Clean work area
Store delivered parts and supplies

Specific Skill Requirements

Knowledge of nomenclature relevant to small gasoline engines
Ability to use simple hand tools and equipment, hand truck
Knowledge of tools, equipment, and simple techniques used in servicing and repairing small gasoline engines
Knowledge of basic routines and procedures of a small engine repair shop
Knowledge of tools and techniques for cleaning parts
Ability to safely lift, carry, and move heavy objects
Knowledge of techniques for cleaning and storing tools and equipment
Knowledge of proper storage techniques for delivered parts and supplies
Knowledge of tools and techniques for cleaning work areas
Knowledge of hazards of tools and equipment, flammables, solvents, and of repair shop settings in general
Knowledge of locations of tools, equipment, storage, and work areas
Ability to work in close cooperation with servicer

Relevant DOT Reference

Automobile Mechanic Helper 620.684-014

Related Jobs

Electric Appliance Repair Helper (job profile E-22)
Motorcycle Subassembly Repairer 620.684-026

JOB PROFILE E-24
Heating and Air-Conditioning Service Helper

General Description

Assists workers engaged in installing, repairing, and servicing industrial, commercial, and domestic heating and air-conditioning systems.

Job Activities

Gather and move tools, equipment, and materials between storage and work areas
Carry parts of system; use hand truck
Cut opening in wall to install system
Assist with assembly and installation of system
Assist with wiring
Assist with piping
Apply packing material in empty space between wall and system
Wrap insulation material around air ducts
Remove and replace simple parts of systems (for example, filters)
Clean and lubricate parts
Assist in checking operation of system
Clean work area, dispose of scrap material, using wheelbarrow

Specific Skill Requirements

Ability to use simple hand and power tools and equipment (especially carpentry and sheet metal tools)
Knowledge of tools and techniques used in the assembly, installation, and repair of heating and air-conditioning systems
Knowledge of routines and procedures of heating and air-conditioning installation and repair
Knowledge of simple carpentry and sheet metal techniques
Knowledge of simple wiring and piping techniques
Knowledge of tools and techniques for installing insulation materials
Knowledge of tools and techniques for cleaning work areas and removing trash
Ability to use hand truck, wheelbarrow, ladder
Ability to work in close cooperation with co-workers
Ability to safely lift, carry, and move heavy objects
Knowledge of hazards of hand and power tools and equipment, electricity, heating gas, and of construction/installation settings in general

Relevant DOT Reference

Air Conditioning Mechanic Helper 637.664-010

Related Jobs

Gas Appliance Service Helper 637.684-010
Air Conditioning Installer-Service Helper (Window Unit) 637.687-010
Refrigeration Mechanic Helper 637.687-014

JOB PROFILE E-25
Swimming-Pool Service Helper

General Description

Assists swimming-pool servicer in cleaning and making minor repairs to swimming pools and equipment. Employment opportunities may be seasonal. The work setting is principally outdoors, although some activities may take place in the repair shop.

Job Activities

Gather and move tools and equipment between service truck and pool work area
Clean bottom and sides of pool, using various vacuum systems, brushes and nets
Clean tile and pool fixtures
Clean filter system
Assist in maintaining and repairing heating and pumping equipment, at pool and in repair shop
Add chemicals to pool in directed amounts
Replace damaged tile
Assist in the installation of new pool equipment (plumbing, wiring, assembly)
Clean and perform simple maintenance upon tools and equipment
Move dry and liquid pool chemicals from storage area to truck to customer's pool

Specific Skill Requirements

Ability to use simple hand and power tools and equipment, hand truck
Knowledge of the routines and procedures for pool servicing
Knowledge of tools, techniques and supplies used in the maintenance/repair of swimming pool pumping and heating equipment
Knowledge of tools and techniques for cleaning pool sides, bottom, tile, and fixtures
Knowledge of tools and techniques for replacing damaged tile
Ability to assist with wiring, plumbing, and assembly for installation of new equipment
Ability to safely and accurately add dry and liquid chemicals to pools as directed

Knowledge of simple cleaning and maintenance techniques for tools and equipment
Ability to safely lift, carry, and move heavy objects
Knowledge of the hazards of hand and power tools and equipment, pool chemicals and cleaners, electricity, heating gas, and of swimming pool and repair shop settings in general
Knowledge of locations of tools, equipment, supplies, chemicals, repair parts, and of work areas
Ability to swim

Relevant DOT Reference

Swimming-pool Serviceman (Servicer) 891.684-018

Related Jobs

Sewage Treatment Worker (job profile C-41)
Dockhand (Ship and Boat Building) 891.684-010
Tank Cleaner (Any Industry) 891.687-022

JOB PROFILE E-26
Upholstery Shop Helper

General Description

Assists in upholstering and reupholstering tasks; may also assist in pickup and delivery. The upholstery shop may be an industrial or retail business. If delivery is part of the job, see job profile A-15.

Job Activities

Gather and move tools, equipment, and materials between storage and work areas
Perform simple disassembly and assembly of furniture
Remove old webbing, defective springs
Assist in measuring, cutting, sewing, and fastening fabric
Drive nails, staple wood, or insert wood screws
Operate sewing machine to seam cushions
Assist in repairing or refinishing wooden surfaces

Store delivered materials and supplies
Move furniture pieces during pickup and delivery
Clean work area

Specific Skill Requirements

Knowledge of nomenclature related to upholstery
Ability to use simple hand and power upholstery tools, sewing machine
Knowledge of routines and procedures of an upholstery shop
Knowledge of basic techniques used in upholstery (measuring, cutting, sewing, fastening); familiarity with fabrics
Ability to make fine, coordinated movements
Knowledge of basic furniture disassembly and assembly techniques
Knowledge of storage techniques for delivered materials and supplies
Ability to safely lift, carry, and move heavy objects
Knowledge of cleaning techniques for work areas
Knowledge of hazards of hand and power upholstery tools and equipment, sharp objects, glues, and of shop settings in general
Knowledge of locations of tools, equipment, materials, supplies, and work areas

Relevant DOT Reference

(Helper to) Furniture Upholsterer 780.381-018

Related Jobs

Furniture Refinishing Helper (job profile E-27)
Upholsterer, Inside (Furniture) 780.681-010

JOB PROFILE E-27
Furniture Refinishing Helper

General Description

Assists furniture refinisher in refinishing damaged, worn, or used furniture by preparing materials and furniture surfaces. If delivery is part of the job, see job profile A-15.

Job Activities

Gather equipment and supplies and set up at the work station
Use simple and power tools and equipment
Disassemble and reassemble furniture
Mask areas not to be refinished
Remove knobs, hinges
Apply solutions
Sandpaper
Scrape or steel wool finish
Apply putty
Mix finishes
Wax and polish finish
Clean work area
Clean and store equipment
Store delivered supplies and materials
Move furniture pieces during pickup and delivery
Assist in pickup and delivery of furniture, if required

Specific Skill Requirements

Ability to use simple hand and power refinishing tools and equipment
Knowledge of routines and procedures of a furniture refinishing shop
Knowledge of tools and techniques for disassembly and reassembly of work pieces
Knowledge of tools, techniques and supplies used in the preparation, refinishing, and waxing/polishing of furniture surfaces
Knowledge of special mixing procedures for stripping and staining solutions
Knowledge of storage techniques for delivered materials and supplies
Knowledge of cleaning techniques for work areas
Knowledge of hazards of hand and power tools, equipment, refinishing solvents and finishes, flammables, and of refinishing shop settings in general
Ability to safely lift, carry, and move heavy objects
Knowledge of locations of tools, equipment, supplies, and work areas
Ability to make fine, coordinated movements

Relevant DOT Reference

(Helper to) Furniture Finisher 763.381-010

Related Jobs

Upholstery Shop Helper (job profile E-26)
Cabinet Assembler 763.684-014
Furniture Assembler 763.684-038

JOB PROFILE E-28
Shoe Repair Helper

General Description

Helps shoe repairer to repair and shine shoes. May perform other duties, such as light cleaning, in the repair shop. May assist in taking orders from customers and issuing claim checks, or in packaging completed work for customers.

Job Activites

Rip worn soles and heels from shoes
Assist in tacking soles and heels in place
Trim leather
Sand sole edges
Shine, stain and dye shoes
Place completed work on shelf or rack, according to claim check system
Clean work area and shop
Clean and perform simple maintenance upon tools and equipment
Store delivered supplies and merchandise
Issue claim check for shoes left by customer for repair
Bag or wrap finished shoes for customer

Specific Skill Requirements

Knowledge of routines and procedures of a shoe repair shop
Ability to use shoe repair hand tools and power equipment
Knowledge of shoe repair techniques
Ability to make fine, coordinated movements using tools and power equipment

Ability to clean and perform simple maintenance upon shop tools and equipment
Ability to clean work and shop areas
Ability to store delivered supplies and merchandise
Knowledge of the hazards of sharp tools, power equipment, chemicals, glues, and of shop setting in general
Knowledge of locations of tools, equipment, supplies, and work areas
Ability to interact well with the public
Ability to make simple notations on claim check or repair receipt tags

Relevant DOT Reference

Shoe Repairer Helper 365.674-010

Related Jobs

(Helper to) Luggage Repairer 365.361-010
Shoe Shiner 366.677-010

JOB PROFILE E-29
Meter Repair Helper

General Description

Assists meter repairer in installing, repairing, and maintaining gas, oil, or water meters. Work is performed both in- and outdoors. Emergency installations and repairs may require exposure to adverse weather conditions.

Job Activities

Gather and move tools, equipment, supplies, or meters between truck and work areas
Assist in disassembly and reassembly of meters
Connect meters to testing apparatus for inspection and adjustment by meter repairer
Clean and repair parts
Replace defective parts
Assist in the assembly and installation of equipment
Clean and perform simple maintenance on tools and equipment
Clean work area

Specific Skill Requirements

Knowledge of tools, equipment, materials, and techniques used in the assembly, repair, and installation of meters
Ability to safely use common hand and power repair tools
Ability to clean and perform simple maintenance upon tools and equipment
Ability to clean work areas
Ability to safely lift, carry, and move heavy objects using handtruck, cart, and hoist
Ability to make fine, coordinated movements for instrument assembly and servicing
Knowledge of locations of tools, equipment, materials, and work areas
Willingness to work in adverse weather conditions
Ability to work in close coordination with meter repairer

Relevant DOT Reference

Meter Repairer Helper 710.684-034

Related Jobs

(Helper to) Parking Meter Servicer 710.384-026
Instrument Technician Helper 710.684-030

JOB PROFILE E-30
Newspaper Production Worker

General Description

Assists in activities relating to the preparation and distribution of a daily newspaper. If messenger or delivery services are part of the job, see job profiles A-14 (Merchandise Deliverer), B-2 (General Office Messenger) and B-4 (Copy Messenger).

Job Activities

Clean press rollers and platens
Fill presses with ink, fluid

Help replace newsprint rolls in presses
Fold and bundle printed papers for distribution
Label (stencil) bundled papers
Count or weigh bundled papers
Keep simple records of bundle distributions
Perform messenger duties within building, and to and from advertisers
Clean printing and distribution areas
Store delivered printing supplies

Specific Skill Requirements

Knowledge of newspaper production routines, procedures, nomenclature
Knowledge of tools, techniques, and materials used for simple cleaning or maintenance of large presses
Knowledge of procedure for replacing newsprint rolls in presses
Ability to operate bundling machine
Ability to stencil, count/weigh, and keep simple records of bundles for distribution
Ability to perform messenger duties within and outside the building
Ability to drive, bicycle, or use public transportation for outside messenger work
Ability to clean work areas
Ability to properly store delivered supplies
Ability to lift, carry, and move heavy objects, using hand truck, dolly
Knowledge of the hazards of printing presses, bundling machine, solvents, flammables, and of printing room settings in general
Knowledge of locations of tools, equipment, materials, storage and work areas, office areas, and of advertisers

Relevant DOT Reference

Print-shop Helper 979.684-026

Related Jobs

Print Shop Worker (job profile E-31)
Stationery Manufacturing Worker (job profile F-18)

JOB PROFILE E-31
Print Shop Worker

General Description

Assists in tasks of handling and assembling books and magazines. May assist in reproduction, layout or paste-up work. If deliveries are part of the job, see job profile B-2 for in-house deliveries; A-14 and A-15 for outside deliveries.

Job Activities

Clean rollers and platens
Burnish multilith plates
Hand wash plates in developer fluid
Fill machines: ink, fluid
Monitor rollers
Gather or collate papers
Stack paper (jogging)
Staple (machine)
Fold paper
Package or wrap, tie bundles with rope or string
Label (stencils)
Count or weigh bundles
Keep simple records of bundle distributions
Prepare purchase requisitions
Take and transmit telephone messages
Make deliveries
Clean work areas
Store delivered supplies and materials
Assist in darkroom and in stripping
Operate varitype machine

Specific Skill Requirements

Knowledge of print shop routines and procedures
Knowledge of tools and techniques for cleaning, preparing, and monitoring press rollers, platens, and multilith plates
Knowledge of tools and techniques for maintaining proper ink and fluid levels
Ability to stencil, count/weigh, and keep simple records of bundles

Ability to perform messenger duties within and outside the building
Ability to use public transportation or company vehicle to make deliveries
Ability to safely lift, carry, and move heavy objects, using hand truck/dolly
Ability to clean work areas
Ability to store delivered supplies and materials
Knowledge of the hazards of print shop machinery and tools, solvents, flammables, and of the shop setting in general
Knowledge of locations of tools, equipment, materials, supplies, and storage and work areas

Relevant DOT Reference

Print Shop Helper 979.684-026

Related Jobs

Newspaper Production Worker (job profile E-30)
Bindery Worker (job profile E-32)
Stationery Manufacturing Worker (job profile F-18)
Blueprinting Machine Operator 979.682-014

JOB PROFILE E-32
Bindery Worker

General Description

Assists in binding books and magazines. Tends or operates a variety of automatic and manual bindery equipment.

Job Activities

Gather or collate papers
Stack paper (jogging)
Drill/punch holes in paper
Stamp numbers on sheets by hand or machine
Crease and compress signatures with hand press before affixing covers
Fasten sheets or signatures using hand or machine stapler
Feed automatic binding machines
Tend or operate binding machines (for example, wire stitching, plastic rings, plastic strips, stapling)

Unload finished products from machines
Place paper jackets on finished books
Package or wrap bound products
Label packages
Keep simple records of bundle distributions
Clean work areas
Store delivered supplies and materials

Specific Skill Requirements

Knowledge of bindery shop routines and procedures
Ability to safely operate hand and power bindery machines
Ability to keep simple records of bundles for distribution
Ability to safely lift, carry, and move heavy objects, using hand truck, dolly
Ability to clean work areas
Ability to store delivered supplies and materials
Ability to make coordinated movements using bindery machinery
Knowledge of the hazards of bindery shop machinery and tools, and of the shop settings in general
Knowledge of locations of tools, equipment, materials, supplies, and storage and work areas

Relevant DOT Reference

Bindery Worker 653.685-010

Related Jobs

Newspaper Production Worker (job profile E-30)
Print Shop Worker (job profile E-31)
Book Repairer 997.684-010
Hand Stitcher, Printing and Publishing 977.684-022
Hand Collator, Printing and Publishing 977.687-010

Master Profile F: **Processing and Manufacturing Occupations**

General Description

Jobs in this category generally are found in industries which rely on semiskilled or unskilled workers to perform a large part of the necessary tasks. Two main types of jobs in this category are those found in local shops or moderate-sized businesses, and those found in factories or manufacturing plants. Many of these jobs require considerable physical strength and stamina. Some production jobs, on the other hand, involve light physical work but require the worker to remain in one place and perform a given task for an extended period of time. The jobs in this category generally require either physical strength or fine motor coordination, but not necessarily both of these capabilities.

Workers in processing and manufacturing jobs will receive fairly constant supervision. In small businesses they will be working closely with other employees and may have some customer contact. In factories or large plants, employees probably will be working on an assembly line or performing material handling and clean-up tasks. The work on an assembly line is repetitive, requiring periodic shifting to other stations to reduce fatigue.

Many hazards exist for workers in these jobs, including glass, knives, explosives, hot rivets, welding torches, ovens, kilns, hot water, automated machinery, heavy powered machinery, and heavy loads to be transported. The worker also must exercise caution in handling fragile and perishable products.

Job Profiles (See pages immediately following this master profile.)

F-1 Riveter Helper
F-2 Welder Helper
F-3 Grinder Operator
F-4 Glass Production Helper
F-5 Cannery Worker
F-6 Bakery Worker
F-7 Baker Helper
F-8 Candy Maker Helper
F-9 Dairy Plant Worker
F-10 Poultry Processing Worker
F-11 Slaughterhouse Worker
F-12 Nut Processing Worker
F-13 Framing Shop Helper
F-14 Furniture Factory Worker
F-15 Small Products Assembler
F-16 Production Worker, Transportation Equipment Plant
F-17 Production Worker, Electrical/Electronic Equipment
F-18 Stationery Manufacturing Worker
F-19 Bag Cutter
F-20 Cloth Folder, Textile Manufacturing
F-21 Clothing Manufacturing Worker
F-22 Sewing Machine Operator

F-23 Leather Handle Maker
F-24 Shoe or Boot Manufacturing Worker
F-25 Toy Factory Worker
F-26 Pottery Worker
F-27 Pulp Mill Worker
F-28 Tannery Worker
F-29 Brickyard Worker
F-30 Cement Block Production Worker
F-31 Stone Quarry Worker
F-32 Plastics Molder Helper
F-33 Packer
F-34 Material Handler Helper
F-35 Forklift Operator
F-36 Factory Equipment Cleaner
F-37 Recycling Bin Attendant

Skill Requirements

The following basic, core, and personal/social skills are considered to apply generally to all the jobs in the processing and manufacturing occupations. In addition to these, each job profile lists specific skill requirements relevant to that particular job.

Basic skills The numbers in parentheses refer to the sequence of the skills listed in the basic skills chart beginning on page 43, which defines the individual skills and cites applications for each one.

Read (labels, patterns, directions) (1)
Write (keep simple records) (2)
Count and record numbers (3)
Perform simple calculations (4)
Sort by category (6)
Repeat a visual pattern (7)
Locate (collect supplies and materials) (9)
Communicate verbally (observations, needs, messages) (10)
Tell time (13)
Measure (length, weight, volume) (14)
Read dials, gauges, meters and record readings (15)
Manipulate small objects (17)
Trace (use stencil) (18)
Tie with string or rope (19)
Secure with tape (20)

Core skills The numbers in parentheses refer to the sequence of the skills listed in the core skills chart, beginning on page 47, which defines the individual skills and cites applications for each one.

Fold (fabrics, paper) (1)
Bundle (fabrics, leather, produce) (2)
Assemble (3)
Fasten (glue, nails, clips) (4)
Package or wrap (5)
Cut (fabrics, paper, leather, metal) (6)
Lift and carry (7)
Load and unload (8)
Transport (hand truck, cart, dolly) (9)
Stack and shelve (10)
Pack or crate (11)
Open and unpack (12)
Stamp and label (13)
Mix and blend (22)
Perform indoor cleaning (24)
Handle dangerous substances (30)
Stitch (31)
Iron (minimal) (32)
Use hand tools (33)

Personal/social skills Skills which are required to a major extent in the processing and manufacturing occupations are indicated in the following profile. Punctuality and reliability of attendance usually are stressed in this type of organization, as the worker generally performs in close coordination with others who are counting on his presence.

Communication skills are very important; the employee must be able to understand directions, to pose questions and to report defects in the product, malfunction of equipment, or other discrepancies.

Often the environment in a processing or manufacturing plant is subject to significant variations in temperature and noise levels. It is necessary for the worker to become adapted to these changes and it is important in many of the jobs (e.g., those employing heavy power equipment) that the worker concentrate on the task despite these environmental distractions.

As in the agricultural job group, trainees in meat processing occupations should be able to accept the killing and dressing of poultry and livestock.

Master Profile: **F. Processing and Manufacturing Occupations**

Personal/Social Skill Requirements		Extent Required: Minimal	Extent Required: Moderate	Extent Required: Major
Social Skills	1. *SELF EXPRESSION* - communicate, ask for assistance, question			●
	2. *SOCIABILITY* - interact with other employees or public		●	
	3. *WORK INDEPENDENCE* - work without supervision or guidance		●	
	4. *APPEARANCE/HYGIENE* - cleanliness, good manners, neatness in appearance		●	
	5. *TEAMWORK* - perform in close coordination with other jobs			●
Time Factors	6. *PACE* - perform at a consistent rate of speed			●
	7. *ATTENDANCE* - be reliable in attendance and punctuality			●
	8. *SIMULTANEITY* - perform several activities at near same time			●
	9. *TIMING* - perform timed, scheduled activities; be aware of time		●	
Performance Skills	10. *ACCURACY* - perform within well-defined tolerances			●
	11. *DEXTERITY* - make fine manipulations, coordinated movements			●
	12. *CHOICES* - select among alternatives, make decisions		●	
	13. *DIRECTION* - follow procedures, instructions or directions			●
	14. *MEMORY* - remember locations, procedures, nomenclatures, etc.		●	
	15. *CAUTION* - use care in activities which pose personal hazard			●
	16. *NEATNESS* - work in a neat, orderly manner		●	
	17. *CONCENTRATION* - attend to task despite environmental distraction			●
Tolerance	18. *REPETITION* - tolerate repetitive work assignments			●
	19. *PERSEVERANCE* - perform continuously, over normal periods			●
	20. *STAMINA* - have physical stamina, strength, resist fatigue			●

JOB PROFILE F-1
Riveter Helper

General Description

Assists journey-level riveter in a variety of tasks related to metal fabrication. Work may be either indoors or outdoors, in such settings as building frame assembly, ship construction, or factory assembly line.

Job Activities

Gather and move workpieces manually, by handtruck and/or by hoist
Gather and move tools, equipment, and supplies between storage and work areas
Position parts to align rivet holes
Fasten aligned parts together using clamps, or bolts and impact wrench
Place rivets in holes
Ream misaligned rivet holes
Remove unsatisfactory rivets using hand tools
Remove, mark, and transport finished work
Keep simple records of number of items processed
Replenish supplies to work or storage areas
Clean tools, equipment
Clean work areas, remove scrap
Assist in operating hoist or crane to move heavy objects

Specific Skill Requirements

Knowledge of use of riveting tools, equipment, and supplies
Ability to safely lift and move heavy objects manually and by handtruck
Knowledge of locations of work areas, supplies, tools, and equipment
Knowledge of procedures and routines characteristic of specific job setting
Knowledge of hazards of riveting tools, equipment, and job setting
Knowledge of cleaning techniques for tools, equipment, and work areas
Ability to properly attach crane or hoist grappling equipment for moving heavy objects

Relevant DOT Reference

Riveter Helper 800.687-010

Related Job

Welder Helper (job profile F-2)

JOB PROFILE F-2
Welder Helper

General Description

Assists journey-level welder in a variety of tasks revolving around manufacturing or maintenance welding. Work may be either indoors or outdoors, in a number of different settings, such as building frame assembly, heavy equipment maintenance, factory assembly line, and shipyard work.

Job Activities

Gather and move workpieces manually, by handtruck, and/or by hoist
Gather and move tools, equipment and supplies between storage and work areas
Fasten workpieces to table or into jigs, or hold in position as directed
Remove impurities from workpieces, using mechanical and/or chemical means
Connect gas hoses or electrical cables onto equipment for use by welder
Place workpieces into preheating furnace prior to welding
Keep simple records of number of items produced
Remove, mark, and transport finished work
Replenish supplies from central supply to work or storage areas
Clean tools, equipment
Clean work areas, remove scrap
Assist in operating hoist or crane to move heavy objects

Specific Skill Requirements

Knowledge of use of welding tools, preheating furnace, and other equipment
Ability to safely lift and move heavy objects manually and by handtruck
Knowledge of techniques for removing slag, rust, grease, or other impurities from workpieces

Ability to properly use wire brush, portable grinder, hand scraper, and chemical solutions
Knowledge of gas and electrical connections for welding equipment
Knowledge of locations of work areas, supplies, tools and equipment
Knowledge of procedures and routines characteristic of specific job setting
Knowledge of hazards of welding tools, equipment, cleaning solvents, and job setting
Knowledge of cleaning techniques for tools, equipment, and work areas
Ability to properly attach crane or hoist grappling equipment for moving heavy objects

Relevant DOT Reference

Welder Helper 819.687-014

Related Jobs

Riveter Helper (job profile F-1)
Welding Machine Helper 819.666-010
Welding Machine Feeder 819.686-010

JOB PROFILE F-3
Grinder Operator

General Description

Uses hand tools and power equipment to clean, polish, or grind metal and plastic parts. This job excludes those grinding operations that are performed by production machines.

Job Activities

Mount and grind parts on revolving spindle
Scrape parts with hand tools or buffing cloth
Use reamer to clean inside surfaces of holes
Clean or polish parts on revolving spindle
Clean and perform simple maintenance upon tools and equipment
Clean work areas

Specific Skill Requirements

Ability to grind and polish with revolving spindle and hand tools
Knowledge of hand scraping techniques
Ability to use hand tools (chipping hammer, buffer, deburring tool, hand pick)
Ability to use reamer
Ability to use abrasive compounds for polishing
Ability to clean and perform simple maintenance upon tools and equipment
Ability to maintain a clean work area
Knowledge of hazards of hand and power tools and equipment, and of work settings in general
Knowledge of locations of tools, equipment, and storage and work areas

Relevant DOT Reference

Laborer, Grinding and Polishing 705.687-014

Related Jobs

Buffing-Machine Tender 603.665-010
Hand Scraper, Machine Shop 705.384-010

JOB PROFILE F-4
Glass Production Helper

General Description

Assists highly skilled glass workers by performing setup and handling tasks. This employee also may do some product finishing tasks. Products might include bottles, containers, and other glass items as well as plate glass.

Job Activities

Transport molds and machine parts about the plant
Supply machine operators with necessary solutions and equipment
Operate grinder
Polish, buff, and wax glass surfaces

Weigh or weigh-count items produced
Assist in keeping simple production records
Pack (in straw or excelsior) and crate finished items, label crates
Transport products to shipping department
Clean tools, equipment, and work areas
Dispose of waste glass
Perform minor maintenance/lubrication on equipment
Store delivered supplies and materials

Specific Skill Requirements

Knowledge of routines and procedures of a glass-producing plant
Ability to use simple hand and power glass production and finishing tools or equipment
Knowledge of tools and techniques for packing, crating, and labeling glass items
Ability to make coordinated movements by hand and using power equipment
Awareness of personal hazard in working with glass and of need for caution to prevent breakage
Knowledge of techniques for cleaning tools, equipment, and work areas
Ability to safely and carefully lift, carry, and move glass and other heavy objects
Ability to use forklift or hand truck for transporting products
Knowledge of the hazards of hand and power tools and equipment, glass production machinery, and of the work setting in general
Knowledge of locations of tools, equipment, materials, and storage and work areas

Relevant DOT Reference

Floor Attendant, Glass Manufacturing 579.687-018

Related Jobs

Porcelain-Enamel Laborer 509.687-014
Glass Cleaning Machine Tender 579.685-018

JOB PROFILE F-5
Cannery Worker

General Description

Assists in commercial preparation of canned and frozen food. Tasks in a cannery or frozen food plant are quite varied, and an individual work assignment would include only a limited number of the job activities listed.

Job Activities

Wash produce
Sort and grade produce by size, quality, color
Dump or place raw produce in hoppers or conveyors
Feed products into processing equipment (such as peeler, corer, pitter)
Cut and slice fruits and vegetables by hand
Feed empty containers onto conveyors
Fill containers by hand
Monitor packing or bottling machine
Wash utensils and containers
Weigh filled containers and be sure weight conforms to specified standard
Keep simple records of production
Move and stack containers by hand or by hand truck

Specific Skill Requirements

Ability to correctly load, unload, and monitor automated equipment
Ability to safely use cutting tools to slice fruits and vegetables
Ability to use handtruck to transport containers and cases
Knowledge of cleaning procedures for utensils and equipment
Knowledge of health and hygiene practices for food preparation workers
Observance of safety precautions near hazardous equipment
Ability to tolerate repetitive activities

Relevant DOT Reference

Cannery Worker (Canning and Preserving) 529.686-014

Related Jobs

Freezing Room Worker (Canning and Preserving) 523.587-018

Packer, Agricultural Produce 920.687-134

JOB PROFILE F-6
Bakery Worker

General Description

Bakery workers are employed in large, commercial bakeries, attending conveyor belts which finish and package baked goods. This job does not require training in dough preparation or baking (see Baker Helper, job profile F-7).

Job Activities

Place baked items on conveyor for slicing, stacking, weighing
Guide, separate, stack, or count items on conveyor
Load and unload machines (filling, slicing, wrapping, sealing)
Monitor the machines
Check packages of baked goods for correct weight
Remove paper liners from baked cakes
Assemble cartons for baked goods
Place labels on filled bags or cartons
Transport cartons to storage or shipping area
Clean work area

Specific Skill Requirements

Ability to correctly load conveyors for various operations
Ability to tend conveyor and recognize malfunction
Ability to sort and combine items as directed
Ability to operate sealing and labeling devices
Ability to use handtruck for transporting finished products
Knowledge of careful handling techniques for baked goods
Knowledge of health and hygiene practices for food workers
Observance of safety precautions near ovens, hot water, or automated equipment

Relevant DOT Reference

Bakery Worker 929.686-010

Related Jobs

Candy Maker Helper (job profile F-8)
Laborer, Pie Bakery 529.686-054

JOB PROFILE F-7
Baker Helper

General Description

Assists in the production of baked goods in a large commercial bakery or local bakeshop. A major part of the job is handling raw materials and prepared dough, and cleaning utensils and equipment.

Job Activities

Move and distribute supplies and products throughout bakery
Weigh and measure ingredients
Pour ingredients into mixers
Feed dough into processing machines
Load and unload machines, bins, racks, and ovens
Prepare pans or boards for baking
Clean mixing and baking equipment
Clean ovens

Specific Skill Requirements

Ability to use handtruck and conveyors to move supplies and baked goods
Awareness of hazards while working near ovens and conveyors
Ability to lift heavy sacks and containers
Knowledge of sanitary dough handling procedures
Ability to feed and tend dough processing machines
Ability to grease, line, and flour baking pans and boards
Knowledge of techniques, equipment, and supplies used in cleaning baking utensils and equipment

Relevant DOT Reference

Baker Helper 526.686-010

Related Jobs

Candy Maker Helper (job profile F-8)
Cannery Worker (job profile F-5)
Baker Helper (Hotel and Rest.) 313.684-010
Laborer, Pie Bakery 529.686-054

JOB PROFILE F-8
Candy Maker Helper

General Description

Assists in operations related to the making and packing of candy. Many of the operations are performed by semi-automatic machinery, but some candies may be formed or pulled by hand.

Job Activities

Unpack and shelve ingredients and wrapping supplies
Weigh, measure and mix ingredients
Tend mixing machine
Fill cooking utensils and monitor cooking time
Cast candy into molds or fill extruder
Assist in forming candies by hand
Cut candy by hand or with machine knife
Assemble boxes for packing
Hand pack candies into boxes
Check that weight of filled boxes is correct
Label filled boxes
Transport product to storage or shipping
Wash utensils, kettles, cookers, other equipment
Clean workroom and work tables

Specific Skill Requirements

Knowledge of candy making procedures
Ability to make coordinated movements in handling fragile candy
Ability to use handtruck for transporting finished products
Awareness of hazards (hot candy mix, automatic equipment)
Knowledge of health and hygiene practices for food workers
Knowledge of locations of work areas, supplies, and equipment
Ability to tolerate repetitive activities

Relevant DOT Reference

Candy Maker Helper (Confection.) 520.685-050

Related Jobs

Baker Helper (job profile F-7)
Icing Mixer (Bake Prod.) 520.685-114
Candy Molder, Hand 520.687-018
Candy Spreader 520.687-022

JOB PROFILE F-9
Dairy Plant Worker

General Description

Assists in activities related to bottling or packaging of milk and other dairy products.

Job Activities

Scrub bottles, pipes, fittings, and machines with chemical solution
Dump milk, cream into machine hoppers
Tend pasteurizing machine
Tend slicing, packaging, or bottling machines and conveyors
Cut butter and cheese
Wrap and seal butter prints

Fill cartons or bags with milk, powdered milk, butter, or cheese
Wrap and/or seal cartons
Weigh or count filled containers
Pack cases and transport to storage
Maintain cool temperature in storage area
Clean workroom and work tables

Specific Skill Requirements

Ability to use brush and chemicals for cleaning dairy equipment
Knowledge of sanitary cleaning procedures for work areas and equipment
Ability to lift and handle large containers in a safe manner
Ability to load and unload automated processing equipment
Ability to monitor processing machines and conveyors and report malfunctions
Ability to use wrench and screwdriver to attach fittings
Ability to hand-pack cases of dairy products
Knowledge of health and hygiene practices for food workers
Observance of safety precautions near pasteurizing machine and automated bottling machine

Relevant DOT Reference

Dairy Helper (Dairy Products) 529.686-026

Related Jobs

Cannery Worker (job profile F-5)
Laborer, Cheesemaking 529.686-050

JOB PROFILE F-10
Poultry Processing Worker

General Description

Assists in dressing and preparing poultry for delivery to markets. The worker functions in this job as a helper to the skilled poultry dresser. The job also includes performance of cleaning activities in the work areas.

Job Activities

Pluck fowls
Suspend live poultry from conveyor hooks
Load and transport dressed poultry in hand carts
Wrap and pack dressed poultry for shipping
Weigh poultry and mark weight on container
Sack feathers
Dispose of inedible waste
Stack cases in cold storage room
Maintain temperature in cold storage room; replenish ice if required
Load and unload crates from delivery trucks
Wash equipment, utensils
Clean work areas
Assist in cutting up poultry

Specific Skill Requirements

Ability to handle live poultry with ease
Ability to attach live poultry to processing conveyor
Ability to use specialized wrapping and packing techniques
Ability to use scales and record weights on tags and containers
Ability to work in below-normal temperatures
Ability to lift and carry crates of live or dressed poultry
Knowledge of health and hygiene practices for food workers
Awareness of importance of cleanliness in the work area
Toleration of tasks involving slaughtering of poultry or handling of dead poultry

Relevant DOT Reference

Poultry-Dressing Worker 525.687-082

Related Jobs

Slaughterhouse Worker (job profile F-11)
Poultry Hanger 525.687-078

JOB PROFILE F-11
Slaughterhouse Worker

General Description

Assists in the slaughtering and dressing operations of beef, hogs and sheep. This worker's responsibility is to help the skilled meat handlers and to perform housekeeping duties in the work areas.

Job Activities

Unload carcasses and carry from shipping platform to truck
Hang carcass on conveyor
Wash carcasses on conveyor line
Hold meat while it is being cut
Stamp predetermined grade on meat; attach date tag
Distribute meat to various departments for further processing
Push conveyor racks, carcasses or meat cuts down conveyor line
Load meat onto conveyor, carts, tables or trucks, using hook
Dispose of inedible carcass waste
Fill ice trucks
Wrap meat, seal packages and weigh
Label packages of meat
Wash utensils; clean and grease conveyor rails
Clean work room and work tables
Spread sawdust on floor
May assist in cutting meat, trimming fat, shrouding carcasses, or other tasks

Specific Skill Requirements

Ability to lift and handle heavy loads
Ability to work in below-normal temperatures
Awareness of safety hazards (knives, cleavers, heavy carcasses)
Knowledge of health and hygiene practices for food workers
Knowledge of special techniques of meat handling
Knowledge of locations of equipment, various departments
Acceptance of tasks involving handling of dead animals

Relevant DOT Reference

Laborer (Slaughtering and Meat Packing) 529.687-130

Related Jobs

Poultry Processing Worker (job profile F-10)
Cooler Room Worker (Slaughtering and Meat Packing) 525.687-022
Washer, Carcass (Slaughtering and Meat Packing) 525.687-122

JOB PROFILE F-12
Nut Processing Worker

General Description

Assists in activities related to the processing and packaging of nuts. Employment opportunities may be seasonal in some geographic regions.

Job Activities

Sort nuts by size and quality
Weigh or weigh-count nuts
Fill bins or conveyor feeders, using shovel
Tend shell-softening bath
Operate nut-cracking machine
Insert and remove trays from ovens
Monitor packing machine
Pack products into cartons
Change barrels in nut-cracking machine, using hand tools
Wash utensils
Perform simple maintenance on machines
Move materials and supplies between work areas

Specific Skill Requirements

Ability to safely lift and carry heavy loads
Ability to use forklift or handtruck to move materials
Knowledge of packing techniques
Knowledge of locations of tools, equipment, materials, and storage and work areas
Awareness of saftey hazards in working with semiautomated equipment, ovens, and hot water baths
Ability to tolerate repetitive activities

Relevant DOT Reference

Nut Process Helper 529.486-010

Related Jobs

Cannery Worker (job profile F-5)
Nut Grinder 521.685-234
Nut Sorter Operator 521.685-238

JOB PROFILE F-13
Framing Shop Helper

General Description

Perform tasks related to construction of windows, picture frames and door frames. Parts may be prefabricated or precut, or it may be necessary to cut the framing material to the desired lengths.

Job Activities

Sort wood cuts
Sort nails, screws, and other small hardware
Fill wood (paste rub)
Put putty in holes
Wipe stained or filled wood
Perform simple assembly, using nails, staples, screws, and/or glue and clamps
Measure (rule) and cut wood to size
Pack or crate, label
Store delivered supplies and materials
Clean work areas

Specific Skill Requirements

Knowledge of framing shop routines and procedures
Ability to use simple hand and power framing tools, equipment, and supplies
Knowledge of techniques for preparing, assembling, and finishing frames

Knowledge of tools and techniques for frame packing, crating, and labeling
Ability to store delivered supplies and materials, using handtruck or forklift
Knowledge of the hazards of hand and power tools and equipment, flammables, and solvents
Knowledge of locations of tools, equipment, materials, and of storage and work areas

Relevant DOT Reference

Woodenware Assembler 762.687-070

Related Jobs

Furniture Factory Worker (job profile F-14)
Picture Framer 739.684-146

JOB PROFILE F-14
Furniture Factory Worker

General Description

Performs tasks in furniture manufacture, using hands or light tools. This job emphasizes the woodworking aspect of furniture manufacturing. The employee in an upholstered furniture manufacturing plant will require training in handling a variety of fabrics and in techniques specific to upholstering. (See job profile E-26.)

Job Activities

Gather and move tools and equipment between storage and work areas
Drill, sand, saw
Perform simple assembly, using nails, screws, staples, and/or glue and clamps
Put putty in holes
Fill wood (paste, rub)
Wipe stained or filled wood
Paint or varnish by hand or machine

Monitor automatic or semiautomatic wood finishers
Polish
Attach hardware, such as drawer pulls, drawer guides, catches, and latches
Measure with square and tape measure, to check accuracy of specified dimensions
Pack or crate, label (stencil) containers
Clean and perform simple maintenance upon tools and equipment
Clean work areas
Store delivered materials and supplies
Perform cutting and fastening operations in upholstering of furniture

Specific Skill Requirements

Knowledge of tools and techniques used in furniture assembly and finishing and in upholstering techniques
Ability to make coordinated movements by hand or with power tools
Knowledge of tools and techniques for packing, crating, and labeling completed products
Ability to monitor automated wood finishing machines
Ability to clean and perform simple maintenance upon tools and equipment
Ability to maintain a clean work area
Ability to safely lift, carry and move heavy objects, using handtruck or cart
Knowledge of the hazards of hand and power tools and equipment, flammables, solvents, and automated machines
Knowledge of locations of tools, equipment, materials and storage and work areas

Relevant DOT Reference

Furniture Assembler 763.684-038

Related Jobs

Upholstery Shop Helper (job profile E-26)
Framing Shop Helper (job profile F-13)
Hardware Assembler 763.684-042
Blow-off Worker (Furniture) 763.687-010

JOB PROFILE F-15
Small Products Assembler

General Description

Performs simple assembly in mass production of various plastic, wood, metal or rubber items. May work in a variety of manufacturing settings such as toys, musical instruments, automotive, or household products.

Job Activities

Perform simple assembly, using bolts, screws, clips, cement, or staples
Load and unload automated preset machines
Tend setup machines that punch, press, rivet or cut
Apply stencils or decals
Pack or crate products

Specific Skill Requirements

Ability to select parts by color, type
Ability to position parts together correctly
Ability to use hand or power tools for bolting, clipping, and cementing
Fine motor coordination for using tweezers, tongs for positioning and inserting parts
Ability to load, unload and monitor preset equipment
Ability to tolerate repetitive activities

Relevant DOT Reference

Assembler, Small Products 739.687-030

Related Jobs

Toy Factory Worker (job profile F-25)
Tie-up Worker 710.687-034
Vacuum Bottle Assembler 739.687-194
Hardware Assembler 762.687-046
Motorcycle Subassembler 806.684-094

JOB PROFILE F-16

Production Worker, Transportation Equipment Plant

General Description

Assists in tasks related to the production of heavy transportation equipment and their subassemblies. Equipment would be for railroad, truck, shipping, aircraft, and construction industries.

Job Activities

Clean metal assemblies
Chip slag and spaul from welding
Grind metal parts
Mate and align parts
Install bolts
Insert screws and cold rivets
Buck rivets
Install connectors
Paint by hand or machine
Oil and grease machine parts
Assemble crating
Pack and crate finished subassemblies
Stamp or stencil labels
Transport by cart, handtruck, hoist
Clean work areas
Perform simple maintenance upon tools and equipment
Store delivered parts and supplies

Specific Skill Requirements

Ability to use simple hand and power assembly, grinding, and jointing tools and equipment
Knowledge of techniques used in assembly, grinding, and painting of heavy transportation equipment
Knowledge of tools and techniques for packing, crating, and labeling finished subassemblies
Ability to lift, carry, and move heavy objects by hoist, handtruck, and cart
Ability to clean and perform simple maintenance upon tools and equipment
Ability to make coordinated movements by hand and with power tools

Knowledge of the hazards of hand and power tools and equipment, flammables, and solvents
Knowledge of locations of tools, equipment, supplies, parts, and of storage and work areas

Relevant DOT Reference

Utility Worker (Transportation Equipment) 869.684-074

Related Jobs

Riveter Helper (job profile F-1)
(Helper to) Trailer Assembler (Automobile Manufacturing) 806.381-058
Shipfitter Helper 806.687-050

JOB PROFILE F-17
Production Worker, Electrical/Electronic Equipment

General Description

Assists in tasks relating to the production of electrical devices (for example, irons, telephones), or electronic subassemblies (such as circuit speakers, antennas).

Job Activities

Use simple hand and power tools and equipment
Use simple electronic testing devices to locate defective parts
Perform simple assemblies
Solder, bolt simple connections
Thread wire, bundle wires to form cables
Crimp wire or metal (machine)
Glue or bolt units together
Sort hardware, parts
Transport by tray or cart
Fill cartons or pack, label containers
Store delivered parts, supplies, and materials
Clean work area

Specific Skill Requirements

Ability to use simple hand and power electrical assembly tools and equipment
Ability to use simple electrical/electronic testing equipment, such as ohmmeter, ammeter, voltmeter, oscilloscope
Knowledge of techniques for electrical assembly and testing
Ability to make fine, coordinated movements by hand and with power tools
Knowledge of tools and techniques for packing, crating, and labeling (stenciling) finished products
Ability to safely lift, carry, and move heavy objects by handtruck or cart
Care in handling delicate items
Knowledge of the hazards of hand and power tools and equipment, solvents, and glues
Knowledge of location of tools, equipments, supplies, and storage and work areas
Ability to tolerate repetitive activities
Ability to work in close coordination with other workers

Relevant DOT Reference

Electronics Worker 726.687-010
Subassembler, Electronic Products 729.684-054

Related Jobs

Electrode Cleaner 729.687-014
Assembler, Dry Cell and Battery 727.687-022

JOB PROFILE F-18
Stationery Manufacturing Worker

General Description

Assists in the handling of paper stock through the various processes in the production of stationery and related paper products.

Job Activities

Cut or trim paper, using cutting machine
Start folding machine
Feed papers into machine
Remove completed items from machine
Stack or handle papers
Pack paper in boxes or cartons
Wrap cartons
Seal cartons with glue or tape
Label cartons or rolls (stencils)
Count or weigh cartons
Keep simple records of cartons
Load, unload, and transport by cart, handtruck
Make in-house deliveries
Tie bundles of paper, by hand or using strapping machine
Shred waste paper for disposal or recycling
Operate power bailer
Monitor automatic machinery
Store delivered supplies and materials
Clean work areas

Specific Skill Requirements

Ability to operate paper folding, cutting, shredding, and bailing machines
Ability to clean and perform simple maintenance upon shop's paper machines
Ability to bundle papers by hand and using power strapping machine
Ability to safely lift, carry, and move heavy objects, using handtruck and cart
Ability to monitor automated machines as directed
Knowledge of the hazards of shop machinery and tools, solvents, and flammables (if shop also has printing activities)
Knowledge of locations of tools, machinery, supplies, materials, and of storage and work areas

Relevant DOT Reference

Folding Machine Feeder 641.685-050

Related Jobs

Newspaper Production Worker (job profile E-30)
Print Shop Worker (job profile E-31)
Bindery Worker (job profile E-32)

JOB PROFILE F-19
Bag Cutter

General Description

Reclaims usable material from defective textile bags in textile bag factory. May use hand sewing machine to repair rips in cloth bags.

Job Activities

Open bags by removing stitching
Locate defects in bag material
Cut out defective section
Cut usable material into largest possible bag dimension
Sort and stack reclaimed cloth by size
Use hand sewing machine to repair small tears
Keep work area neat and clean

Specific Skill Requirements

Ability to use hand scissors, thread pullers, and power shears
Ability to cut or pull thread to open seams
Ability to recognize defects in cloth
Ability to remove defect with power shears, leaving largest possible remnant
Ability to sort remnants by size
Ability to operate hand sewing machine and to mend straight rips in cloth

Relevant DOT Reference

Bag Cutter (Textile Scrap Salvager) 789.687-010

Related Jobs

Cloth Folder, Textile Manufacturing (job profile F-20)
Cutter Helper 781.687-022
Mender 787.682-030
Bag and Sack Sewer 787.682-042

JOB PROFILE F-20
Cloth Folder, Textile Manufacturing

General Description

Folds cloth by hand in preparation for further processing or for packaging and shipment. This worker is usually employed in a factory which manufactures cloth or household items such as sheets, blankets, or tablecloths.

Job Activities

Offload cloth from work station or storage area
Inspect cloth for defects
Cut cloth at specified length
Fold fabric, aligning edges and matching pattern
Form cloth into a pile by lapping at intervals
Trim ends of cloth
Examine cloth for uniformity of color, texture
Bind folded cloth with rope
Record yardage of cloth; keep simple records
Transport cloth to next work station or to storage
Collect and dispose of waste
Clean up work area

Specific Skill Requirements

Ability to recognize defects in dyeing, printing, or finishing of the fabric and route the material correctly
Knowledge of procedures and routines characteristic of specific job setting
Knowledge of location of work areas, supplies, equipment, and storage
Awareness of safety hazards in working around power machinery

Relevant DOT Reference

Cloth Folder, Hand (Textile) 589.687-014

Related Jobs

Clothing Manufacturing Worker (job profile F-21)
Cloth Folder, Machine 689.685-078
Yarn Sorter 689.687-086

JOB PROFILE F-21
Clothing Manufacturing Worker

General Description

Performs tasks in clothing production either by hand or using simple tools. The tasks may encompass many aspects of clothing production; for example, cutting from a pattern, sewing, setting pockets, making buttonholes. The worker may assist more skilled workers in production tasks and is responsible for cleanup and other housekeeping duties.

Job Activities

Supply workers with materials
Keep storage area neatly stocked
Offload work stations and transport materials to other stations, to storage, or to shipping
Sort thread, lace, and other materials by specified type, size, weight, or color
Operate or tend sewing machine
Sew by hand to join, hem, or reinforce garments
Press
Fold clothing
Mark for buttonholes
Cut material at specified length of cloth
Observe sewn garment to detect defect in stitching
Keep simple records of movement of materials
Oil machines; perform other routine preventive maintenance
Collect and dispose of waste
Sweep; keep work areas clean

Specific Skill Requirements

Ability to recognize defects in sewing and to route the garment correctly
Knowledge of procedures and routines characteristic of specific job setting
Knowledge of locations of work areas, supplies, equipment, storage
Knowledge of routine maintenance procedures for sewing machines
Awareness of safety hazards in working with powered equipment
Ability to make fine, coordinated hand movements in sewing

Relevant DOT Reference

Utility Operator (Garment) 786.682-262
Hand Sewer 782.684-058

Related Jobs

Sewing Machine Operator (job profile F-22)
Bias Cutting Machine Operator 686.682-014
Cutter Helper 781.687-022
Thread Marker 782.687-058
Garment Folder 789.687-066

JOB PROFILE F-22
Sewing Machine Operator

General Description

Operates power sewing machine in the manufacture of such items as clothing, linens, draperies, leather goods, or home furnishings.

Job Activities

Prepare machine for operation
Select pieces of fabric to be joined
Sew pieces of fabric together as required
Perform daily maintenance of machine
Report machine malfunction

Specific Skill Requirements

Ability to thread machine, thread and insert bobbin, change needle
Ability to start, stop, and control speed of machine
Ability to position and join fabric parts correctly
Ability to oil and clean machine
Ability to recognize common machine malfunctions
Observance of safety precautions in using a powered machine

Relevant DOT Reference

Sewing Machine Operator, Any Industry 787.682-046

Related Jobs

Sewing Machine Operator, Trim and Embroidery 787.682-070
Utility Operator (Garment) 786.682-262
Sewing Machine Operator, Semi-automatic 786.685-030

JOB PROFILE F-23
Leather Handle Maker

General Description

Assembles parts of luggage handles in preparation for stitching and attaching to pieces of luggage.

Job Activities

Clean leather
Sort leather by size
Apply glue to individual metal handle frames
Wrap handle frames with cardboard and shape with hand press
Staple precut leather to cardboard around frame
Stack handles for stitching

Specific Skill Requirements

Ability to use automatic glue applicator or glue pot and brush
Ability to operate hand press for shaping handles

Ability to correctly position precut leather handle on cardboard frame
Ability to use large stapler safely

Relevant DOT Reference

Assembler, Leather Goods II 783.687-010

Related Jobs

Leather Belt Maker 690.685-266
Table Worker, Leather Products 783.687-030

JOB PROFILE F-24
Shoe or Boot Manufacturing Worker

General Description

Assists in the production, handling, and transporting of shoes and boots at different stages of fabrication.

Job Activities

Remove lasts from assembled shoes
Sort and store lasts in bins
Punch leather
Install grommets
Stamp designs by hand or machine
Cut or trim by hand
Assist in assembly and sewing
Gather leather scraps for salvage
Sort and stock salvaged leather
Remove shoe parts from automatic cutting and shaping machines
Sand shoe heels
Polish finished products
Move products from area to area for further processing
Wrap or bail leather
Sweep floors
Clean work benches

Specific Skill Requirements

Ability to hand-release lasts from shoes
Ability to sort leather pieces by size and shape
Ability to stack leather scraps neatly
Ability to tend automatic machines used in plant
Ability to operate heel-sanding machine, sewing machine, grommet-installing machine
Ability to use handtruck for transporting products about plant
Knowledge of plant areas by name and location
Ability to make fine, coordinated hand movements in working with leather

Relevant DOT Reference

Laborer, Boot and Shoe 788.687-066

Related Jobs

Boot Trimmer 690.685-434
Boot Turner 788.687-130
Leather Belt Maker 690.685-266
Leather Cutter 783.684-022

JOB PROFILE F-25
Toy Factory Worker

General Description

Performs simple assembly in mass production of toys, or toy parts; may also do finishing work such as stencil painting.

Job Activities

Select part by color, type
Fit parts together, using hands, tweezers, or pliers
Fasten parts together, using clips, glue, screws, dowels, nails, or staples
Sand by hand
Paint toys
Apply stencils or decals

Operate or tend power equipment, such as drill press or punch press
Inspect toy to ensure operation
Pack or crate products
Clean up work area

Specific Skill Requirements

Fine motor coordination for positioning and inserting parts
Ability to follow a specified pattern in assembling parts
Knowledge of routines, procedures, and locations in the specific job setting
Ability to exercise safety precautions when working with power presses
Ability to tolerate repetitive activities
Ability to work in close coordination with other workers

Relevant DOT Reference

Toy Assembler (Toys and Games) 731.687-034

Related Jobs

Small Products Assembler (job profile F-15)
Water Sports Equipment Assembler 732.684-014
Assembler, Mechanical Pencils and Ball Point Pens 733.687-014

JOB PROFILE F-26
Pottery Worker

General Description

Assists in the factory production of pottery and porcelain dishware, using manual or light machine labor.

Job Activities

Gather and supply wet clay, other materials, and tools to pottery makers
Clean equipment and work area
Assist in stamping designs
Assist in glazing, applying decals
Place pottery in drying racks and remove when dry

Fill bins with clay
Transport finished pottery in plant
Pack pottery for shipment
Load and unload trucks or railroad cars

Specific Skill Requirements

Knowledge of slip, clay, and special tools used in making dishware
Knowledge of cleaning procedures to be used with jigs and equipment in plant
Ability to handle wet or dry pottery cautiously to prevent damage
Ability to lift heavy loads of clay
Knowledge of packing procedures for standard pottery items
Knowledge of various plant areas and departments

Relevant DOT Reference

(Helper to) Pottery Machine Operator 774.382-010

Related Jobs

Glass Production Helper (job profile F-4)
Kiln Burner Helper 573.687-026
Brick and Tile Sorter 573.687-034
Hand Molder, Brick or Tile 575.684-042

JOB PROFILE F-27
Pulp Mill Worker

General Description

Performs a variety of tasks in making paper and other pulp products from rough logs. Work may include heavy labor in the handling of logs, portable bins, and finished products.

Job Activities

Load, unload, and stack logs
Transport materials by hand cart
Tend hydraulic press

Tend pulp processing machines
Clean vats and machinery

Specific Skill Requirements

Ability to lift, handle, and stack logs in a team with other workers
Ability to use pulley, cable, cart hook, and peavey in log handling
Ability to use hammer, wrench, screwdriver
Ability to load, unload, and tend specific automated processing machines as required by job (turn valves, pull levers, tend conveyors, fill and empty vats)
Knowledge of hazards in plant and ability to follow safety procedures
Physical strength; ability to perform strenuous tasks over extended periods of time

Relevant DOT Reference

Pulp-Press Tender 532.685-026

Related Jobs

Pulp Piler 922.687-082
Digester-Operator Helper 532.686-010

JOB PROFILE F-28
Tannery Worker

General Description

Assists in the preparation of hides and leather for making leather goods. The individual worker will probably perform only a few of the diverse activities listed and may assist in any task related to cleaning, drying, processing, and bundling hides for shipment to leather goods manufacturers.

Job Activities

Unload bundles of hides from railroad cars or trucks
Count and tie hides into bundles for processing
Clip wet hides onto drying frames
Place framed hides in drying tunnel

Feed dried hides into finishing machines
Clean and disinfect vats and processing areas

Specific Skill Requirements

Ability to lift and carry heavy bundles of hides
Ability to count hides correctly for bundling
Ability to use awl and cord for punching and tying hides together
Knowledge of purposes of various chemical vats
Ability to stretch and clip hides on drying frames
Ability to tend automatic finishing machines (pressing, brushing, vacuuming)
Knowledge of specialized tools, chemicals, and procedures for cleaning tannery equipment

Relevant DOT Reference

Laborer, General 589.686-026

Related Jobs

Stainer 589.687-034
Rackloader 590.687-018

JOB PROFILE F-29
Brickyard Worker

General Description

Performs handling tasks required in firing clay products in large quantities.

Job Activities

Clean kilns
Load and unload kilns
Move finished items to storage areas and stack
Weigh or weigh-count finished products
Assist in keeping production records
Sort bricks and other products

Transport wet clay by cart
Fill bins with clay
Perform simple carpentry
Clean work areas
Clean and perform simple maintenance on tools and equipment

Specific Skill Requirements

Knowledge of routines and procedures of a brickyard
Ability to use simple hand and power tools and equipment used in a brickyard
Knowledge of techniques used in firing and handling clay products
Ability to clean and perform simple maintenance upon kilns, tools, and equipment
Ability to safely lift, carry, and move heavy objects, using handtruck, cart, and hoists
Knowledge of the hazards of hand and power tools and equipment and kilns
Knowledge of locations of tools, equipment, materials, and storage and work areas
Physical strength; ability to perform strenuous activities over extended periods

Relevant DOT Reference

Kiln-Burner Helper 573.687-026

Related Jobs

Cement Block Production Worker (job profile F-30)
Kiln Placer 573.686-026
Kiln Drawer 929.687-014

JOB PROFILE F-30
Cement Block Production Worker

General Description

Assists in activities related to the molding, storage, and delivery of cement blocks; could also apply to production of concrete vaults or tanks.

Job Activities

Fill molds
Scrape off excess concrete
Strip finished block from mold
Assist in setting up automatic machine
Tend automatic machine that casts blocks
Weigh or weigh-count finished products
Assist in keeping production records
Stack blocks onto pallets
Assist with loading truck or rail cars
Shovel sand and other materials
Clean work area
Clean and perform simple maintenance upon tools, molds, and automatic machine

Specific Skill Requirements

Knowledge of routines and procedures of a cement block plant
Ability to use hand and power tools and equipment used in the production of cement blocks and related items
Ability to monitor, clean, and perform simple maintenance upon automatic block-making machines
Ability to safely lift, carry, or move heavy objects using handtruck, cart, and hoist
Ability to clean tools, molds, and work areas
Ability to shovel, move, and mix raw materials
Knowledge of the hazards of tools, equipment, and machinery, and of the work setting in general
Knowledge of locations of tools, materials, and work areas
Physical strength; ability to perform strenuous activities over extended periods

Relevant DOT Reference

Block-Making Machine Operator 575.685-014

Related Jobs

Brickyard Worker (job profile F-29)
Hand Molder, Brick or Tile 575.684-042
Terrazo Tile Maker 575.684-046

JOB PROFILE F-31
Stone Quarry Worker

General Description

Assists in tasks related to blasting, cutting, and transporting of quarried stone or rock. Employment opportunities may be seasonal in some geographic regions.

Job Activities

Mark desired dimensions on stone
Remove mud from surface of stone
Chip irregularities from stone slabs
Loosen blasted stone and skid into position for breaking
Break stone into pieces
Polish and buff
Operate grinder
Cut notches in block of stone and attach cable or hook
Load broken rock into boxes for removal
Pack (in straw or excelsior)
Perform simple carpentry
String blast wire
Make chain or cable hitch
Gather and move tools and equipment between storage and work areas

Specific Skill Requirements

Ability to perform simple maintenance upon tools and equipment
Knowledge of routines and procedures of a stone quarry
Ability to use simple hand and power quarrying and construction tools
Knowledge of techniques for blasting, preparing, and transporting quarried materials
Ability to load or crate for shipment various quarried materials
Ability to lift, carry, and move heavy objects, using cart or hoist
Ability to perform simple maintenance upon tools and equipment
Knowledge of the hazards of tools, equipment, machinery, explosives, and of the work setting in general
Knowledge of locations of tools, equipment, supplies, and work areas
Willingness to perform dirty, repetitive, strenuous tasks
Physical strength; ability to perform strenuous activities over extended periods

Relevant DOT Reference

Quarry Worker 939.667-014

Related Jobs

Brickyard Worker (job profile F-29)
Cement Block Production Worker (job profile F-30)
Placer Miner 939.684-014

JOB PROFILE F-32
Plastics Molder Helper

General Description

Assists in construction of plastic forms using molds, liquid plastic, and glass fiber cloth.

Job Activities

Coat mold interiors with wax to facilitate form removal
Brush liquids in mold
Lay strips of fiber in mold
Clamp halves of mold together
Remove dried forms from mold
Clean work area
Clean tools
Sort forms
Store delivered supplies and materials

Specific Skill Requirements

Knowledge of routines and procedures of plastics-molding shop
Knowledge of tools, equipment, materials, and techniques used in molding plastic forms
Ability to work within well-defined tolerances
Knowledge of tools, solvents, and techniques used to clean and maintain tools and molds
Knowledge of tools and techniques for cleaning work areas

Ability to store delivered supplies and materials
Ability to safely lift, carry, and move heavy objects, using handtruck and cart
Knowledge of hazards of tools, equipment, plastics, solvents, and of molding shop setting in general
Knowledge of locations of tools, equipment, supplies, materials, and storage and work areas

Relevant DOT Reference

Plastics Molder 779.684-050

Related Jobs

Mold Closer 518.684-018
Molder, Fiber Glass Luggage 575.685-066

JOB PROFILE F-33
Packer

General Description

Packages materials and finished products by hand or machine. Duties may vary considerably depending upon the products, which range from food and textiles to electronic and mechanical parts.

Job Activities

Assemble crates and cartons
Wrap products with protective material
Fill containers
Close and seal containers
Label filled containers
Assemble and wrap bundles of filled containers
Replenish packaging supplies
Record number of units packaged
Tend conveyor or automatic packaging device
Transport bundled containers to shipping area
Clean work area

Specific Skill Requirements

Knowledge of packing routines and procedures
Ability to use hand and power tools to assemble, pack, and seal containers
Knowledge of proper techniques for assembling, packing, sealing, and labeling containers
Ability to monitor automatic packaging and conveying equipment
Ability to keep simple records
Ability to safely lift, carry, and move heavy objects using handtruck and cart
Knowledge of hazards of packing tools and equipment, and automatic machinery
Knowledge of locations of tools, equipment, supplies, and storage and work areas

Relevant DOT Reference

Packager, Hand 920.587-018

Related Jobs

Carton Packaging Machine Operator 920.665-010
Marker 920.687-126
Packer, Agricultural Produce 920.687-134

JOB PROFILE F-34
Material Handler Helper

General Description

Loads, unloads, and conveys materials within or near plant, yard, or worksite; uses tools and equipment to open or seal containers or bundles of material. This worker may be responsible for cleaning and maintaining an orderly storage area.

Job Activities

Load or unload materials by hand
Use hand tools to open containers

Convey materials from one area to another by hand cart or moving bin
Stack incoming material on pallets or in storage area as directed
Apply identifying markings to cartons using tags, labels, or stencil as directed
Use banding machine and clincher
Tend conveyor system, removing loose material
Aid machine operators by moving objects by hand as directed
Use brooms, rags, vacuum, and cleaning compounds to clean work area

Specific Skill Requirements

Ability to use hand tools (hammer, crowbar, metal cutter) to open crates and boxes
Ability to operate manual or motorized equipment as required (handtruck, banding machine, forklift)
Ability to safely lift, carry, and move heavy objects
Ability to accurately apply identifying markings
Ability to tolerate temperature variations, noise, and physical hazards
Ability to maintain a clean work area
Knowledge of hazards of hand and power tools or equipment, and of work setting in general
Knowledge of locations of tools, equipment, and work areas
Physical strength; ability to perform strenuous activities over extended periods

Relevant DOT Reference

Material Handler 929.687-030

Related Jobs

Packer (job profile F-33)
Forklift Operator (job profile F-35)
Laborer, Stores 922.687-058

JOB PROFILE F-35
Forklift Operator

General Description

Operates a forklift tractor in a warehouse, storage yard, or factory. Moves and stacks material on pallets or skids; delivers materials to workers and picks up finished products for storage or shipping. This employee also may tow a trailer and operate a power scoop.

Job Activities

Start and operate electric or gasoline-powered forklift
Load and unload skids, pallets, or boxes
Tow trailer
Use power scoop to move loose material
Manually load and unload lifting mechanisms
Perform daily vehicle maintenance
Fill requisition orders
Keep record of hours of vehicle operation

Specific Skill Requirements

Ability to operate electric and gasoline-powered forklifts
Ability to observe limit regulations of equipment
Ability to perform simple maintenance procedures upon equipment
Ability to read and fill out requisitions
Tolerance for a wide range of temperature and noise
Ability to keep simple records
Ability to safely lift, carry, and move heavy objects
Knowledge of the hazards of electric and gas-operated forklifts and scoops, and of the work setting in general
Knowledge of locations of tools, equipment, and work areas

Relevant DOT Reference

Industrial-Truck Operator 921.683-050

Related Jobs

Laborer, Hoisting 921.667-022
Road-Roller Operator 859.683-030

JOB PROFILE F-36
Factory Equipment Cleaner

General Description

Cleans and sterilizes machinery, utensils, and equipment used to process or store products.

Job Activities

Gather and move tools and equipment between storage and work areas
Use hand and power tools and cleaning equipment, and cleaning solutions
Turn valves to drain machinery
Connect and disconnect pipes, hoses
Spray machinery, work area with water, steam, and/or cleaning solutions
Scrub machinery, floors, walls, pipes, valves
Dry machinery with compressed air
Mix cleaning solutions to specific concentrations
Draw samples of cleaning solution for lab analysis
Lubricate machinery
Clean and perform simple maintenance upon cleaning tools and equipment
Store delivered cleaning supplies

Specific Skill Requirements

Knowledge of cleaning routines and procedures for particular work settings
Ability to use hand and power cleaning tools and equipment, and cleaning solutions
Knowledge of techniques for cleaning various kinds of work settings and machinery
Ability to safely and accurately mix cleaning solutions
Ability to take cleaning solution samples for lab analysis
Knowledge of tools and techniques for lubricating machinery
Ability to clean and perform simple maintenance upon cleaning equipment
Knowledge of the hazards of cleaning tools, equipment, solutions, steam, and of the work setting and its machinery in general
Knowledge of locations of tools, equipment, supplies, and of storage and work areas

Relevant DOT Reference

Equipment Cleaner 599.684-010

Related Jobs

Laborer, General (Plastics Production) 754.687-010
Helper, Manufacturing (Aircraft Manufacturing) 809.687-014

JOB PROFILE F-37
Recycling Bin Attendant

General Description

Performs attendant duties at a center which recycles materials such as paper, aluminum, or glass. At a small center the worker may simply transport and sort materials. Workers at larger centers may be required to operate automated equipment, weigh incoming materials, and keep records.

Job Activities

Load and unload paper, aluminum, and glass from donors' vehicles
Sort and stack incoming material in proper bin or space
Load cans onto conveyor for sorting and weighing
Operate conveyor and automated sorting equipment
Report weight of material to supervisor
Maintain simple records of materials received
Meet and direct donors to appropriate recycling area
Maintain clean and orderly receiving and processing areas

Specific Skill Requirements

Ability to lift heavy bundles or containers of salvaged materials
Ability to use handtruck or dolly
Ability to sort materials by type (aluminum, glass, newspapers, magazines)
Knowledge of organization and layout of recycling areas
Ability to load and operate conveyors and automated equipment
Ability to maintain simple records of materials received
Neat appearance and ability to relate to the public

Ability to wait for extended periods without supervision when business is slow

Relevant DOT Reference

Laborer, Salvage 929.687-022

Related Jobs

(Helper to) Sorter-Pricer, Non-Profit Organization 222.387-054
Garment Sorter 222.687-014

C. Index to Types of Employing Organizations

References

Barker, E. Current and significant: ENCORE—a community's alternative to institutionalization. *Education and Training of the Mentally Retarded,* December 1971, *6*(4), 185-90.

Begab, M. The mentally retarded and society: Trends and issues. *The mentally retarded and society: A social science perspective.* Edited by M. Begab and S. Richardson. Baltimore, Md.: University Park Press, 1975.

Brolin, D.; Durand, R.; Kromer, K.; and Muller, P. Post-school adjustment of educable retarded students. *Education and Training of the Mentally Retarded,* October 1975, *10*(3), 144-49.

Brolin, D. *Vocational preparation of retarded citizens.* Columbus, Ohio: Charles E. Merrill Publishing Co., 1976.

Clark, A. T. No "open sesames" in rural rehabilitation. *Rehabilitation Literature,* July 1973, *34*(7), 207-9, 223.

Commission on Accreditation of Rehabilitation Facilities (CARF). *Standards manual for rehabilitation facilities.* Chicago, Ill.: Commission on Accreditation of Rehabilitation Facilities, 1976.

Conley, R. *The economics of mental retardation.* Baltimore, Md.: Johns Hopkins University Press, 1973.

Edgerton, R. Issues relating to the quality of life among mentally retarded persons. *The mentally retarded and society: A social science perspective.* Edited by M. Begab and S. Richardson. Baltimore, Md.: University Park Press, 1975.

Farber, B. *Mental retardation: Its social context and social consequences.* Boston: Houghton-Mifflin, 1968.

Gardner, W. I. *Behavior modification in mental retardation: The education and rehabilitation of the mentally retarded adolescent and adult.* Chicago, Ill.: Oldine, 1971.

Gardner, W. I. Mental retardation: A critical review of personality characteristics. *Mental retardation: Rehabilitation and counseling.* Edited by P. Browning. Springfield, Ill.: Charles C. Thomas, 1974.

Gold, M. W. Research on the vocational habilitation of the retarded: The present, the future. *International review of research in mental retardation.* Edited by N. R. Ellis. New York: Academic Press, 1973, *6,* 97-147.

Gold, M. W. Task analysis of a complex assembly task by the retarded blind. *Exceptional Children,* October 1976, *43*(2), 78-84.

Goldstein, H. Social and occupational adjustment. *Mental retardation: A review of research.* Edited by H. A. Stevens and R. Heber. Chicago, Ill.: University of Chicago Press, 1964, 214-58.

Goldstein, H. How you can help a retarded patient get a job. *Medical Times,* August 1971, *99*(8), 123-36.

Grossman, H. J. *Manual on terminology and classification in mental retardation.* Washington, D.C.: American Association on Mental Deficiency, 1977.

Katz, E. *The retarded adult in the community.* Springfield, Ill.: Charles C. Thomas, 1968.

Kelly, J. and Simon, A. The mentally handicapped as workers—a survey of company experience. *Personnel,* Sept-Oct 1969, *46*(5), 58–64.

Kirk, S. A. *Early education of the mentally retarded: An experimental study.* Urbana, Ill.: University of Illinois Press, 1958.

Nirje, B. The normalization principle and its human management implications. *Changing patterns in services for the mentally retarded.* Edited by R. Kugel and W. Wolfensberger. Washington, D.C.: President's Committee on Mental Retardation, 1969.

O'Connor, G.; Justice, R. S.; and Warren, N. The aged mentally retarded: Institution or community care? *American Journal of Mental Deficiency,* November 1970, *75*(3), 354–360.

Olshansky, S. Changing vocational behavior through normalization. *The principle of normalization in human services.* Edited by W. Wolfensberger. Toronto, Canada: National Institute on Mental Retardation, 1972.

Olshansky, S. Work samples: Another view. *Rehabilitation Literature.* February, 1975, *36*(2), 48–49.

Olshansky, S. and Beach, D. A five year follow-up of mentally retarded clients. *Rehabilitation Literature,* 1974, *35*(2), 48–49.

Parnell, D. Career education and the school curriculum. *Essays on career education.* Edited by L. McClure and C. Brian. Portland, Oregon: Northwest Regional Educational Laboratory, 1973.

Peterson, R. O. and Jones, E. M. *Development of a system of job activity elements for the mentally retarded.* Pittsburgh: American Institutes for Research, 1959.

Peterson, R. O. and Jones, E. M. *Guide to jobs for the mentally retarded.* Pittsburgh: American Institutes for Research, 1960.

President's Committee on Mental Retardation. *These two must be equal: America's needs in habilitation and employment of the mentally retarded.* Washington, D.C.: U.S. Government Printing Office, 1969.

Richardson, J. B. A survey of the present status of vocational training in state institutions for the mentally retarded. *Mental Retardation,* Feb. 1975, *13*(1), 16–19.

Rosen, M. and Kivitz, M. S. Psychological evaluation of the mentally retarded adult. *Handbook of measurement and evaluation in rehabilitation.* Edited by B. Bolton. Baltimore, Md.: University Park Press, 1976.

Rosen, M.; Clark, G. R.; and Kivitz, M. S. *Habilitation of the handicapped: New dimensions in programs for the developmentally disabled.* Baltimore, Md.: University Park Press, 1977.

Sakata, R. and Sinick, D. Do work samples work? *Rehabilitation Counseling Bulletin,* 1965, *8,* 121–24.

Skeels, H. M. and Dye, H. B. A study of the effects of differential stimulation on mentally retarded children. *Proceedings and Addresses of the American Association on Mental Deficiency,* 1939, *44,* 114–36.

Skeels, H. M. and Skodak, M. "Adult status of individuals who experienced early intervention." Paper presented at a meeting of the American Association on Mental Deficiency, Chicago, 1966.

Stanfield, J. Graduation: What happens to the retarded child when he grows up? *Exceptional Children,* Apr. 1973, *39*(7), 548–52.

Tobias, J. Vocational adjustment of young retarded adults. *Mental Retardation,* 1970, *8*(3), 13–16.

United States Employment Service, *Dictionary of occupational titles*. 4th ed. Washington, D.C.: U.S. Government Printing Office, 1977.

Usdane, W. M. The placement process in the rehabilitation of the severely handicapped. *Rehabilitation Literature,* June 1976, *37*(6), 162–67.

Wehman, P. Vocational training of the severely retarded: Expectations and potential. *Rehabilitation Literature,* 1976, *37,* 233–36.

Weld, R. A. A procedure for behavior management. *Handbook for home training specialists and day care personnel.* Edited by D. Brolin. Proceedings of the Home Trainer's Workshop, Northern Wisconsin Colony and Training School, Chippewa Falls, Wisconsin, June 21–25, 1971.

Wolfensberger, W. *Citizen advocacy for the handicapped, impaired and disadvantaged: An overview*. Washington, D.C.: U.S. Government Printing Office, 1972.

Index